# The Borders of Europe

# The Borders of Europe
## Hegemony, Aesthetics and Border Poetics

*Helge Vidar Holm,*
*Sissel Lægreid,*
*Torgeir Skorgen (eds.)*

Aarhus University Press |

*The Borders of Europe*

© the authors and Aarhus University Press

Typeset by Narayana Press

Cover design by Jørgen Sparre

Front cover illustration: *The Rape of Europe*, 1910, by Valentin Aleksandrovich Serov.
 Private Collection/The Bridgeman Art Library. BAL 75869

Printed by Narayana Press, Denmark

Printed in Denmark 2012

ISBN 978 87 7934 552 2


Aarhus University Press

*Aarhus*

Langelandsgade 177

DK – 8200 Aarhus N


*Copenhagen*

Tuborgvej 164

DK – 2400 Copenhagen NV

www.unipress.dk


Published with the financial support of

The Bergen University Fund and

OFNEC (L'Office Franco-Norvégien d'Echanges et de Coopération) at the

University of Caen Basse-Normandie


INTERNATIONAL DISTRIBUTORS:


White Cross Mills

Hightown, Lancaster, LA1 4XS

United Kingdom

www.gazellebookservices.co.uk


ISD

70 Enterprise Drive

Bristol, CT 06010

USA

www.isdistribution.com

# Content

First section:
Aesthetic Hegemonies and Conceptions
of Centre and Periphery in Europe

## Second section:
## Constructions of National, Regional and Artistic Identity in Literature and Art

## Third section:
## Poetics and Aeshetics of Borders and Border Crossing in Contemporary Literature and Art

# Introduction:
# The Notion of Europe, its Origins and Imaginaries

*Helge Vidar Holm, Sissel Lægreid & Torgeir Skorgen*

*A pilgrim on a pilgrimage*
*Walked across the Brooklyn Bridge*
*His sneakers torn*
*In the hour when the homeless move their cardboard blankets*
*And the new day is born*
*Folded in his backpack pocket*
*The questions that he copied from his heart*
*Who am I in this lonely world?*
*And where will I make my bed tonight?*
*When twilight turns to dark*
*Who believes in angels?*
*Fools do*
*Fools and pilgrims all over the world*

This song from Paul Simon's latest album, *So Beautiful or So What* (2011), may serve as an entrance to our book. Simon's lyrics illustrate what it is about: the aesthetics and poetics of borders, both interior and exterior, the time-spatiality of border zones and frontiers, the aesthetics of border crossing and the implications of being in transit, the aesthetics and experience of exile and of being excluded as opposed to being included. In short, the focus is on the strategies of identity rooted in the dynamics of identity and alterity (otherness), both related to the idea of Europe based on hegemonic power structures and strategies used throughout history in a continuous quest for the European identity. Today, in the post-national state of cultural and economic globalization with its multiplicities of disappearing old and emerging new identities both on a personal and collective level, this quest has proved increasingly challenging.

Much of this is foreshadowed in the quoted lyrics from Paul Simon, both from a historical perspective and metaphorically speaking. Being on a pilgrimage means being on a journey in search of a place of importance to a person's beliefs or faith, such as the place of birth or death of founders or saints. In other words, it implies both searching for a place of origin, or in the Christian sense of the word, where life is seen as a journey between birth and death on the way to paradise, searching for the promised land of life after death.

From the perspective of the pilgrim this means being in the time-spatial state of transition, on the move here and now, between what was in the past and what will be in the future, when or if he reaches his place of destination, something that requires moving across both cultural and geographical borders. At the same time the pilgrim, as a stranger, is conceived of as the Other, which implies moving like a migrant and exile through foreign territories after having left his home territory and cradle of origin, being on the way to the unknown and yet promised territory.

The time-spatial dimension of the kind of border-crossing practice described by Paul Simon is also metaphorically indicated by the image of the torn sneakers, which may be read as signs of time passing as well as of the pilgrim's journey through time and space. In view of the complexity of the aesthetics and poetics of borders, the torn sneakers, with their surface holes and miserable soles, may serve as potential points or spaces of contact and communication both in a concrete and symbolic sense. They are spots where the pilgrim's feet get in touch with the ground on which he walks, so they may be said to represent a border zone and border-crossing practices on different levels.

Furthermore, in a more concrete sense the torn sneakers may be seen as containing traces and reminders of the places the pilgrim has been. In this sense they are virtual ingredients of his personal memory, and as such they may help him compose the narrative of who he is, of his personal identity. In other words, on the surface they will most likely contain some fragments of the answer to the question "Who am I in this lonely world?".

The fact that he has copied this question from his heart and carries it with him in his backpack pocket may be read as an indication implying that identity and place of belonging, on many levels, is what the song is about. This reading, supported by the fact that the constitution of identity as a strategy is based on the dynamics of exclusion and inclusion, also finds its expression in the image of the homeless, moving their cardboard blankets, in as much as they, as a group living on the outside of society, are conceived of as the social Other, excluded from the collective identity framework of society. And yet the pilgrim moves towards them "in the hour … when the new day is born". In other words, in the border zone between night and day, on the bridge connecting the two banks of the river, he performs a time-spatial border-crossing act. And as he asks "… where will I make my bed tonight?", he seems to seek their company, thus both identifying with them and looking upon them as an entity constituting a social outcast group of society.

From a perspective of the aesthetics and poetics of borders and border crossing as outlined above, the bridge, both as a border zone and as a threshold and possible entrance, represents a means of communication. It is both a passage way and a zone possibly bringing two opposites into dialogue. And last but not least, as is the case with the pilgrim, it symbolizes the state of being in transit.

In a more specific and concrete sense of the bridge image, the fact that Brooklyn Bridge crosses East River gives both the song and the image a historical and topographical dimension. Topographically it connects two boroughs of New York: Brooklyn, traditionally a part of the city with the biggest community of Norwegian immigrants, now taken over mostly by other ethnic minorities, and Manhattan, New York's oldest borough, originally called Mana hatta by the Delaware Indians, who lived there until the Europeans came and established their cultural and territorial hegemony.

Thus the historical dimension and dynamics of cultural hegemonic strategies indicated in the song may be said to be revealed. Furthermore, if we add to this reading some elements from the biography of Paul Simon, the passage back to Europe and to the question of origins, identity and transformation may be retraced. As the son of Hungarian Jews, who in order to survive had to leave Europe and emigrate to America in the 1930s, Paul Simon himself may be said to personify, by his family heritage, the complexity of some of the issues treated in this book.

Towards the end of this introduction, we shall come back to the individual treatment of these issues by the authors of the various chapters in the following three sections. However, first we shall be discussing the notion of Europe in general, its origins and its imaginaries.

Anyone trying to define the notion of Europe geographically will almost automatically be confronted with considerable difficulties. The notion of Europe does not seem to refer to a clearly limited continent, as one might think, but rather to an imagined cultural realm, or simply to an idea with a historically and semantically unstable content. From nature's hand, Europe is not a readily defined part of the world: it is not defined by oceans in every direction like other continents. When an Englishman says that he wants to go to Europe, he usually refers to the European mainland reaching eastwards to Asia or the Orient. And normally it is the question of the contested Eastern border which causes real challenges. As an example, the debates about Central Europe among exiled writers and intellectuals at the end of the Cold War were largely concerned with the question of whether Russia should be considered a part of Europe or not. And what about Azerbaijan – the winner of the Eurovision Song Contest in 2011? When did we start to think of the Caucasus as a part of Europe?

In his lecture "Vilnius, Lithuania: An Ethnic Agglomerate", the Polish writer and emigrant Cslaw Milosz tried to launch the notion of Central Europe as an alternative to the division between Eastern and Western Europe. Milosz defined this realm as Estonia, Lithuania, Poland and the current Czechoslovakia. However, Milosz admitted that the existence of such a Central Europe was contested by colleagues like Josif Brodsky, who preferred the notion of Western Asia (cf. Swiderski 1988: 140). According to his Hungarian colleague, the sociologist Georgy Konrad, the border-crossing dissidents and exile writers represented the true Central Europeans, raising their voices against the officially established cultural and political hierarchies and divisions of the East and West. To Conrad, the notion of Central Europe does not refer to any geographical border, but rather to a certain cultural practice; namely border-crossing.

Being a Central European implies a border-crossing attitude or such a state of mind.

In other words, the notion of Central Europe appears to be an imagined historical and cultural realm, i.e. a mental map signified by flexible and permeable borders and a cultural attitude of crossing borders among its inhabitants. On the other hand, the pretension of being Central European implies, although unspokenly, that other Europeans are peripheral. From a French or German perspective, the Baltic peoples are themselves viewed as peripheral, in contrast with inhabitants of Berlin or Paris. This illustrates the perspectivist aspect of the notion of Europe: it tends to change focus and meaning according to the geographical situation of the speaker. To most people on the continent today, "Europe" means the European Union, whereas to most Norwegians it means a geographical area surrounded and divided by national borders.

During the Cold War, the notion of Europe could refer to a humanist and modernist Utopia contrasting with subjugation and oppression experienced by exiled writers like Konrad or Kundera. Later on, the legal actions taken against Orhan Pamuk, who was prosecuted for his political views by the Turkish government in the 1990s, could give rise to similar views. If the homeland authorities appear oppressive, the Europeans are viewed as liberal. And if the homeland regime is reactionary, the Europeans seem progressive. Confronted with the exile experience of the Western European societies, this high esteem could however sometimes be turned into ambivalence and disappointment, as expressed in Pamuk's novel *Ka* and in his essayistic encounter with Europe as an exclusionary political and cultural system (cf. Pamuk 2011).

Being raised with the image of Europe as the paradigm of humanism, modernity and progress, Pamuk points to a certain shift in the view of Europe among Turkish intellectuals, who seem rather disappointed with a European Union which seems incapable of accepting a major Islamic nation as part of the union. The EU's restrictive attitude towards an inclusion of the Turkish nation in the union does not seem to have only economic or constitutional reasons. It also seems like an echo from the Renaissance notion of Europe as a slogan for Christianity. To Pamuk, the restrictive policy of the European countries towards poor immigrants from Africa and Asia seems to contradict the French ideals of liberty, equality and brotherhood, which he once embraced as a young student.

Despite the continuing process of secularisation, religion still seems to play an important part in defining Europe and its borders. Hence Europe is not merely a space, nor is it merely a historical or cultural/religious community. It is an imagined region defined by historical memories, narratives and interpretations of cultural, religious, economic and political traits. These narratives and traits are sometimes uniting and sometimes dividing border markers, but they always depend on the way their interpreters are situated in time and space and on whom they relate to as their "Others". The Norwegian assassin and terrorist who on 22 July 2011 caused the death of 77 innocent people (many of whom were children) was guided by the utopian vision of a culturally homogenous Christian Aryan Europe.

Accordingly, the mass-murderer saw himself in the glorious act of a modern Temple Knight crusader, defending the threatened purity of both national and European culture against jihadism, feminism, multiculturalism and "cultural marxism". To him the extermination of 69 members of the youth organisation of the Norwegian Labour Party was a painful but necessary response to this imagined historical threat. Further investigation and psychiatric examination will have to reveal the extent to which the terrorist was representing a pathologically paranoid mindset of his own, and the extent to which he was an extreme symptom of a certain exclusionary, in some cases even hateful, European historical imaginary.

We propose to establish some major assertions regarding the epistemological and historico-semantic status of the notion of Europe:

- Semantically speaking, the notion of Europe refers to a field of meanings which is dependent on the situations or the relations in which it is used and interpreted.
- Epistemologically speaking, Europe may be viewed as an imagined spatial realm with flexible, permeable and disputable borders, and as an imagined historical realm, a "time-place" or a *chronotope* (Bakhtin 2008), to which certain defining cultural, religious and political narratives, memories and practices may be ascribed.
- The notion of Europe is a complex cultural system, integrating several imagined cultural, religious, economic and political communities into a larger and more complex regional community, constituted by different levels of inclusion and exclusion along various border markers, such as those between culturally dominating and dominated, centre and periphery, natives and exiled, settled and nomads.

To the ancient Greeks, "Europe" could refer either to the homelands of the "hyperborean" Barbarians or to the myth of the abduction of princess Europe, the daughter of king Agenor in the land of the Phoenicians. According to the myth, Zeus fell in love with her and seduced her in the shape of a white bull and persuaded her to sit on his back. Carrying her like this, Zeus swam to Crete, where they bred the son Minos. Thereafter Zeus married Europe to Asterion, who adopted her sons, who thus became emperors of the island. Apparently, the ancient Greeks gave this name to parts of the continents both to the South as well as to today's Central Europe and Northern Africa, "the land of the sunset", which is one possible meaning of Semitic origin of the word "Europe", "Maghreb" being another synonym (in Arabic: al-Magrib, or "where the sun goes down").

In other words, the original "Europe" never was European in our modern meaning of the word, whether as a royal, mythological person or as geographical area defined by the position of the sun (and of the speaker): Phoenicia was situated approximately where we find Lebanon, Syria and Israel today, and the Maghreb countries include Tunisia, Algeria and Morocco. Originally, "Europe" referred both to a certain realm of the world and to the name of the Phoenician princess who was seduced by Zeus (cf. Stråth 2003).

Much later Europe was launched as political-religious slogan or notion. Hence Europe is a situational notion as well as a relational one. Related to almost every epochal or main political shift, the implications of being European, and the borders of *Europeanness*, have been questioned in new ways. Since the 18th century, when the modern notion of Europe came into being by offering a definite replacement of the old parameters like that of Christianity and the Occident, questions regarding its contents, borders and political constitution have been continuously discussed. Following the end of the Cold War, these issues have been especially recurrent in political speeches and academic publications (cf. Eggel & Wehinger 2008).

This modern notion of Europe may be considered to be a construction based on a kind of collective identity. As a consequence of the prevailing concept of national cultural identities, which in the wake of the 19th century nation-building process linked culture with territory, attempts at deciding on a common foundation of a European cultural identity have proved to be extremely challenging. Two strategies of identification have clearly been at work: that of building European identity on a common history such as the Second World War; and that of a strong, opposing image of the Other, e.g. the Oriental Other. In the first case, Europe is conceived of as a project for peace and reconciliation, whereas the notion in the second case is based on a common consciousness of "Europeanism" involving "a political consciousness of the West". This idea came into being after the Ottoman conquest of Constantinople in 1453, when Europe was conceived of as an "active community of Christians" (Mastnak 1997: 16-17).

Attempts are still being made to reconstruct a European "essence" with reference to different cultural, historical and political border markers, such as the heritage from Greek Antiquity, *Lex Romanum*, the Enlightenment or the English and the French revolutions. However, historical experience shows that the borders of this mental map are culturally and politically constructed and hence fluctuating and changeable. It was only in the 18th century that the notion of Europe commonly replaced the notion of Christianity, and only in the early 19th century that the Europeans would start to refer to themselves as Europeans.

This was also the age of emerging nationalism, which in accordance with the idea of Europeanism faced the challenge of finding a historical and rhetorical system of interpretation that could integrate past memory with present experience and future expectations. In our days, we ask ourselves if the European Union basically is political and economic, or if it may be conceived of as a cultural entity where borders tend to disappear. As to the few European states that still have not joined the Union, are their frontiers of another kind than those that constitute the member nations? Is Paris more European than Bucharest? To which European nation does a German-speaking, Jewish author like Kafka belong?

In one of his 18th century epigrams, Goethe wrote: "*Germany, but where is it? I cannot seem to find it on the map*" (Goethe 1908). At the time most Europeans did not consider themselves as such, nor did they see themselves as a part of a national community. Germany was not yet a national state and could only be anticipated by poets and thinkers. It only existed as a complex of feudal states, conducting state affairs against each other. Its external territorial borders were undefined, its culture in reality complex and contradictory. While Goethe was witnessing the battle of Valmy, the first republican victory over the joint European royal forces by the French army in September 1792, he wrote in his notebook that a new era in world history had started: Celebrating his army's victory over the Prussians, the French general Kellermann spurred his stallion, lifted his feather-decorated, military helmet up on top of his impressive sword and shouted: "Vive la nation!". The soldiers copied General Kellermann's example and started repeating loudly and proudly his cry of victory instead of the usual "Vive le roi!" (Boll-Johansen 1992: 19).

The world had changed its idol, Goethe wrote. People had found a new concept to worship and celebrate, a mutual image in which everybody could participate and feel like part of a new grandeur. The idea of a nation, as an imagined community, including all social layers of citizens, was born.

What used to be the most important identity framework for people in Europe is now generally considered outdated. Does the idea of a nation, as discussed by historians and philosophers from Herder, Kliuchevski and Renan to Narochnitskaia and Anderson, belong to our past? In some cases nation-building movements have regarded themselves as emancipating movements opposing established cultural and political forms of hegemony (e.g. hegemonic interpretations of ancient Greek or Roman culture, Italian Renaissance or French Enlightenment culture). But they could also, in given contexts, define themselves as "modern classic", in accordance with inherited and nationally adapted myths and topoi like that of the Golden Age.

When the concept of a nation was launched, it was in many ways formed as an "imagined community". Through media and public education, the grand narratives of the people and its history were presented. In his major work on the origin of nationalism, *Imagined communities*, Benedict Anderson issues warnings against the confusion between imagination and fabrication or falsity:

> In fact, all communities larger than primordial villages of face-to-face contact (and perhaps even these) are imagined. Communities are to be distinguished, not by their falsity/genuineness, but by the style in which they are imagined (Anderson 1991: 6).

So according to Anderson, the modern nation is signified by three features. Firstly by the fact that it is imagined, in the sense that most of its members do not know each other from face-to-face meetings. Secondly the modern nation is imagined as sovereign, which means that the power of deciding the national state's internal and external affairs should belong to the people, and no longer to kings or emperors, as expressed by Kellermann's slogan at Valmy. And thirdly, the modern nation is imagined to be limited by borders, which are sometimes firm, sometimes fluctuating:

> The nation is imagined as limited because even the largest of them, encompassing perhaps a billion living human beings, has finite, if elastic, boundaries, beyond which lie other nations. No nation imagines itself coterminous with mankind (Anderson 1991: 6).

The fluctuating nature of national borders and the need for historical and rhetorical systems of interpretation are features of great relevance to the construction of Europeanness. But while most modern nations have been created on the basis of the political, legal and economic institutions of the national state, a similar development has taken place in Europe through the successive foundations of the forerunners of the EU after World War II, like the ESCS (European Coal and Steel Community) and the EEC (European Economic Community), established by the Treaties of Paris and Rome.

Interestingly enough, Anderson mentions both the dynastic state and the Catholic church as important forerunners of the modern nation. Accordingly, the Catholic church and its community may be viewed as an institutional religious paradigm of Europeanness. During the pilgrimages, travellers were received by Catholic priests in the monitories, who guided the commonly illiterate pilgrims into a correct understanding of the Holy Scripture. But they were also exposed to other Christian pilgrims from various European regions and kingdoms, who could now imagine themselves as part of a larger Christian Europeanness. This sense of belonging could later on be mobilized and turned into a powerful church slogan, as Pope Pius called upon the Christian kings and princes to join forces in the holy battle against the Turks.

Emphasizing the fact that the notion of Europe and of being European refers to an imagined community with historically and semantically unstable border markers does not mean that this notion is sheer fabrication or fiction. The fact that the notion of Europe and Europeanness has turned out to be historically and semantically unstable does not mean that it is useless or "false". Like the uniting narratives of the modern nation, the competing narratives of Europeanness needed to appeal to some cultural ideas and historical experiences that were recognizable to the audience, encouraging a sense of community and belonging and offering them a trustworthy interpretation of the current historical situation. In this sense, the concept of Europe and Europeanness represents a kind of cultural and linguistic *poiesis*: a production of religious, historical and political meaning which in turn anticipated some actual European institutions and historically acting collectives. Bearing this in mind, the notion of Europe and being European will thus be used as an operational and reflexive term in this anthology.

Some kind of mental maps had to be constructed for the modern nation as well as Europe, containing not only past memory but also present experience and future hopes. In his essay on the chronotope and the historical and aesthetic development of the novel genre, Mikhail Bakhtin points to the chronotope as a kind of time-place, where time is visualized as space and space is intensified by the movement of time. In this way, flowing time is limited by spatial borders.

Bakhtin's description of the chronotope has striking parallels with the imaginaries of nationality and Europeanness. In both cases, the national borders not only define geographical realms, they also give meaning and direction to historical memory and experience. Hence modern patriot and nationalist movements were challenged to find a system of interpretation capable of integrating their experience of present decay, their conceptions of "imagined antiquity" (Hobsbawm) and their utopian hopes of future prosperity in a recognizable fashion.

Such temporary processes of cultural change and self-interpretation were partly reflected by the emerging philosophy of history, allowing the nation-building elites to ask for the inner necessity of cultural change and national traditions, which now might be conceived of as the nation's history.

A major precondition for the emergence of this new philosophical discipline, and along with it the rise of modern nationalism, was a fundamental shift of the European time conception, which Walter Benjamin has described as a turn from the Messianic time conception of the Middle Ages to the modern conception of time as "empty" and "homogenous" (cf. Benjamin 1997: 700-703). According to the Messianic time conception, time was inseparably linked to the place and to the expectation that Messiah would return at any point of time. It was therefore unnecessary to conceive of time in more extensive historical lines. To the medieval mind, there was a "now" that was inseparably linked to a "here". Time only existed if it "took place" and was conceived of as an expandable moment which was inseparably tied to the locality in which it was experienced. Places far away were accordingly projected far back in time.

In the wake of new 18<sup>th</sup> century discoveries and technical inventions, such as the invention of the chronometer and the synchronization of the homogenous global time by the division of time meridians, time could be gradually separated from space, and a new conception of time as empty and homogenous emerged (cf. Anderson 1996: 22-36). To the medieval mind, time had been filled with mythological and religious meaning and stories, serving as moral examples. In the new homogenous time conception, these stories were replaced by history, which in turn was filled with new meanings and narratives, such as the concept of progress.

The European experiences with non-European civilisations had confirmed a certain feeling of accelerating progress among the Europeans, allowing them to think of history in a linear or helical scheme of technical, scientific and political progress, for instance in terms of Enlightenment, freedom and human rights. Within this new historical scheme of self-interpretation, some cultures could be thought of as modern and progressive, while others were conceived of as backward. The German historian Reinhart Koselleck has also referred to this period as *Sattelzeit* (saddle time) or *Schwellenzeit* (threshold time); that is a time in which the Europeans experienced a growing gap between the current realm of experience and their horizon of future expectation, allowing new political ideologies and utopian narratives such as those of the national community and its future prosperity to emerge. Accordingly, Voltaire and Kant launched competing utopian drafts of a future European League of Nations, ruled by democratically elected governments, thereby securing the welfare of their citizens and striving towards the regulative ideal of the perpetual peace and happiness of mankind by mutual agreements and obligations. Kant's liberal Utopia of a democratic League of Nations would later on be disputed by the German poet Novalis, or Fredrich von Hardenberg, who in his essay "Christianity or Europe" idolized the Christian medieval culture as a state of religious-aesthetic harmony, hoping that the alienating process of modernization would eventually dissolve itself and make room for a new religious spirituality in a future Europe.

In our time, the definition of Europe as being synonymous with medieval Catholic Christianity has been relaunched and radicalized in a rather dangerous and martial manner inside the anti-jihad movement, which brought fuel to the fire that exploded so tragically in Norway on 22 July 2011.

These modern historical interpretation systems could also integrate inherited religious myths and traditions and popular stereotypes and self-images of the people as a "collective subject" (Koselleck) and climate theories (e.g. the patriot myth of the Norwegians as descendants of bold Giants, or Hermann the Cherusc as the founding father of the modern German cultural nation, etc.)

In both cases, the national myths of origin eventually had to be confronted or sometimes harmonized with civic ideas of European *Bildung* (educational culture), emerging along with nationalism in the late 18th and early 19th centuries.

This transnational, educational ideology was oriented towards both ancient Greek and Roman culture and aesthetics and a utopian Christian humanism as dividing lines excluding from the aesthetic, religious and utopian realm of Europe not only the uneducated "Barbarians" from within but also the "Orientals" from the outside. Thus the concepts of Europe and Europeanness were launched by romanticist poets like Novalis and Chateaubriand in the early 19th century, drawing on the 15th century application of the notion of Europe as a Christian Church slogan directed against the Muslim Ottomans on the one hand. On the other hand, the conception of Europe was temporalized and virtualized through their romanticist philosophy of history, projecting Europe into a future spiritual and aesthetic state of harmony, unity and dissolved alienation.

In the age of Enlightenment and early colonialism, Europe was conceived of as a chronotope of progress (Bakhtin), i.e. as a symbolic spatialization of a historically temporalized and individualized project (Koselleck). On the outskirts of this chronotope of progress, the Orient was imagined as the chronotope of stasis and invariability (Saïd). In this way, emerging colonialism and capitalism provided the Europeans with an outside view on themselves, affirming their experience of accelerating technical, financial and political progress and scientific enlightenment.

This outside perspective or *exotopi* (Bakhtin) generated a certain critical self-reflection (Diderot, Herder, Forster), and sometimes even cultural pessimism (Rousseau). From an outside point of view, European civilisation appeared to be rational and progressive, but also fragmented and alienated.

Within such aesthetic, cultural and ideological frameworks, the notion of Europe was nourished by romanticist aesthetics, making new transcendental division lines between nature and freedom, the limited and the unlimited, instrumental and "pure" art as self-purpose, and between original and imitating culture. The romantic concept of originality, launched by Herder, contained a certain ambiguity, drawing on both a linguistic conception of the individuality of the "people" and its popular traditions (poetry, music, dance etc.) on the one hand. On the other hand, the concept of originality could refer to the cultural achievements of the artist's genius, both expressing the individuality of his "people's voice" and exhausting the human possibilities.

The Herderian concept of national and cultural individuality was clearly a reaction against the cultural hegemony of both ancient Greek and Roman, French Enlightenment culture and European colonialism. Herder was underlining the necessity of evaluating each nation, people and culture by its inherent standards. The Herderian differential conception of culture, which was opposed to Rousseau's and Kant's universalistic conceptions, has been a major inspiration to modern conceptions of multiculturalist politics and minority rights (Taylor). However, the Herderian relativistic concept of national individuality was also embedded in a universalistic conception of a common humanity, stressing each nation's and culture's ability to contribute by making the best of its given conditions and by learning from other cultures.

In his major historico-philosophical work *Ideen zur Philosophie der Geschichte der Menschheit,* Johann Gottfried Herder depicts the progress of historical epochs as a relay between hegemonic civilisations, with the torch of culture being handed over from one nation to another. Starting with the ancient Sumerians and Egyptians, the "mother torch" was handed over to the Babylonians, Persians and Greeks, who in turn handed it over to the Romans and so on (cf. Herder 1967: 227ff.).

What does this torch of civilisation illuminate, and what does it leave in darkness? First of all it sheds light on a certain historical and cultural concept of hegemony and hegemonic heritage: the idea that certain ethnic groups and civilisations throughout history have been politically dominant and given more significant contributions to civilisation and Europeanness than others. It also means that some cultures lost their hegemonic status once they had handed over the torch of civilisation and thereby left their age of glory behind.

The Herderian concept of cultural didactics and hybridization by intercultural and historical learning processes drew on the classical humanist conception of *translatio studii,* (i.e. the transfer of knowledge or learning from one geographical place and time to another), by way of translating the inheritance of hegemonic classical traditions. Herder wanted to emancipate young nations and cultures from the restraining weight of hegemonic traditions, thereby establishing a dialectics between national cultural self-maintenance and a common humanity.

Hence romanticist aesthetics, nationalist ideology and the philosophy of history were responding to certain early modernity "threshold experiences" (Koselleck) like the growing gap between the realm of experience and the horizon of expectation (cf. Koselleck 1989a). In this realm the notions of nation and Europeanness were temporalized and received political, historical, ideological and utopian meaning and tension. According to Reinhart Koselleck, this semantic change was also significant to the structural development of collective identities through asymmetric counter-conceptions like the division between citizens and barbarians, Christians and pagans, Europeans and Non-Europeans, Occidentals and Orientals (cf. Koselleck 1989b).

In the early 19th century, when the Europeans first really started referring to themselves as Europeans, the national idea regarding political and cultural hegemony and colonization reached its peak. In this situation, culturally constructed conceptions of "race" could in some cases further a sense of European unity (the Aryan myth), and in other cases affirm linguistic and cultural division lines (Slavonic vs. Germanic vs. Gallic vs. Semite vs. Celtic etc.) The aesthetic and anthropological division lines would sometimes affirm, sometimes question the religious dividing lines between European Christianity, and the Islamic or Jewish Orient.

Some European artists and intellectuals (including Herder, Goethe, Schlegel, Nerval, Flaubert, Renan, Loti and Strindberg) also sought vitalizing cultural impulses from Arab, Turkish, Jewish or Indian culture, opposing the sublime Orient to the decadent Occident.

Through travel descriptions and other literature, the impression of cultural hegemonic centres associated with old and new hegemonic capitals (London, Paris, Rome) or powers like England, France and Italy was confirmed. At the same time, travelling writers and intellectuals like Wolstonecraft, Loti and Renan took interest in the outskirts of Europe. In Russian literature, the image of the progressive and rational Russia was cultivated on the one hand, while the Caucasus region was regarded as wild, untamed but vital on the other. Accordingly, the Balkans were often regarded as an unruly, chaotic conflict region ("Balkanism").

Scandinavia, Scotland and Switzerland could also be subjects of utopian projections and exoticism. Artists and writers from these regions, like Ibsen and Hamsun, could act as travelling and writing Orientalists, thereby referring to themselves as Europeans through the asymmetric division line towards the Oriental Other. Barents, Shetland, Greenland and Scotland could be conceived of in exotic terms as part of the Ultima Thule myth of the endless landscapes of the European outskirts and their freedom-loving inhabitants (cf. Sagmo 1998). In some cases, like Wolstonecraft's travel description from Norway, the inhabitants could be described as rude or simply as the negation of urban European *Bildung* culture (cf. Wolstonecraft 1796). In other cases, like the travel description of the German professor Theodor Mügge or the novels of Pierre Loti, Norway and Iceland were conceived of as a zone in which ancient Germanic virtues had wintered and survived. Bearing such liberating and revitalizing potentials, these countries were more closely associated with the "universal history" (Kant, Hegel) of colonialism. At the same time, the European periphery could represent a kind of outside perspective with regard to the inherited colonial conception of European culture as progressive and historically rational.

During the 18th century, the topographical realistic travel description was disparaged in favour of subjective, fictional travel literature, as in the cases of Wolstonecraft, Loti and Hamsun. In our days, travel literature is experiencing a cultural reappraisal, whereby the romanticist division between "higher" literary fiction and "lower" non-fiction is challenged and partly overcome. In this situation aesthetics is challenged to redefine and extend its realm to include wider parts of our sensual world and culture, allowing new discourses on Europeanness to develop. In contrast with the inherited "continental" *Bildung* culture and its exclusionary attitude towards "low", "provincial" culture, imitating culture, popular culture, carnevalesque culture etc., the new discourses of Europeanness tend to embrace border crossings between artistic genres and media, between "high" and "low" culture and assumed national traditions.

In modernist aesthetics, responding to new historical ruptures and threshold experiences, the transcendental division lines of romanticist aesthetics have gradually been replaced by more concrete borders, thresholds and division lines. Elaborating the experience of war, crisis and rupture, modernist aesthetics from Baudelaire to Benjamin emphasizes modern urban experience and architecture, borders and transgressions between dream and consciousness, language and experience, launching new discourses of Europeanness. Historical and aesthetic manifestations of borders and thresholds contribute to the configuration of a modernist and postmodernist aesthetics. This configuration has also foregrounded a metropolitan trend in lifestyle and architecture, which has called attention to the borders between dream and reality, language and experience, synaesthesia and synecdoche. A new aesthetic framework is now emerging for the reinterpretation of the distinctively *European* in art, literature and philosophy.

This book is divided into three sections which have been subdivided into thematically related chapters. As individual contributions they are in some cases placed in dialogue with each other working in pairs on similar geographical or thematic contexts.

Thus, following this introduction, the first section treats the aesthetics of hegemony and conceptions of centre and periphery in Europe. The second section presents and discusses various conceptions and constructions of national, regional and artistic identity in European literature and art, whereas the third section contains discussions of the aesthetics and poetics of borders and border crossing in contemporary art and fiction.

Opening the first section, Siri Skjold Lexau gives in her chapter, "Hegemonic Ideals – Turkish Architecture of the 20th Century", a thorough description of modernism and the use of historicist Ottoman styles in its political and cultural context, especially in the period following the proclamation of the Turkish republic in 1923. She argues that the architectural styles discussed are dictated by political-cultural hegemonies formed in order to modernize Turkey by instilling specific values in the population, and that modern architecture, urban planning and design had central roles in this project. Lexau details the involvement of German and French architects in various periods, along with German-trained Turkish architects, and argues that Ottoman style influences, reread as a Turkish style of architecture, mainly appear on building exteriors, with the use of interior space formed more in line with Western modernist ideals.

In the second chapter, Steven Ellis provides a detailed historical presentation of the creation of the English Pale in Ireland in the late Middle Ages, the process of bordering the Pale on discursive and material levels, and the gradual institutionalisation of internal zones of "marches" (a border zone) and "maghery" (an internal zone of peace) within the Pale. The chapter refers to an ongoing debate involving different theories of historical Irish and English identity in Ireland. It also addresses the relevance of agricultural, political and legal changes affecting the border zone, taking as its focus historical bordering practices connected to a dominant nation in Europe. It both provides a historiographical contribution to the book as a whole and contextualizes this within contemporary concerns as expressed within Irish historiography.

In the third chapter of this section, Kåre Johan Mjør gives a narrative and historical analysis of Vasilii O. Kliuchevskii's history of Russia, with particular emphasis on his notion of Russia as both unique ("individual") and European. In addition, Mjør examines Kliuchevskii's historical thinking in the contexts of European nineteenth-century historicism and Russian historiography in general. Mjør argues that the liberal Kliuchevskii belonged neither to the "westerner" nor to the "slavophile" schools of Russian thought, but rather was seeing Russia as unique and not belatedly following Western European models of development, thus he was clearly placing it between Europe and Asia.

The chapter's main involvement in the theme of the borders of Europe is its focus on how Kliuchevskii (and by extension different Russian historians and thinkers) set the borders of Europe and of Russia, and thus it points to the following chapter on Narochnitskaia, where Jardar Østbø succinct discussion arguing that the "romantic realism" (Morozov) of Nataliia Narochnitskaia's idealist portrayal of Russian/European geopolitics is deeply based on a cultural essentialization of religion, which in turn forms the basis for the idea of Russia being the true Europe. According to this chapter, this world-view is both nationalist and universalist, the latter countering any desires for dialogue expressed in Narochnitskaia's cultural initiatives in Western Europe. The "Borders of Europe" theme is retained in the implications of cultural definitions of Narochnitskaia's type, both in their play on simultaneous inclusion and exclusion and their focus on the geopolitical dimensions of the Baltic-to-Black-Sea border zone ("The Eastern Question").

In chapter five, Per Olav Folgerø examines details in the frescoes in early Sanctuary of S. Maria Antiqua in Rome. He argues that they show evidence of not only Byzantine culture but also Palestinian theology and iconography in 7th-8th century Rome. Folgerø continues to discuss various possible places and ways in which this cultural cross-over may have happened, concluding that at the very least, Rome was in this period a cultural melting pot.

In chapter six, Knut Ove Arntzen suggests an image of the border as a dialogic space based on the network of triangulation points which envelope Friedrich Georg Wilhelm von Struve's pioneering mapping of a geodetic arc (1816-1855) from the Black Sea to North Norway: i.e. along and within the border zone often imagined as dividing Western Europe from Russia. This suggestion is followed by a combined philosophical meditation and appraisal of current tendencies in art, especially theatre. The chapter gives a tour of contemporary theatre projects located roughly along the line of Struve's arc.

Chapter seven, "Multiple dimension and multiple borderlines – cultural work and borderline experience", describes several examples of crossing borders in performing arts practice. Artists who boldly open up different territories, independently of whether their borders are of an aesthetic, geographical or political nature, enrich their experience by diverse cultural influences and innovate artistic forms on many levels as is shown by particular projects created in the European periphery with a special focus on Eastern Europe. In this chapter, Gordana Vruk gives an overview and an analysis of the tendency to cross formal and geographical borders in art in the new Europe, as seen from a "periphery" perspective.

Lillian Jorunn Helle opens the second section with a chapter on the orientalized Caucasus as an alter and alternative ego in Russian classical literature. Her chapter focuses upon the relationship between the colonizer and the colonized as depicted in the so-called Caucasus texts of Russian literature. It aims to show the flexibility and the shifting constellations of this relationship, ranging from rigid binary oppositions to complex forms of cultural interaction. The chapter gives an account of different forms of Orientalist and colonialist imaging of the Caucasus in Russian literature of the 19th century, showing how the imagined Caucasus relates to Russian self-imaging both as an Eastern other and as a border-destabilizing inner and alternative self. The chapter is related to the borders of Europe theme through its focus on the nature of the cultural bordering going on in these literary texts, and also relates to the discussion of Russia's place in relationship to European borders in the chapters on Kliuchevskii and Narochnitskaia.

In this section's second chapter, Helge Vidar Holm uses theories from Koselleck and Bakhtin to discuss Edward Saïd's readings of two novels by Gustave Flaubert, *Salammbô* and *Bouvard et Pécuchet*. While recognizing Flaubert's critique of Orientalism, Saïd still emphasizes the orientalizing effect of the novels. But he also recognizes the contrasts between Flaubert's handlings of time and a hegemonic historiography of time, a mainly orientalist historiography, exemplified by that of the French historian Jules Michelet. Like most of the other chapters in this section, Holm's chapter addresses aesthetic versions of cultural East-West borderings. Like the previous chapter, it has a specific focus on us/them-relationships, bringing in the German historian Reinhart Koselleck's writings on historical concepts in a rather unusual combination of theoretical references. The chapter's use of Bakhtin focuses on his late work on "creative chronotopes".

In the third chapter, Torgeir Skorgen reads Mozart's opera "The Abduction from the Seraglio" especially for its implications in its national political context, for its use of the adventure chronotope and for its carnivalesque aspects, thus implying several Bakhtinian concepts. Skorgen makes observations on Mozart's opinion that the text should be subservient to the music in opera, and uses the Catelanian Calixtio Bieito's production of the opera to develop his discussion of orientalist borderings. The chapter suggests that looking at the borders of Europe in a narrative makes it possible to scale down the perspective and look at individual border crossings in the work (religious conversion, infiltration of the harem, and abduction).

The fourth chapter, by Sigrun Åsebø, examines the work of two contemporary Norwegian woman artists, A K Dolven and Mari Slaatelid, against the background of theories of landscape art and a Norwegian history of art. It argues that the focus on the body in the work of these women artists (e.g. placing naked female bodies in a landscape) disrupts the disembodied gaze of the male Romantic landscape and thus standard national histories of art, deeply connected as they are to the power of landscape art to create national imaginaries. This argument involves the border theme of the book at various points: among them the connection between the borders of the landscape (or the composite landscape of a canon of landscape art), national identification among viewers, and the actual borders of the nation; and the foregrounding of bodily borders as a way of disrupting the gaze. The European dimension is left implied by the subject matter, art traditions in a European nation on the edge of Europe, and the gendering of European identities.

The book's third and last section, dedicated to border aesthetics and poetics, opens by a chapter on the borders between different media. Jørgen Bruhn's "On the Borders of Poetry and Art: The Destructive Search for Media Purity from Lessing to Post Modernity" addresses the way in which medial borders have been conceived within different traditions of aesthetics and (inter)media theory. The chapter begins with a brief sketch of the history of aesthetic borders, leading to an important question in contemporary cultural theory: What is a medium, and what is exactly a border of a medium? The chapter's attempt to define a medium, and its borders, leads to a terminological suggestion that may prompt new ways of thinking about media and media borders.

In the second chapter of this section, Øyunn Hestetun aims to show how Eva Hoffman's memoir of exile from Poland to Canada *Lost in Translation: Life in a New Language* (1989) is a work of self-definition and "finding at-homeness". Eva Hoffman writes *as* an exile, and *of* exile from her lost home in post-war Europe. By foregrounding the way in which the crossing of geographical borders is paralleled by cultural transplantation and linguistic transposition, Hoffman's tale contributes to our understanding of the experience of border crossing. The discussion focuses on structures, tropes and the representation of the liminal position of border crossing, and how the memoir – in "writing exile, writing home" – presents a meditation on language, self-knowledge and identity.

Inspired by Julia Kristeva's writing on identity and exile, Sissel Lægreid argues in the section's third chapter that three central poets of German-Jewish exile, Paul Celan, Rose Ausländer and Nelly Sachs, address in their poetry the "fragile boundaries and temporal equilibrums" of their exile situation. Their poetry is caught in Ernst Bloch's simultaneous-non-simultaneous ("Gleichzeitigkeit des Ungleichzeitigen") and in an aesthetics of the transitory. The chapter aims thus to examine the aesthetic effects of exile and estrangement, not unlike the chapter on Eva Hoffman's exile experience, and reaches a similar conclusion: these experiences prove productive to writing. The chapter analyses poetry connected to a central border experience in European historical memory, and makes a good argument for the relevance of Deleuze and Guattari's concepts of deterritorialization and reterritorialization to the aesthetic effects.

In the book's last chapter, Jørgen Lund investigates the concept of the threshold as formulated by Walter Benjamin for its potential "thingly" resistance to a posited border discipline based on a disembodied view of space. In doing so, it develops new perspectives for a border aesthetics which go beyond clichéed avantgardist aesthetics of transgression.

Lund shows that Benjamin's aesthetically informed reflections on borders come together in a certain concept of the threshold. Marking a transition from a way of thinking in mathematically accountable localities and significances to a certain materiality or "thingness", the threshold offers an alternative to present conceptions of border aesthetics. Although itself a kind of border, it represents a sort of bodily event, a sensibility or animation coming about precisely as a departure from "border discipline".

Let us now summarise the complex aim of this book in a complex question: In what ways has the configuration of new aesthetic motif clusters along with the thematization of threshold experiences, crisis, and fragmentation influenced the concept and discursive formulations of the distinctively *European*? In order to describe the processes indicated in this question, the answers suggested in this book draw on a differentiated conception of borders. Important references are the works of modernist thinkers such as Ernst Cassirer and Walter Benjamin, who have developed theories of the border as a threshold ("Schwelle"). Their theorizing, when brought together with concepts borrowed from thinkers who have developed theories of modernity in the age of globalization, provide important aesthetic, hermeneutic and cultural-poetic tools of analysis for studies aiming to establish a better understanding of why European borders are conceived not only as borders of territorial demarcation, but also, increasingly, as membranes for dialogue and exchange.

# Bibliography

Anderson, B. (1991). *Imagined Communities. Reflections on the Origin and Spread of Nationalism.* London & New York: Verso.

Bakhtin, M. (2008). "Forms of time and chronotope in the novel". *The Dialogical Imagination. Four essays by M.M. Bakhtin,* trans. Emerson, C. & Holquist, M. Austin: University of Texas Press.

Boll-Johansen, H. (1992). *De franske. Fransk identitet – myte og virkelighed.* Copenhagen: Gyldendal.

Eggel, D. and Wehinger, B. (2008). "Zur Europaidee im 18. Jahrhunders" in: Eggel, D. & Wehinger, B. (eds.) *Europavorstellungen des 18. Jahrhunderts. Imagining Europe in the 18th century.* Berlin: Wehrmann Verlag.

Goethe, J.W. (1908). *Sprüche in Reimen; zahme Xenien und Invektiven,* ed. by Max Hecker. Leipzig: Insel-Verlag.

Herder, J.G. (1967). "Ideen zur Philosophie der Geschichte der Menschheit" in: Suphan, B. (ed.). *Herders Sämtliche Werke.* Hildesheim, vol. 14, 227 ff.

Koselleck, R. (1989a). "'Erfahrungsraum' und 'Erwartungshorizont' – Zwei historische Kategorien" in: Koselleck, R. *Vergangene Zukunft. Zur Semantik geschichtlicher Zeiten.* Frankfurt a.M.: Suhrkamp Verlag.

Koselleck, R. (1989b). "Zur historisch-politischen Semantik asymmetrischer Gegenbegriffe" in: Koselleck, R. *Vergangene Zukunft. Zur Semantik geschichtlicher Zeiten.* Frankfurt a.M.: Suhrkamp Verlag.

Pamuk, O. (2011). "Drømmen om Europa". *Aftenposten,* 08.01.2011.

Renan, E. (1882). Qu'est-ce qu'une nation? Conférence faite en Sorbonne, le 11 Mars 1882 http://fr.wikisource.org/wiki/Qu%E2%80%99est-ce_qu%E2%80%99une_nation_%3F. Accessed January 13, 2011.

Sagmo, I. (1998). "Norge – et forbilde eller et utviklingsland? Folk og land i første halvdel av 1800-tallet – sett med tyske reisendes øyne" in: Sørensen, Ø. (ed.). *Jakten på det norske. Perspektiver på utviklingen av en norsk nasjonal identitet på 1800-tallet.* Oslo: Ad Notam Gyldendal.

Saïd, E.W. (1978). *Orientalism. Western Conceptions of the Orient.* New York: Pantheon Books.

Simon P. (2011). *So Beautiful or So What.* Hear Music/Concord Music Group.

Stråth, B. (2003). The Meaning of Europe. http://www.helsinki.fi/nes/the%20meanings%20 of%20europe%20helsinki.pdf.

Swiderski, B. (1988). "Østeuropæernes Europa". *Europas opdagelse: Historien om en idé.* Copenhagen: Christian Ejlers.

Wolstonecraft, M. (1796). *Letters Written during a Short Residence in Sweden, Norway and Denmark.* London: Joseph Johnson.

# First section:
# Aesthetic Hegemonies and Conceptions of Centre and Periphery in Europe

# Hegemonic Ideals: Turkish Architecture of the 20th Century

*Siri Skjold Lexau*

## Politics and architecture

Political opposition, the founding of the Committee of Union and Progress (CUP) in 1913, and political processes in the wake of World War I all led to the proclamation of the Republic of Turkey on 29 October 1923, with the war hero and nationalist Mustafa Kemal as its president. After 1913, the Turkish people's main criterion of identity was to be its sense of nationality, of what it means to be *Turkish*, as opposed to the earlier Ottoman *Islamic* identity. Kemal was honoured with the title *Gazi* (war hero and fighter for the Islamic faith) in 1921, and adopted the name *Atatürk* (Turkey's father) in 1934. He led Turkey's only political party, the Republican People's Party (RPP), which had just one principal aim on its agenda: the modernisation of society, on structural, social and cultural levels.

The Swiss-French architect Le Corbusier (pseudonym for Charles-Édouard Jeanneret-Gris, 1887-1965) was a central spokesman for the ideology of modernism in Europe. His enquiring gaze and the notes he made during his *grand tours* to many of Europe's important historical towns constituted a type of architectural research which he used systematically as a basis for his own architectural theory and practice. Visiting Istanbul for the first time in 1911, he documented his trip by means of a diary and sketchbooks (Le Corbusier 2002). The observations Le Corbusier made on that journey offer a valuable insight into Istanbul during the first decade of the 20th century: "Wooden houses with large spread-out roofs warm their purple colours amidst fresh greenery and within enclosures whose mystery delights me, [although] they group themselves quite harmoniously around all these summits formed by really enormous mosques ..." (Le Corbusier 2007: 90). The fact that this urban structure was so ruthlessly obliterated in the course of the 20th century was something even the modernist Le Corbusier characterised as catastrophic (Le Corbusier 2007: 160). He also described with great sorrow a massive fire that reduced 9,000 houses to ashes. It is precisely because of all the fires which still destroy the traditional, Turkish timber houses that even Le Corbusier

*Fig. 1. Amcazade Hüseyin Paşa Yalısı, Asian shore of Bosporus north of Anadolu, probably from the 17ᵗʰ century. Considered one of the most important examples of Ottoman wooden architecture. D-DAI-IST-KB9404 (photographer and year unknown).*

recognised as masterpieces that the city is constantly being renewed, albeit rarely for the better.

A further source of pressure on the architectural heritage was the new, Western-inspired architecture that the so-called Young Turks wanted for their new country. The Young Turks (*Jön Türkler*), a movement of dissent founded largely by military cadets in 1889, attracted support from artistic circles as well as among civil servants and scientists. The Young Turks, who opposed the Otto-man sultanate in general and the rule of Sultan Hamid II in particular, became a significant political force in 1908, providing a springboard for Atatürk's rise to power a few years later. Le Corbusier warned Atatürk that the new archi-tectural ideals threatened to undermine appreciation of the masterpieces of earlier architects, which included mosques, hammams, and the original and richly varied Ottoman timber architecture. He later regretted that this posi-tion had thrust him onto the sidelines, as recorded in an interview of 1949:

> If I had not committed the most strategic mistake of my life in the letter I wrote to Atatürk,
> I would be planning the beautiful city of Istanbul, instead of my competitor Henri Prost.

In this notorious letter, I foolishly recommended to the greatest revolutionary hero of a new nation to leave Istanbul as it was, in the dirt and dust of centuries (Bozdoğan: 67).

I shall take Le Corbusier's perspective as a point of departure for this article, which will explore some of the architectural ideals of the young Turkish nation during its first half century as a republic. Le Corbusier also drew attention to what will concern us in the following: architecture as a marker of political hegemony. In taking a closer look at the dynamics of architectural developments in 20th century Turkey, it is important to note the nuances and geographical differences affecting the concept of "modernism". Architectural history was dominated by the Euro-centric and North American perspective until late in the 20th century. The past three decades, however, have seen the publication of considerable academic material that explores many different histories and expressive idioms associated with modernism in non-Western societies.

Traditionally, studies of non-Western cultures have aimed to explore the exotic. Cultures outside the industrialised regions were seen as interesting primarily because they represented the unfamiliar, often a culture that was viewed as underdeveloped relative to that of the West, to the extent that the latter could be treated as a single entity. Modernity was regarded as a European-American category, which "others" could import, accept, or perhaps oppose, but which they could not reproduce from within their own cultural sphere. Edward W. Saïd gives a detailed account of this cultural "asymmetry" in his reference work *Orientalism* from 1978.

In countries outside the regions of Western Europe and North America, the phenomenon of "modernisation" did not always have far-reaching social consequences, unlike the profound social changes of the 19th century and the transition to industrialised, urban and market-oriented structures. In some places modernisation constituted an official programme, developed and implemented either by a colonial power or by an ambitious elite in authoritarian nations, by regimes that placed great emphasis on architecture and urban planning as a kind of physical embodiment of policy. A full consideration of the architectural idioms that were regarded as modern takes us far beyond conventional notions of modernist architecture as the expression of an international style, stripped bare of national or traditional features.

By the time Atatürk turned his full attention to the construction of modern Turkey, he had already outmanoeuvred the central power holders of Ottoman society in favour of the idea of Turkey as a nation-state. The Sultan was deposed as head of the Empire in 1922, while the top religious leader of all Muslims, the Caliph of Istanbul, was dismissed in 1924. Admittedly, Atatürk installed leading members of the former political and religious bodies in new positions of authority, but it is still remarkable that one leading individual could succeed in binding the loyalty of such an ethnically diverse population to a single national identity, that of Turkey.

In order to make such radical, centrally imposed reforms appear fundamental and worth striving for, and in order to render this value set functional on an individual level, it was necessary to establish a range of ideals and concepts concerning what was best suited to serve the nation and the individual as *hegemonic* and *legitimate*. Whereas the substance of the former can be determined and implemented by the state, the latter poses a far greater challenge. In a non-authoritarian society at least, values must be recognised as morally and legally valid. Originally, the concept of hegemony was applied to those Greek city-states that dominated other city-states, and by analogy the term has been used to describe any state that exercises dominance or leadership over another. The dominance of an empire over its component and subordinate states can also be characterised as hegemonic.

The Italian politician and philosopher Antonio Gramsci (1891-1937) developed a revised and expanded definition of the concept of hegemony that could be applied to social classes. Where society is characterised by *cultural* diversity, it can be dominated by one social class and its set of values, norms and practices. This in turn forms the basis for a complex system of political, social and economic values that establish themselves as *dominant* (Gramsci: 10, Adamson: 149). Gramsci describes social groups that do not initially represent a hegemony. But when individuals organise themselves into social classes or class alliances in response to foregoing class struggles, they are able to achieve a legitimate consensus in civil society, and thus to attain a dominant and frequently "hegemonic" position. Thus a *cultural hegemony* is formed. Given Gramsci's analysis and reasoning, it might seem to be straining a point to adopt the term as a central principle in the current study. In Turkey it was single individuals as members of the new regime rather than oppressed classes who established a new hegemony, not least through the use of architecture as a crucial instrument. In other words, the term is not applied here as directly analogous to Gramsci's concept, although I still consider it applicable to any newly established power configuration that encompasses as much ethnic diversity as we find in Turkey. Over the years, however, this regime showed an ambivalence about how to project its own status to the outside world. It is possible to identify clear but changing architectural preferences among the major national construction projects that have been implemented in Turkey.

Atatürk's programme of modernisation entailed radical changes to society on many levels, affecting government, power structures, and people's everyday lives down to the finest detail. In 1926, Islamic law (*sharia*) was replaced with a new legal system based on that of Swiss legal practice, and in 1927 Arabic script was replaced with the Latin alphabet. A completely new form of civilisation was to be introduced, which meant a fundamental change from the ethnic and organisationally fragmented Ottoman Empire to a new, Western and secular nation. Considerable emphasis was placed on the outward aesthetics of everything from clothing and hairstyles to architecture and urban planning as a way of providing momentum for this change.

The development of what we might call leading architectural cultures, in the plural and evolving, in the young Turkey says a lot about the directions and architectural styles that established themselves as hegemonic. Turkey has always been a transition zone between West and East, between Occidental and Oriental cultures, both within the very different bounds of the Ottoman Empire, and today within the country's current borders. This is clearly reflected in its architecture, not least in the period we will explore here. When we consider the buildings in Ankara, which was proclaimed capital in 1923, it is as if Western-inspired architecture, with its elements of international style, became the norm from one day to the next. Even so, it is interesting to study how the cultures of Ottoman and Western modernist architecture were introduced and how they were balanced with each other over time, and how preferences for both national and international styles established hegemonies and influenced developments. Those at the forefront of the hectic construction of a new capital, thanks not least to their intellectual ballast, made crucial contributions to the design of Ankara's central districts. Both France and Germany had played leading parts in building up the art academies where architects had been educated since the mid-18th century. Architects from these two countries in particular also set their stamp on architectural developments both before and after the founding of the new Republic of Turkey.

## Ottoman-European architecture as the façade of modernity

In the period 1908-18, prior to the proclamation of Ankara as Turkey's new capital, the Young Turks initiated a modernisation of Istanbul's technical infrastructure. By that time, moves to improve sanitation systems and the transport network were already underway in an effort to revitalise the Empire physically and restore the "sick man" of Europe, the Sultanate, to health. In the same period, new architectural aesthetics also began to appear in Turkey, an idiom which in many ways symbolised both the ideological aspirations and the cultural complexities of the Empire in its final years. Istanbul was still the capital of the Ottoman Empire, and it was there that a form of architecture emerged that was at one and the same time European, to some extent modern, and Ottoman. In the political climate of the period, it was also essential that architecture could be defined as *Turkish*.

Around the turn of the 20th century, foreign architects were hired to tackle major projects in Istanbul. For instance, Alexander Vallaury (1850-1921), a Franco-Turkish architectural graduate of the Beaux-Arts Academy in Paris, designed the government building for public debt (*Düyun-i Umumiye Idaresi*, 1899) in Cağaloğlu, Eminönü; while the German architect August Jachmund designed the Sirkeci railway station, which was built in 1888-90.

This station was the terminus for the famous Orient Express, which ran between various European cities and Istanbul from 1883, initially with the support of interlinking forms of transport. The station building's main façade is strictly symmetrical, with a portal motif that rises all the way to the cornice. The design of this motif is familiar from Ottoman palaces. The window openings have horseshoe arches and are shaped in a way that immediately evokes associations with Arabic architecture, while the whole structure is crowned with a type of roof that was common in both the French and the German baroque. The corners are emphasised with towers that are similarly reminiscent of Ottoman architecture. Both Vallaury and Jachmund used Islamic-Ottoman elements, especially in the building's exterior. The two architects latched on to trends in the political climate that had the potential to be reflected in architecture: people preferred to speak of building upon and modernising the existing regime and the culture of the Ottoman Empire, rather than starting an architectural revolution and throwing all traditional values overboard.

The architecture represented institutions that were meant to serve Istanbul's international relations, so it was not unnatural that it played on both European and Ottoman associations. Functional aspects and the treatment of volumes were influenced by Western architecture; while arches, columns, articulating features and wide overhanging eaves were inspired by the Ottoman architectural heritage. Even so, none of these buildings when viewed as a whole resembles the architecture we associate with pre-19th century Ottoman society. New construction methods allowed for new shapes, a different organisation of architectural elements, and larger openings to let in light. Not least, there were innovations in the use of iron and glass in the construction of railway stations, shopping arcades, greenhouses and exhibition buildings in particular. In Istanbul this hybrid architecture with partly local roots was employed especially for buildings associated with Western culture and the development of international communications.

Turkish architecture of the early 20th century bore many features of Ottoman influence, but it was also constructed using contemporary technology: reinforced concrete, iron and glass. In this sense it could also be called *modern*. One of the earliest examples is the Central Post Office in Sirkeci, Istanbul, designed by Mehmet Vedat Bey (1873-1942) and erected in 1908-09 – just as the European-educated Young Turks were rising to power in what was still the Ottoman Empire. To the extent that these buildings were meant to meet international standards and the needs of the modern era, the internal organisation of space and the distribution of functional areas generally reflected what was common practice for such buildings elsewhere in the Western and industrialised world.

## The First National Style

From this foundation grew what architectural historians have since dubbed "the First National Style", a style referred to at the time and by Turks themselves as "Neo-classical Turkish Style" or the "National Architecture Renaissance". Vallaury taught at the Art Academy (*Sanayi-i Nefise Mektebi*), and Jachmund at the School of Civil Engineering (*Hendese-i Mülkiye*), both in Istanbul. Kemalettin Bey (1870-1927), who had studied under Jachmund and at the Charlottenburg Technische Hochschule in Berlin, would be central in shaping this first national trend in architecture in Turkey. Kemalettin Bey and his fellow countryman Mehmet Vedat Bey (1873-1942) also exerted considerable influence on architectural developments through their teaching at the same schools. Vedat Bey is considered to be the first Turk to undergo formal training as an architect in Turkey and also the first Turk to teach architectural history at the art school starting in 1900 (Yavuz and Özkan: 41).

The architecture that was created in the early decades of the 20th century employed an aesthetic that was clearly indebted to the characteristic features of Ottoman architecture. For centuries Ottoman culture had dominated the geographical region that would become the Republic of Turkey. Mosques, hammams and wooden buildings sported structural and visual features that one immediately associates with the building culture of the Ottoman Empire, a building culture that was clearly hegemonic with regard to the region's architecture, and which cut across the many ethnic divisions in the population.

The foundation of the stylistic vocabulary seen in the National Architecture

*Fig. 2. Ismail Hasif Bey et.al.: The regional centre for the Commitee of Union and Progress/The first Parliaments building in Ankara, 1917-23. Author's photo, 2009.*

Renaissance was established in an architectural treatise from 1873, *The Principles of Ottoman Architecture* (*Usul-i Mimari-yi Osmania*), written by Ibrahim Edhem Pasha (1819-1893) on the occasion of an international exhibition in Vienna in 1873. The principles were developed on the basis of systematic studies and documentation of classical Ottoman buildings, monuments and decorative details. The theoretical models, analytic methods and representational techniques were unmistakably European, and were particularly influenced by the methodology used in the French academies. Both Edhem Pasha and the other Ottoman artists and intellectuals who contributed to the work were educated in France, and this kind of ambivalence between self-identity and an international mindset seems highly characteristic of the nationalism associated with many newly established political systems in non-Western contexts after 1900. The rule set had to be based on architecture that was deemed to possess national characteristics, but it also had to provide the basis for an architecture that could be described as "modern". The authors of the treatise wanted to restore the dignity of the Ottoman architectural culture, while at the same time demonstrating that it was no less worthy than that of Europe (Bozdoğan: 23-24).

The city of Istanbul was closely associated with its Ottoman past, yet was also profoundly marked by centuries of communication with the West and the rest of the world. This partly explains why the capital of the newly established Turkish nation was moved to the area around the town of Angora in Anatolia, which did not have this historical background. The national army had its headquarters during the war of independence here, and, on a more pragmatic level, Angora was centrally situated in what remained of Ottoman Turkey after World War I. Consequently, the regime focused its architectural interests largely on the town that would duly become known as Ankara, which

*Fig. 3. Mehmet Vedat Bey: Headquarters for The Republican People's Party/The second parliament building in Ankara, 1924-26. Author's photo, 2009.*

is where we find many of the most characteristic and seminal examples of the architecture that developed in the 1920s.

The first building to be erected here to serve national interests was a modest, single-storey building designed by Ismail Hasif Bey (1878-1920), on which work began in 1917. It was intended as a regional centre for the Committee of Union and Progress, but was put to use as the new nation's first parliament building as early as 1920. The building had outer walls of natural stone and a low-pitched hipped roof. The wide eaves are heavily cantilevered and covered with decoratively patterned wood panelling underneath. The layout is symmetrical despite comprising a number of volumes, and the windows are high with pointed arches. If we compare this with the wooden building on p. 32, it is evident that many features of Ottoman architecture have been incorporated in this central building of the new nation. Today it houses a museum commemorating the war of independence.

Just one year after the first parliament building was inaugurated, the architect Vedat Bey was summoned from Istanbul to design two important buildings in the new city: a new and larger building for the national assembly, and the Ankara Palas Hotel. The buildings would stand facing each other near the city's new main traffic artery, Atatürk Boulevard, which runs from the railway station to the old citadel. The second parliament building was initially conceived as the headquarters for the Republican People's Party, but it was decided that it was more suitable as a parliament building (Yavuz and Özkan: 53). The building is a two-storey, rectangular volume, set side-on to the street. The main façade with the entrance faces a garden that has an elongated fountain on its central axis. The garden slopes down towards the west, culminating in an oval pond with water lilies. The building's strict symmetry is reinforced by the fact that the entrance is projected forward and capped with a different kind of roof. Above the entrance portal is a loggia with three pointed-arched openings, which serves as a tribune at public events. The building is simple and rustic in style, and is clad in local, pinkish stone with details of glazed brick. The main hall was surrounded by offices on two floors. Here we also find some of the stylistic features that can be traced back to the old wooden architecture: a series of hipped roofs, overhanging eaves, and volumes organised along a symmetrical axis. Although it became clear as early as the late 1930s that the building did not meet the state administration's rapidly expanding needs, it remained the seat of the National Assembly for the next 30 years. Today, the building houses the Museum of the Republic.

On the opposite side of Atatürk Boulevard, Vedat Bey erected his second building in Ankara, the Ankara Palas Hotel. Construction began in 1924, but within a year the commission was passed on to Kemalettin Bey, who was brought in from Jerusalem to help build the new capital. His first task was to design a stately portal for the new parliament building, which he embellished with deep mouldings, decorative figures, and an ornamental cornice. In parallel he continued work on the Ankara Palas Hotel, a building that was originally meant to house the health ministry. However, representative accommodation for guests of the government administration was given priority. Outwardly, the hotel's architectural style seems somewhat anachronistic for 1927, although it tells us a lot about the enduring status of the Ottoman architectural heritage. The main façade is symmetrically arranged around an imposing entrance, which is decorated with elegant tiles and a lavishly ornamented cornice. The entrance portal is crowned with a timber-framed onion dome. The earliest sketches show a more coherent treatment of volumes, although the ultimate design enhances the three main elements of the exterior: the central portal with its onion dome, and the pronounced, square corner towers with their wide overhanging eaves. The two-storey side wings between the central section and side towers are set back. The first-floor balconies and the high arched windows on the ground floor are fronted with carved marble balustrades. The hotel was designed as a two-storey, rectangular building with a large ballroom at its centre. The spaces on the ground floor were assigned to functions such as a restaurant, a tea salon, and administrative offices, while the rooms for guests were situated on the upper floor. The original plans indicate that many of the guest rooms were conceived as small, single rooms. In many ways, the organisation of the rooms is reminiscent of Ottoman guesthouses, with a central courtyard surrounded by rooms on two floors. The design of the main façade demonstrates what one might call Ottoman nostalgia. The exaggerated dimensions of the building's central section and side towers give the construction the appearance of exhibition architecture, a staging of the nation that employs imaginative interpretations of national architectural characteristics.

When it opened in 1927, the hotel was praised as a symbol of modern civilisation, albeit mostly on account of the technical facilities with which it was equipped. Ankara Palas was a meeting point and social hub for both Turkish statesmen and foreign diplomats. Here Western lifestyles and dress codes were flaunted; dancing in couples and Western hairstyles and fashion were seen as symbols of modernity and republican westernisation (Bozdoğan: 212). The form in which this Western lifestyle was packaged was, however, both romantic and exotic, and soon it would have to give way to a more modernist public architecture. When both the parliament and the central business district moved further south in the 1950s, attention turned to other architectural ideals. Ankara Palas fell into disrepair, although in 1983 the hotel was restored by the architect Orhan Akyurek and re-emerged as the Neva Palas Hotel Ankara.

Different versions and combinations of Ottoman influence are apparent in several public buildings erected in Ankara in the first decade of the republic. Certainly, they were constructed in part of modern materials, such as reinforced concrete, and were fitted out with modern facilities such as electric lighting, pressurised water systems, and efficient heating systems. Nevertheless, the formal idiom chosen for central institutions, especially those that would serve as the nation's face to the outside world, clearly testify that the crucial aspects of Ottoman architecture still held a hegemonic position. Just as Ottoman culture was repackaged as Turkish culture, the National Architecture Renaissance was defined as a specifically *Turkish* national style, according to Sibel Bozdoğan (Bozdoğan: 21). In her view, it was this "Turkification" of Ottoman architecture that enabled it to survive to a certain degree in the Kemalist architecture of the Republic.

The style of the National Architecture Renaissance was employed primarily in public buildings. But there are exceptions, including a number of apartment buildings in Istanbul by Kemalettin Bey from 1919-22, the Harikzedegân apartments, which also offer one of the earliest examples of the use of reinforced concrete in Turkey; and Vedat Bey's own house in Nişantaşı, Istanbul. Critics have argued, however, that the buildings that used this architectural idiom came across as parodies of mosques, and that the only thing they lacked was the minaret on the outside and the mihrab on the inside (Tekeli: 15). The first National Architecture Renaissance also constitutes a trend that found expression primarily in the style and treatment of the exterior, while the building's internal organisation was determined by the demands of modern functionality.

## Windows to the West and international (state) modernism

Social life and conventions in Ankara in the late 1920s carried the message that international modernist aesthetics was on its way, even though the architectural packaging still had at least one foot in the rich traditional styles of the past. In the decade that followed, almost all construction work, except for that of residential buildings, was initiated by the public sector (Batur: 69). One of the goals was to create orderly conditions in urban environments, an understandable aim when one considers the outward aspect of many Turkish cities even today. As a relatively pristine town, Ankara offered opportunities for systematic planned development, thanks not least to the adoption of a comprehensive master plan in 1928.

It was the German architect Hermann Jansen (1869-1945) who won the international competition to develop a large-scale urban strategy, implemented from 1932. The plan contained important elements that one associates with modernist urban planning: fully paved roads, pavements, parks with fountains and open spaces, the zoning of different functions, and uninterrupted transport lines. Atatürk Boulevard was designed to serve as a principal axis in the north-south direction, with a second axis crossing it at Ulus. Along these axes the new developments would spread out independently of the older building substance, which was to be preserved. The commercial centre would remain in Ulus, while the new administrative centre would be located in Yenisehir. Residential blocks were laid out according to a grid system in the areas to either side of Atatürk Boulevard. Dead-end roads were to be eliminated from the existing districts, a measure that was implemented with little regard for the historical value of the buildings that happened to be standing where the new openings were required (Batur: 70).

In Ankara, the development of republican architecture continued, and in the period 1930-40 the regime consolidated both its Kemalist ideology and the architectural idiom that would constitute its physical, substantive face. According to Afife Batur, the republican middle classes were decisive in conferring approval on the new architectural methods in Ankara. Prominent citizens wanted a new, modern, Western lifestyle with no associations to the past, and they regarded the physical and architectural process of modernisation as a visible and concrete expression of the nation's positive development (Batur: 78). A key socio-economic measure was the promotion of modern industry, and in the region of Anatolia in particular, which had hitherto been a predominantly agrarian society, industrial plants represented an entirely new building type. Some of the constructions from the mid-1920s were among the first to use modernist building techniques and styles: these include the Ankara textile factory and the Alpullu sugar refinery. The former had a flat roof, rectangular volumes, smooth white walls and horizontal ribbon windows.

The Russian Revolution was a clear source of inspiration for the new regime in Turkey, despite their very different origins and historical contexts. The situation was of course special in each of the two countries, albeit in different ways: in Russia a bloody revolution was initiated and pursued by the working class and the peasantry against a hereditary dynasty that had exercised absolute power for centuries. In Turkey the new state apparatus swept aside an equally traditional hereditary dynasty, and the political system underwent an equally fundamental change from a religious to a secular society. In both cases, however, a new hegemony was established. Systematic cooperation between the two nations began after Ismet Inönü, Turkey's prime minister at the time, visited the Soviet Union in 1932. These links resulted in the cooperative body *Turkstroj*, which was meant to take care of industrial development in Turkey (Asiliskender: 216-223). Textile factories were built in response to government initiatives in Kayseri in Anatolia and Nazilli near the Aegean, and a steel plant was constructed in Karabük near the Black Sea coast. In 1933, the first five-year plan for industrial development was implemented, and according to Batur reforms were carried out under an increasingly *dirigiste* system (Batur: 68).

In the first decades, German architects represented a forceful presence in relation to Ankara's major building projects. The three most distinguished, apart from Jansen, who was responsible for the urban master plan, were Theodore Post, Clemens Holzmeister (1886-1983), and Ernst Egli (1893-1974). Holzmeister designed an astonishing number of buildings for central government institutions and banks. With his strict, monumental style he left an indelible stamp on the administrative districts of the new capital. His buildings are of large dimensions, were built using modern construction techniques, and feature natural stone or brick in their façades. Window openings are distributed according to regular, repetitive patterns; and the bodies of his buildings rise from floor plans designed around closed rectangles, U-shapes or T-shapes. There is invariably clear emphasis on symmetry. The presidential palace from 1932, however, is an exception. The building's volumes are organised on a rectangular shape, but one façade is broken up by a series of tall window expanses. The corner is curved and there is a hipped roof with a very low pitch and slightly overhanging eaves, which reflect the influence of Ottoman architecture. The classical idiom is stylised and reduced, indicating that, in its Turkish guise, the modernist aesthetic ideals may have found a certain foothold. Ernst Egli's buildings are considerably more modern, with a freer distribution of building volumes, and clear, horizontal divisions in the façades. The integration of volumes of the kind familiar from early Viennese and Dutch modernism is also a characteristic feature.

Besides industrialisation, one of the main concerns of the Kemalist regime was the construction of homes for a growing population. There was a large and unmet need, both in Ankara and other major cities. Prestige projects for government departments generally went, as we have seen, to foreign architects, while in the early years Turkish architects generally made their mark promoting modernist practices in the context of smaller construction projects. Projects from the 1930s show that young Turkish architects were well informed about international architectural trends, and that they were competent at applying them in practice. Modernism eventually made its mark on the urban architecture of Turkish towns just as it did in the cities of other European countries, although many of the earliest modernist buildings no longer exist.

Naturally, many professionals in the field were unhappy about the fact that large and nationally prestigious projects went to foreign architects. The situation was changed by architects like Seyfettin Nasih Arkan (1902-1966), a major exponent of modernism in the history of Turkish architecture. Arkan was chosen to design the foreign minister's residence and a large house for Atatürk's sister, Makbule Atadan, in Ankara, and the president's summer pavilion at Florya outside Istanbul. Completed in 1934, the foreign minister's residence soon became an icon for the new republic. It was frequently depicted and referred to in foreign-language propaganda, such as *La Turquie Kemaliste*, published by the interior ministry (Akcan: 31). In addition to architectural design, Arkan was also responsible for the selection of fixtures and furnishings, as well as for the landscaping of the surroundings. The estate was not just the private home of a statesman, but also a place for official festivities and a showpiece for the new Turkey. This representative residence was meant to give foreign diplomats a clear impression of the state's ambitions with regard to modernisation and westernisation, while also showing that the new republic was eradicating the oriental traits typical of the Ottoman Empire. The distinction between the private and public spheres was toned down, in strong contrast to the layout of traditional Ottoman-Turkish houses. Many of the features in the foreign minister's residence had their origins in a "Waterfront House" that Arkan had designed during his time as a student at the Charlottenburg Technische Hochschule. There he studied under Hans Poelzig, who presented a modernist approach in his teaching, and Arkan later worked closely with Poelzig at the Prussian Academy of the Arts in Berlin (Akcan: 28). The concept for the waterfront house was further pursued in the residence for Makbule

Fig. 4. Seyfettin Nasih Arkan: The President's summer pavilion at Florya outside Istanbul, 1934-35. Author's photo, 2009.

Atadan in Ankara, built in 1936, and the summer pavilion at Florya, which was completed in 1935.

Both the summer pavilion and the other public residences clearly demonstrate that modernism's structural techniques and aesthetics were preferred for prestigious projects. Arkan was awarded the commission to build the summer pavilion following a closed competition, in which the German architect Martin Wagner also took part. The house was actually situated out in the water on the Marmara coast and connected to the shore by a pier. Atatürk wanted to spend his holidays in contact with the people, and an important specification was that the adjacent beach should remain open to the public. The summer pavilion was meant as a conspicuous reminder that the republican revolution was also the *people's* revolution. The house demonstrated the president's desire for contact with the masses, and was a clear statement that the former regime's hierarchy with its clear distinction between governing and governed classes had been swept aside. Here the president could spend his holidays just a few metres away from the common masses (to the extent that "the masses" were able to choose Florya for their holidays), he could swim and relax with them, and wave to them from the terrace of his boat-like house (Akcan: 42).

Esra Akcan mentions another interesting connection that is rarely considered in contemporary discussions of the pavilion on the Marmara Sea, namely the traditional Ottoman "water baths" that were set up along the Bosporus each summer. In many parts of the world, it was the architects of modernism who introduced the ideals of bodily hygiene and outdoor activities, whereas in Turkey people could just continue the bathing culture they had been practising for centuries. Modernism had come to occupy a leading and hegemonic position, especially in Ankara. It inspired the architecture of a vast number of monumental public buildings, industrial facilities, and residential developments, all of them central building projects that gave the new regime its face.

## Neo-Ottoman brutalism: The Second National Style

Sedat Hakki Eldem (1908-1988) had studied Turkish architecture in Paris in the 1920s, and Ottoman architectural heritage is highly evident in his projects, even though most of them are modernist in their design, use of materials and aesthetics. In the latter half of the inter-war period, many architects turned their attention back to their national "roots" and the architectural heritage of the past, a romantic trend that was also evident in other totalitarian regimes during those years. In Turkey, this era became known as "the Second National Architecture Renaissance". The legacy of Kemalettin Bey and Vedat Bey was continued, and Eldem introduced and formalised the study of Turkish secular architecture in a seminar he held at the art academy. This helped to establish a conceptual framework for further architectural development based on national characteristics.

With an innovative mind, Eldem reinterpreted the Ottoman architectural heritage to yield new idioms, for instance through the use of coarser dimensions rendered in reinforced concrete and glass. Many of his buildings feature the *sofa* element, the central room or hall that was common in traditional Turkish houses. The structuring of the façade and the design of the windows also contain reminiscences of older architecture. This was an approach Eldem would maintain throughout his career, as can also be seen in one of his later works, the Atatürk library near Taxim in Istanbul, built in 1973-75. The vertically proportioned windows, the characteristic overhanging eaves, and the use of wood and tiled panels all provide clear associations to the Ottoman architectural heritage. The floor plan is based on the hexagon, with hexagonal skylights in the roof, while the building sits on a triangular structural system.

As we have seen, the architecture that was built in the first decade of the 20th century adopted many fundamental architectural principles from the Western academic tradition. These were implemented in buildings that were central to the Ottoman Empire's modernisation process. Post offices, railway stations and banks were meant to serve the nation's interests in the broader European community, and it is evident that the architecture of these buildings has many similarities with comparable structures elsewhere in Europe. The theoretical foundations of foreign architecture, in particular that of Germany and France, can also be described as hegemonic within the Western architectural tradition

*Fig. 5. Sedat Hakki Eldem: The Atatürk Library near Taxim, Istanbul, 1973-75. Author's photo, 2009.*

during this period. On the basis of this architectural theory, a state architecture emerged that incorporated influences from the Ottoman heritage, but which was interpreted as Turkish and defined as "national".

Once the Republic had consolidated its ideology, its economic foundation and its political programme, the hegemony shifted from national connotations to the international ideology of modernism. Much the same happened in many other Western nations as well, with other new nation states exploring and reinterpreting their architectural heritage in the decades immediately before and after the turn of the century. The advent of modernism represents a fundamental change. Following the exploration of the defining traits of national styles, the ground was prepared for new social ideals developed in international arenas. The search for national character returned as a source of inspiration after World War II, as is also evident in Turkey's late modernism. Similar phenomena are evident under the influence of postmodernism in the 1980s. New commercial buildings are still being built with traits of postmodern, Ottoman-inspired kitsch at the heart of the major cities, although these now represent little more than nostalgic elements in otherwise diverse cityscapes. Hence an awareness of the characteristics of the national architectural heritage, whether described as Ottoman or Turkish, is still apparent as one of many possible choices. Le Corbusier, who warned Atatürk against the negative aspects of modernisation, would undoubtedly recognise the reverberations of his influential modernist theory in Ankara – even if he himself was not in the position to carry it out. Istanbul's city planners have, as he feared, eradicated much of the city's former architecture without achieving much more than an efficient use of the available space. As far as architecture is concerned, the era of hegemonies is past, not just in Turkey, but in most other countries as well.

# Bibliography

Adamson, W.R. (1980). *Hegemony and Revolution: a study of Antonio Gramsci's political and cultural theory.*

Akcan, E. (2005). "Ambiguities of Transparency and Privacy in Seyfy Arkan's Houses for the New Turkish Republic" in: *METU JFA* no. 2. Ankara: Faculty of Architecture, Middle East Technical University. http://archnet.org/library/sites/one-site.jsp?site_id=685. Accessed 23.03.2009.

Asiliskender, B. (2005). "Installing 'Modern' Life Style with Architecture. A Case of Sumerbank Kayseri Settlement" in: D.C. Papelas. *Revista Semestral de Critica Arquitectonica.* Barcelona: Departament de Composicio Arquitectonica, Universitat Politecnica de Catalunya, vols. 13 & 14, pp. 216-223, October. Also available at http://upcommons.upc.edu/revistes/bitstream/2099/2358/1/216_223_burak. Accessed on 23.09.2008.

Batur, A. (1984). "To be Modern: Search for a Republican Architecture", in: Holod, R. and Ahmet E. (eds.). *Modern Turkish Architecture.* University of Pennsylvania Press.

Bozdoğan, S. (2001). *Modernism and Nation Building. Turkish Architectural Culture in the Early Republic.* Seattle and London: University of Washington Press, referring to an interview with Le Corbusier by S. Demiren in *Arkitekt* 19, nos. 11-12, 1949: 230-31: "Le Corbusier ile Mülakat".

Gramsci, A. (2001). *Lettres de la Prison*, translated by Jean Noaro 1953, edition électronique couple Jean-Marie Tremblay.

Le Corbusier, C-E. (2002). *Voyage d'Orient. Carnets.* Paris: Fondation Le Corbusier. First published as a series of reports for readers of *La Feuille d'Avis* in 1911.

Le Corbusier, C-E. (2007) (1987). *Journey to the East*, translated by Ivan Zaknic, Cambridge Mass. and London: MIT Press from *Le Voyage d'Orient*, Paris, 1966.

Tekeli, I. (1984). "The Social Context of the Development of Architecture in Turkey", in Holod, R. and Ahmet E. (eds.). *Modern Turkish Architecture.* University of Pennsylvania Press.

Yavuz, Y. and S. Özkan. (1984). "Finding a National Idiom: The First National Style", in Holod, R. and Ahmet E. (eds.). *Modern Turkish Architecture.* University of Pennsylvania Press.

# Region and Frontier in the English State: Co. Meath and the English Pale, 1460-1542[1]

*Steven G. Ellis*

The frontier in medieval Ireland has attracted a good deal of attention since Professor James Lydon first explored the problem and sketched its dimensions in a seminal article over forty years ago.[2] Since then, the frontier paradigm has featured quite extensively in studies of Ireland's two nations.[3] Lydon saw the establishment of the Anglo-Gaelic frontier as a deliberate policy by the English government, one which supposedly presented few problems in the age of English expansion (1169-1300), but many more later on. After c.1300 the frontier began to break up, with earlier clear-cut divisions between a *terra pacis* (land of peace) and a *terra guerrae* (land of war) giving way to marchland so that the settlers were "at least partially assimilated to the Gaelic Ireland they found all around them" (Lydon 2008: 329). In the 15th century Lydon detected "a new frontier emerging" in "parts of the four loyal counties" around Dublin; but then "the real frontier contracted once again to the limits of what was known as the Pale". The policy "of separating the races and driving a cultural barrier between them" thus proved "a complete failure", he concluded, so obliging the Tudor monarchs to "face up to the frontier problem in a realistic way" by means of a complete conquest and a new colonization (Lydon 2008: 327, 330-31).

The range of ideas tentatively explored in Lydon's initial sketch of the problem has since the 1960s achieved almost canonical status, with regard to both the distinctive terminology used to analyze the problem and the significance attached to a supposedly continuing English decline in precipitating the Tudor conquest. The medieval frontier is of course a sensitive issue in Irish historio-

---

[1]  The 'English Pale' in Ireland was the name given in the 16th century to the region around Dublin which was directly under English royal administration. The term 'pale' denoted a precisely enclosed area.

[2]  Lydon 1967: 5-22; reprinted in Crooks 2008: 317-31, to which the following references refer.

[3]  Appropriately, frontiers were a key theme of the *Festschrift* presented to Lydon on his retirement: Barry, Frame & Simms (ed.) 1995. For a discussion of writings on the medieval frontier since Lydon's essay, see Crooks 2008: 371-3.

graphy: the island's modern partition between two states shapes the historiography of the frontier – in terms of what is studied, from what perspective,
and in what terms. The late medieval frontier is depicted as a frontier of contact rather than a frontier of separation, or to use the terminology developed
by German geographers, as a *Zusammenwachsgrenze*, not a *Trennungsgrenze*.[4]
In this context, too, the historians' quest to uncover the roots of Irishness also
invites discussion of the growing ties between native and settler while overlooking inherited differences. The national agenda has thus tended to marginalize
the development of the English Pale as a physical frontier and also its essentially English identity: it stresses the thoroughgoing nature of the settlers' dealings
with the Gaelic polity, their supposed Irishness and 'gaelicization', portraying
instead two varieties of Irishmen ('Anglo-Irish' the descendants of the English
settlers and 'Gaelic Irish' the native Irish) interacting across a dissolving frontier.
And attempts to redress the balance by looking more closely at developments in
the English Pale and the settlers' English identity have been dismissed as 'two-
nation theory'(Duffy, Edwards & Fitzpatrick 2001: 30; Nicholls 1999: 22-6).[5]
As this chapter illustrates, however, close attention to the actual evidence – descriptions of the Pale frontier as a physical barrier; the political terminology in
which events there are described – suggests that the English of Ireland were far
from seeing the creation of an English Pale as a failed policy in a failed entity.
But then the Palesmen did not have the benefit of hindsight available to more
nationally-minded historians writing with the recent Troubles in mind. In what
follows, a short description of the origins and development of the English Pale is
first offered, followed by a more detailed analysis of developments in the Pale's
largest shire, Co. Meath, which serves to illustrate these wider developments.

As a distinct region of the English state, the English Pale was a late addition, the product of political change during the course of the 15th century.[6]
(see Map 1)

---

4    For a typology of medieval frontiers, including Ireland, see Power & Standen 1999: 1-31.
     On the whole, however, Irish historians have ignored Lydon's opening suggestion about the
     need for a Turner thesis which would allow the Irish frontier to be viewed comparatively
     in the context of frontiers in medieval Europe: Lydon 2008: 317.
5    'Two-nations theory' is the dismissive phrase coined by modern Irish Nationalists about
     Unionist perspectives on Northern Ireland of which they disapprove. It implies that 'the
     Irish', whether North or South, were one nation, notwithstanding arguments that the
     Unionists in Northern Ireland constituted a separate nation.
6    For conventional views on the emergence of the Pale, see Cosgrove 1987: ch. 18. For a
     different perspective, see Power 2008.

*Map 1. English Ireland c.1525, with the English Pale.*

Geographically, the region was a fertile coastal plain, bounded by the Mourne mountains to the north and, more closely, by the Wicklow mountains to the south, but open to the west. Its emergence as a frontier region reflected the partial nature of medieval English settlement in Ireland and the consequent establishment of a frontier between English and Gaelic Ireland. Attracted by the prospect of good land for agriculture, medieval English colonization of the region had been intensive, with the establishment of manors and a system of mixed farming along English lines. The surrounding uplands were unsuited to tillage, however, and largely remained under Gaelic occupation: English settlement thinned out very quickly to the north and south, but did so more gradually towards the bogs of the midlands. On the whole, though, the regions of English settlement in Ireland formed not one compact block of territory but several smaller areas, interspersed between districts in which Gaelic lordship and rule remained unchallenged; and within the Gaelic parts power was fragmented between numerous small but independent chieftaincies and lordships. Thus, what had emerged by 1300, after the initial English impetus towards conquest had petered out and a broad political equilibrium between the two nations had been established, was "a land of many marches", as Robin Frame memorably described it.[7] And political conditions in each of these marches reflected the shifting balance of power between local Gaelic chiefs and English magnates. Thus, as the Gaelic Revival (the military and cultural resurgence among the native Irish) swept away the more lightly settled districts of English lordship, perceptions of the Pale's borders as a frontier were powerfully reinforced by the close coincidence there of geographical, cultural, political, military, and administrative boundaries. The contrasts were also underlined by the deployment in English official circles of a rhetoric of difference to describe the English and Gaelic parts. This emphasized the 'otherness' of the native Irish living 'beyond the Pale', castigating them as savages. It reflected the politically-fragmented, pastoral and kin-based character of Irish society, living in wooden huts in a dispersed habitat, without towns, in a landscape of mountain, forest and bog, all of which English observers saw as indications of a backward and primitive people.

In terms of economic activity, for instance, the English had already developed in the twelfth century a checklist of the attributes of civility which, in reality, simply replicated conditions in lowland England. These included a well-populated landscape, with a settled society, wealthy towns and nucleated villages, a manorial economy, a cereal-based agriculture, and a well-differentiated social structure with a numerous and vigorous gentry. By contrast, the 'wild' peoples of the British upland zone, notably the Irish, were denigrated as lazy, bestial and barbarous – a shifting population living in idleness and brutality in woods and bogs, eking out a miserable existence from cattle raising and rustling. There were similar checklists of civility and savagery with regard to morals, dress, and physical appearance.[8] English reports divided Ireland rather schematically into a 'land of peace' where lived 'the king's loyal English lieges' in civilized towns and nucleated villages, and a 'land of war' where lurked 'the king's Irish enemies', the 'wild Irish'. Within a few short miles to the south

---

[7]    Frame 1977: 3-33 (quotation, p. 32). 'March' is a *terminus technicus* used in medieval times to denote an extended borderland or frontier zone, as opposed to a border line.

[8]    See Davies 2000: ch. 5; Ellis 2007: 77-92, at pp. 78, 83, and the references there cited.

of Dublin, for instance, the English lowlands gave way to the Gaelic lord-ships of the Wicklow mountains, agriculture to pastoralism, English-speaking gentlemen to Gaelic-speaking clansmen, English cloaks to Gaelic mantles, common law to brehon law, and stone houses to mud huts: in short, 'English civility' gave way to 'Irish savagery'.[9] Legislation, codified in the Statutes of Kilkenny (1366), aimed to preserve the English character of the colonial parts by proscribing the use of Irish law and customs among the English. In truth, though, the Irish were there in their midst because the English settlement had in many parts retained native labourers, often as serfs, to work the land, and the 14th-century labour shortages had encouraged Irish migration into the English districts. The Statutes of Kilkenny, however, also excluded the native Irish from holding freehold land, major office, or ecclesiastical benefice in the English parts unless they had first obtained what was officially described as a "charter of English liberty and freedom from Irish servitude", in other words a grant of denization which accorded them protection at English law. English subjects were expected to speak English, carry English weapons like the bill or longbow, and dress in the English manner. Later, mid-15th-century legis-lation also required Irishmen living in the Englishry to take English names, follow English customs, and generally to adapt their lifestyle to meet official checklists of English civility. Equally, the regular convening of parliament al-lowed Ireland's English ruling elite (nobles, burgesses, knights of the shire) to demonstrate their Englishness by the enactment of law (Parliament roll, 40 Edward III (Berry 1907: 430-69); Smith 1997: 57-65; Ellis 1986: 128-30).

As the Dublin government's control over the lordship's outlying parts de-clined, so marchlands increased: in the early 15th century 'the land of peace' was increasingly identified with the boundaries of 'the four obedient shires', or counties, around the lordship's administrative capital, Dublin, Louth, Meath, and Kildare. Already by the late 14th century this region had emerged as a "recognizable administrative unit" (Richardson & Sayles 1952: 103). By 1428, it had been vaguely divided into "la terre de pees, appelle Maghery" (the land of peace, called Maghery), and the marches (Parliament roll, 8 Henry VI c. 13 (Berry 1910: 34-6). The use of this term 'Maghery', a borrowing and trans-literation of the Gaelic *machaire* ('a plain, or champaign ground'), to describe 'the land of peace' (v. the marches) is revealing. It also occurred, for instance,

---

[9]    Ellis 1999: 155-6. For examples of this rhetoric of difference, see for instance, *Letters & Papers, foreign and domestic, of the reign of Henry VIII* (henceforth *LP*) (21 vols., London, 1862-1932), iv, no. 2405, and the document referenced in note 29 below.

in a statute of 1488, the Act of Marches and Maghery, discussed below (Quinn 1941b: 84; McNeill 1950: 250; National Library of Ireland (henceforth NLI), MS 2507, f. 57v). Its use reflected an emerging distinction, both in terms of land capability, settlement patterns, and political conditions, between a less densely populated, predominantly pastoral, outer defensive ring of the Pale, the marches, and an English heartland, the maghery – an area of mixed farming, nucleated villages, and market towns, in which conditions approximated more closely to those in lowland England and to official perceptions of 'English civility'. This division between marches and maghery, and the essential character of the English Pale as a frontier region, is most readily documented by tracing developments in the shire, or county, of Meath 1460-1542. This was the period from the crown's acquisition of the lordship of Trim on the death of Duke Richard of York to the erection of western Meath as a separate shire by parliamentary statute in 1542.

Meath was geographically much the largest of 'the four obedient shires'. Created in 1297, it stretched over a great swathe of eastern Ireland from the sea to the Shannon. On three sides, Meath had fixed boundaries, with the counties of Kildare to the south, Louth in the north-east, and Dublin and the sea in the east; but to the west, Meath's long frontier lay open to the Gaelic midlands. It ended in an uninhabited wasteland interposed between the English marches and Gaelic Ireland. And until 1460 over half of Meath's geographical area remained a private franchise, the liberty of Trim,[10] distinct from the royal county. Trim was a large block of territory to the north of Kildare, bisecting the royal shire. (Map 2)

Arrangements for government and defence were thus complicated, with responsibilities split between the shire officers (led by the sheriff) and the liberty officials, headed by the lord's seneschal; and for long periods the lord of Trim was not resident there.[11] Added to these difficulties were the problems of defending an extended march from the numerous Gaelic chiefs of the midlands. The English march ran south-westerly from Louth before turning south in a great arc to Kildare's north-west boundary. In the later middle ages it slowly

---

[10] A liberty was a distinct geographical area or district within which English law and local government was administered by special officers appointed by a particular magnate or prelate, the lord of the liberty, instead of by the standard officials appointed by the crown.

[11] Otway-Ruthven 1968: 100, 174, 187; Frame 1982: 52-6, 65, 70-73, 333. And see the map by K.W. Nicholls (Map 3 Counties and Liberties, 1297) in Cosgrove 1987: 174.

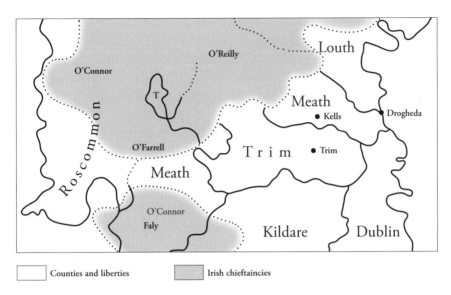

*Map 2: The royal shire of Meath with the lordship of Trim, to 1460. The lordship of Meath had been partitioned in 1244 into two estates, one administered from Trim, the other from Kells.*

crumbled in the face of the Gaelic Revival and the English lordship's internal weaknesses.

If we survey the inherited systems of defence in the region, they were very similar to those of other marchlands of the English monarchy. There was a framework structure of major castles and walled towns, with the land parcelled out into numerous manors normally improved by fortified dwellings and earthworks constructed by the local lord. Where the quality of the land permitted agriculture, the population could be concentrated in nucleated villages, with the cottages of the manorial tenants clustered around the church and the lord's principal dwelling, and the villages located sufficiently close to each other as to offer mutual support and so discourage casual raiding. In the English Pale, this very often also permitted the establishment of a fairly stable frontier, as was the case with the chain of manorial villages to the south-west of Dublin and along sections of the Pale's northern frontier in Co. Louth. Here the contours of the land and intersections between areas of different land capability, between the arable lowlands and the pastoral uplands, also marked the frontier between English and Gaelic Ireland. In such circumstances, the actual march might be a comparatively narrow strip of land only a few miles wide. Along the Pale's western frontier in Co. Meath, however, the champaign ground of the eastern coastal plain simply faded imperceptibly into the bogs of the midlands. These outlying districts of English settlement, where the land was more sparsely populated and given over predominantly to pasture farming, were perforce more reliant on defence in depth. Here the character of the frontier was necessarily rather different, with an extended march many miles wide. If we are looking for medieval European parallels, then the unstable Lithuano-Prussian forest frontier before the boundary was agreed by the Treaty of Melno (1422) might provide one, but English officials – denigrating the Irish as nomads – thought more in terms of a shifting frontier zone between settled and nomadic forms of society, such as that which characterized Russia's frontier with the peoples of the southern steppes and to the east.[12]

The late middle ages, however, was a period of acute labour shortage and economic decline in English Ireland, the successive outbreaks of plague hitting the English towns and cities there much harder than Gaelic Ireland. The result was a decline of tillage in favour of pastoralism as the population declined and labour costs soared, an influx of Gaelic labourers, and increased raiding by the Midland Irish on exposed marchlands as Gaelic chiefs sought to exploit English weakness. These trends hit the English of Meath particularly badly for two main reasons. In the first place, the lower population levels in western Meath – where land quality was poorer, pasture farming more prevalent, and settlement more dispersed – left these districts more vulnerable to Gaelic raids. A description of the united barony of Moyashel and Magheradernon in the 17th century, for instance, noted of the land quality there that it was "arable meadow pasture with great store of red bog and lough and some mountain"; and Corkeree barony to the north was "for a great part arable" but with "many barren mountains and heathy hills not at all profitable" (Simington 1961: 40, 43).[13] Cattle could be moved to safety in the face of impending raids, whereas crops were easily burned; but the switch from tillage, which was more labour intensive, to pastoralism further reduced population levels and exacerbated defence problems. Dispersed settlements, located too far from each other to offer mutual support, were easily picked off in Gaelic raids, and western Meath also lacked the solid framework of market towns further east.

In other circumstances, a resident and active ruling magnate could take charge of defence, so offsetting these difficulties. The second difficulty en-

---

[12]   For the European comparison, see the essays in Power & Standen 1999: 'Introduction', 1-31 (at p. 2); Moreno 1999: 32-54 (35-7); Rowell 1999: 182-208. See also Khodarkovsky 1992: 115-28.

[13]   Here and elsewhere in this paper, I have modernized the spelling of quotations in Tudor English.

countered by the Meath community, however, was the eclipse of the region's ruling magnate in 1460 when Richard Duke of York was killed in the civil war between the rival dynasties of York and Lancaster known as the Wars of the Roses. The lordship passed into crown hands with the accession of his son to the English throne as the Yorkist king, Edward IV. As heir to the earldom of Ulster, and the lordships of Connaught, Trim and Leix, Duke Richard was the crown's only really powerful magnate in Ireland. Richard's most valuable estates lay in Meath and consisted of a block of around eleven fairly large manors comprising the lordship and liberty of Trim, in which the lord also exercised palatine rights of jurisdiction.[14] On his death, they were immediately taken into the king's hand. Without the liberty organization to hold things together and to organize defence, the more exposed of Richard's estates were left in a very vulnerable position. Trim itself and his manors in the Pale maghery were secure enough, but not those in the shire's northern marches, or the sprawling, war-torn manor of Rathwire in the far south-west near the frontier with O'Connor Faly's country. Thus, since all of Meath was now administered as one very large royal shire, extensive changes were needed in the arrangements for the shire's government and defence.

In many ways, the liberty's suppression in 1461 only made a difficult situation worse. Despite the lord's lengthy absences, his seneschal had nonetheless held sweeping powers to organize defence and also enjoyed immediate access to the liberty's not inconsiderable financial resources. In Edward IV's early years sessions of the court of king's bench were often held at Trim as a kind of legal substitute for the liberty jurisdiction, but in other respects the liberty's suppression created a power vacuum (Ellis 1986: 185). A series of military disasters followed, with the shire weakened by internal divisions and Gaelic raids in the early 1460s: a large part of Meath was destroyed in this war, so the Gaelic annals recorded. O'Connor Faly took his opportunity: he and MacRichard Butler, accompanied by a thousand horsemen, symbolically shoe'd their horses at Drumhurlin in Corkeree barony as their raiding parties destroyed the shire.[15] O'Connor had to be bought off. Further east, Mageoghegan launched a series of raids on Delvin barony and also plundered

---

[14] Otway-Ruthven 1968: 181-7; Frame 1982: 24-6, 65, 70-73. A palatinate was a more extensive liberty jurisdiction with power to determine all legal cases except four specific 'pleas' which were reserved to the crown.

[15] A barony was the administrative subdivision of a shire or county in Ireland, akin to a hundred or wapentake in England.

and burned Rathwire. In response, the baron of Delvin mortgaged certain of his lands "en lez frontures dez marches" (in the frontiers of the marches), raising £53 6s. 8d. for defence works, but he had to resort to parliament to force the inhabitants to provide the labour (Parliament roll, 3 Edward IV cc 41-3 (Berry 1914: 134-9); Freeman 1944: 502-7). 1462 also saw a rising in Meath on behalf of the Lancastrian king, Henry VI, led by Philip Bermingham, the future chief justice, and coinciding with an invasion of English Lancastrians led by the Ormond pretender. In the revolt's aftermath, the attainder for treason of leading Meath gentry hardly helped matters;[16] and when in 1463, King Edward's new governor, the earl of Desmond, took office, he immediately faced a new insurrection by 5,000 of the commons of Meath. O'Connor again raided deep into Meath, appearing in Mullingar with a large army to demand the release of a prisoner and exacting a heavy price of 300 cows, droves of pigs, and other goods in return for peace.[17] And when, in 1466, the earl led a retaliatory raid into Offaly, he was defeated and captured, along with many leading Meath landowners. Teig O'Connor, Desmond's brother-in-law, later spirited the prisoners away to Carbury castle, where they were promptly besieged by the O'Connor chief and had to be rescued by levies from Dublin. Meanwhile, the Ulster Irish sacked and burned Meath without opposition, and O'Connor's raiding parties ranged as far north-east as the hill of Tara in the heart of the English Pale, and only fifteen miles from the sea (Freeman 1944: 520-27, 530-33; Ellis 1998: 64-7, 75-80; Ellis 1981: 152-4).

Gradually, however, the military threat was contained. Three developments were important here. The first was the building of standing fortifications. As a statute of 1495 remarked, "the marches of the four shires be open & not [de]fe[n]sible in fastnes [*fortifications*] of ditches and castles, where through Irishmen do great hurts" (Statute roll, 11 Henry VII c. 34 (Conway 1932: 215). The great age of castle building was over by the late 14th century, but in the English borderlands, notably Ireland and the far north, it was followed in the 15th century by an age of towerhouses – free-standing stone keeps, usually three or four stories in height and with battlements. In the English Pale they were concentrated in the marches, including a large cluster in west Meath, and were mainly built by local gentry – often with the encouragement of a small subsidy

---

[16]  Attainder: a conviction for high treason for which the penalty was death by hanging, drawing, and quartering, and forfeiture to the crown of land and goods.

[17]  Parliament roll, 2 Edward IV c. 10, 3 Edward IV c. 68 (Berry 1914: 24-9, 180-87); Freeman 1944: 514-17; Cosgrove 1987: 599; Ellis 1998: 64.

of £10 as authorized by the Irish parliament in a statute of 1429 (Ellis 1995: 30-32; Parliament roll, 8 Henry VI c. 12 (Berry 1910: 32-5). Thus, the marches of Meath were gradually strengthened during the 15th century by the building of these towers or small castles at key points of entry into the English Pale, and also by fortifying bridges. In 1462 a large tower was built at the ford at Kinnegad, O'Connor's most convenient entry into Meath, and in 1468 orders were given for the sure custody of five border castles there, and to build a new tower at the ford of Agane.[18] Similarly, the town of Kells, described as lying in the frontier of the marches near the O'Reillys, was authorized in 1468 to levy customs duties on goods sold there to finance the strengthening of its walls; and in 1472 a subsidy of £10 was granted to build a castle at Laracor, again in the marches.[19] A little later, the value of these fortifications was extended through the construction of earthen dikes and ditches so as to inhibit cattle rustling. For instance, in 1477, following the erection of a tower to protect the open road between Rathconnell and Culleen, the construction of a ditch was authorized. Finally, small-scale initiatives were systematized by the statute of 1495, which required English marchers to "build & make a double ditch of six foot of earth above the ground at the end side or part of the said land that he doth so occupy which joineth next unto Irishmen" and also to construct other "ditches in the wastes or fasaghe[20] lands w[i]t[h]out [=*outside*] the said marches".[21] The Pale marches thus gradually became a distinct and defended frontier, not just a psychological barrier with no physical reality.

Second, the crown needed to ensure that landowners were resident, with troops at hand, to repel border raids. Particularly in frontier conditions, and to save money, English kings relied heavily on the nobles to maintain good rule and defence – the Fitzgerald earls to organize Kildare's defence, for instance. Vigorous marcher lordship was equally necessary to defend Meath's exposed western marches: so in the absence of a resident lord Edward IV set about

---

[18]  Parliament roll, 27 Henry VI c. 16 (Berry 1910: 176); Parliament rolls, 2 Edward IV cc 8, 13, 7 & 8 Edward IV c. 74 (Berry 1914: 22-3, 30-33, 626-7).

[19]  Parliament rolls, 7 & 8 Edward IV c. 84, 11 & 12 Edward IV c. 16 (Berry 1914: 644-9, 742-7).

[20]  Fasaghe: an Anglicization of the Gaelic *fásach*, meaning 'a waste, or uninhabited, uncultivated place'.

[21]  Parliament rolls, 32 Henry VI cc 47-50 (Berry 1910: 299), 16 & 17 Edward IV c. 35 (Morrissey 1939: 518-19); Statute roll, 11 Henry VII c. 34 (Conway 1932: 215-16). In Hiberno-English, the term 'ditch' often refers to the earthen rampart or dike rather than the channel or watercourse from which earth has been scooped.

building up some local gentry as replacements, creating three new peers: Lords Portlester, Trimblestone, and Ratoath.[22] And in western Meath the earls of Kildare began to fill the power vacuum created by Duke Richard's demise. By 1534, Kildare had built up from scratch a rental of £150 a year among the Gaelic and English marcher lineages there.[23] His growing influence was already apparent by 1492 when those Meath gentry who failed to follow his lead found that "as soon as the earl abandoned them, they were universally burned and plundered from every quarter by the Irish" (O'Donovan 1851: iv, 1197-9).

Another, more general weakness facing the Pale arose from the gradual phasing out of military subventions from England. To support their governor's authority in Ireland, English kings had traditionally financed a retinue of 300 English archers; but this policy was gradually curtailed after 1460 in favour of increased reliance on locally-born governors who were expected to manage out of their own resources. Eventually, the Pale community was persuaded, through a new tax called poundage, to pay for a retinue to support the governor. After various experiments, the system which emerged in 1474 involved a corporation of thirteen leading Pale landowners, the Brotherhood of Arms of St George – four from Meath, three each from the other three shires, who would annually elect from among themselves a captain for this new retinue of 120 archers and 40 horsemen.[24] In this context, the invocation of St George, England's patron saint, and the battle cry of English arms in Ireland, tells its own story. More tangibly, the experiment's success left the English Pale now militarily and financially self-sufficient.

Thirdly, the earlier loose division of the English Pale into an inner 'land of peace', or maghery, and the marches which lay open to Gaelic raids was institutionalized: the boundaries between them were precisely delineated and also tied in to the population's obligation to militia service so as to create a cordon sanitaire. In any given region the particular arrangements for defence also reflected in some measure the topography of the land and the prevailing patterns of settlement there. The eastern baronies of Meath, with their numerous market towns, resident gentry and smaller holdings, supported higher

---

[22] *Calendar of the patent rolls preserved in the Public Record Office, 1461-1467*, pp. 84, 117, 178, 188; Parliament roll, 7 & 8 Edward IV c. 72 (Berry 1914: 622-5).

[23] The National Archives (henceforth TNA), SP 60/5, ff 148-9 (*LP*, xii (ii), no. 1317); Mac Niocaill 1992: 126-9, 232-302 *passim*; Ellis 1995: 114-16, 122.

[24] Parliament rolls, 12 & 13 Edward IV c. 60, 14 Edward IV c. 3, 19 & 20 Edward IV c. 27 (Morrissey 1939: 130-37, 188-95, 740-47).

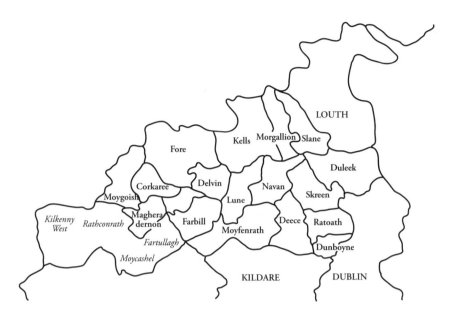

*Map 3. Baronies in Co. Meath, with the new baronies of Westmeath (marked in italics).*

levels of population, particularly where the land was given over to tillage; and in these districts, where the classic English manorial system of mixed farming obtained, the population could be concentrated in clusters of villages positioned sufficiently close to each other to offer mutual support and discourage casual raiding. (Map 3)

By contrast, the more sparsely populated, chiefly pastoral western baronies, with few towns or resident gentry, perforce relied on defence in depth. In part, this contrast between Meath's western marches and eastern maghery reflected the shire's earlier feudal settlement. A predominance of larger holdings in the western parts contrasted with some much smaller tenancies in the east. In 1431, before the union with Trim, the crown had seventy-five knight-service tenants in Meath, mainly in the east: but these tenancies were mostly quite small.[25] More knight-service tenants were acquired in 1460 when Trim fell in, but probably not many in western Meath where holdings were larger. The basic pattern is clear from a list of landowners by barony (plus market towns) prepared in 1511 by Christopher Cusack, the sheriff, ready to summon them for militia service to hostings. In all, 159 lords and gentry were listed in seventeen

---

25  Trinity College Dublin (henceforth TCD), MS 569, ff 47-8v (a copy of the Pipe Roll for 10 Henry VI). Cf. Ellis 1977: 5-28; Otway-Ruthven 1968: 107.

baronies, but resident gentry were more numerous in eastern baronies such as Duleek (18 landowners listed) or Navan (14), and the large barony of Kells (23) on the shire's northern frontier than in western baronies like Corkeree (6) or Moygoish (4). Exceptionally, Magheradernon had no resident landowner.[26] While the landowners were all English, however, many of the peasants who worked the land were native Irish, especially in the marches. Even in a well-insulated eastern barony like Skreen, in 1510 nearly half the tenants on the estates of one of the leading gentry, Christopher Cusack of Gerardstown, had Gaelic names (TCD, MS 594, ff 23-4v). Others of Irish origin may well have taken English names in response to the legislation. Though necessarily English subjects, 10% of those from Meath taking legal cases in the central courts in the 1460s, and a much higher proportion of the jurors, had Gaelic names.[27] The system of military defences thus probably also made it easier to exert anglicizing pressures on the native Irish living within the Pale, but even so a very visible Gaelic subculture still survived behind the Pale's new fortifications.[28]

In the mid-15th century the boundary between marches and maghery was more precisely delineated, in accordance with farming practices and settlement patterns, and was eventually fixed by statute in 1477 (TNA, MS E.30/1548, f. 18 (Conway 1932: 215-16). To the east of the boundary line, tillage predominated, so that the maghery was also protected by a ring of nucleated villages. This region also included nearly all the market towns: Sheriff Cusack's list noted fourteen towns, but only two of these lay in the marches (TCD, MS 594, ff 29-9v). The next step was to ensure that, in the maghery, local arrangements for defence rested on traditional English weaponry and the obligation of militia service, so reducing reliance on the much disliked quasi-Gaelic custom of coign and livery (free billeting of Gaelic troops on tenants). In 1488, the Dublin administration passed the Act of Marches and Maghery. This made it a felony for anyone to impose coign and livery anywhere in the English Pale, except landlords on their own tenants in the marches (Quinn 1941b: 84; McNeill 1950: 250; NLI, MS 2507, f. 57v).

---

[26]   TCD, MS 594, ff 25v-9v. The list includes 160 names, but four are later additions, and one is the archbishop of Armagh.

[27]   National Archives of Ireland, EX 3/1 (Estreat roll, Co. Meath, 1463-8).

[28]   The nature of the surviving evidence means that it is very difficult to look at the English Pale from the outside, from a Gaelic perspective, and almost impossible to view English rule 'from below', through the eyes of the landowners' Gaelic tenantry. For a pioneering attempt to look at things from the 'other side', see Maginn 2010: 173-90.

The division between marches and maghery was thus reflected in the obligation of militia service. Whenever a hosting (military expedition) was proclaimed against the Irish, the gentry were to "elect a captain for the spears of their shire", but in the marches the gentry were to "cess on their march lands six score [120] kerne of their own kerne ... and a captain to be elected for them". Each marcher landowner was to send to each hosting one horseman for every 10 marks (£6 13s. 4d.) of income a year; but in the maghery each landowner had to send an able man with jack (leather coat), sallet (helmet), bow and arrows for every £20 of income.[29] In 1520, when the king's council considered asking for a double subsidy or tax in return for abolishing coign and livery, the proposal was seen as impracticable: the English marchers, compelled to keep kerne and galloglass to defend their lands, could not maintain them without coign and livery; while maghery landowners would be unwilling to grant the subsidy because they were now seldom oppressed with coign. By this date, too, the maghery was so secure from Gaelic raids that, as one official complained, the major landowners there kept "little ordinary houses, as [if] they were in a land of peace", leaving the burden of defence to the poor march gentlemen (TNA, SP 60/1, f. 71 (*LP*, iii, no. 670ii); *LP*, iv, no. 2405 (quotation).

One result of this military reorganization was more stable political conditions, particularly in the Pale maghery, where there was a striking increase in the amount of land under cultivation at this time. (Crops were easily burned during Gaelic raids, whereas cattle and sheep could be moved out of harm's way.) This change may be discerned from evidence concerning the incidence of the parliamentary subsidy, the chief form of direct taxation in late medieval Ireland, which was levied on ploughlands of cultivated arable land.[30] Earlier, some of these tax assessments had clearly been notional, but by the 1470s they were adjusted to reflect more precisely the amount of land actually under cultivation. That for Louth, a small shire, was twice reduced;[31] but the overall trend in tax assessments was firmly upwards. In 1479 the Pale's overall assess-

---

[29]   Patrick Finglas, baron, 'A Breviate of the gettyng of Ireland and of the decaye of the same.' The copy I am using here is from the Marquess of Salisbury's MSS, Hatfield House, CP144, ff 1-15v (at ff 11v-12). There is an inaccurate printed copy in Harris 1747: 39-52.

[30]   The ploughland was a medieval measure of land, equivalent to 120 medieval acres (or 300 statute acres) and supposedly as much land as could be tilled with one plough.

[31]   Parliament roll, 16 & 17 Edward IV c. 17 (Morrissey 1939: 484-7); TCD, MS 594, f. 20.

ment was 793 ploughlands, but by 1500 it had risen to 831.[32] The changes in tax assessments almost certainly reflect the impact of official measures to strengthen the marches and stamp out coign and livery in the Pale maghery.

Turning to the subsidy assessments for Meath, the importance of the division between marches and maghery is immediately apparent. Of the shire's eighteen baronies, eleven lay predominantly within the maghery. Some of these eastern baronies were assessed at thirty ploughlands or more, whereas the western baronies (where political conditions were more turbulent and the land often poorer and given over mainly to pasture) were assessed at just six, or even four ploughlands.[33] In the later 14th century, the shire had been assessed at 366 ploughlands overall. Initially, this assessment held up well, despite the lordship's overall decline: in 1413, the shire was still assessed at 342 ploughlands. But by then, three far western baronies (Moygoish, Corkaree and Magheradernon) had disappeared. The shire's assessment for 1479 (40 ploughlands for the seven western baronies, 'all in the march'; plus 236 ploughlands for the eleven eastern baronies) was well down on this total, with sharp reductions for all the eastern baronies; but the fact that the three 'missing' western baronies had reappeared suggests that Meath was already recovering from a mid-15th century trough. By the late 1490s the shire's overall assessment had risen from 276 to 299 ploughlands, and by 1508 it had risen again to 315 ploughlands – not that far short of the levels a century earlier.[34] Broadly, the assessments of the western baronies in the marches remained fairly stable, but those in the maghery showed striking increases. Evidence concerning the actual subsidy yields bears out this picture. The standard parliamentary grant in the early 16th century was one mark (13s. 4d., or two-thirds of a pound) per ploughland, which, on an assessment of 330 ploughlands, should have yielded £220. In the year 1521-22, the exchequer collected altogether £219 15s. 9d from the eighteen baronies (TNA, E 101/248, no. 21; Quinn 1935: 226). By 1533-34 the actual yield had risen once again to £229 6s. 8d., indi-

---

[32]   The subsidy extents for 1479 are included in British Library (henceforth BL), Royal MS 18C, XIV, ff 105-5v, 107v. The extents for c.1500 are in TCD, MS 594, ff 18v-21v. See also Quinn 1935: 219-46; Richardson and Sayles 1952: ch. 15.

[33]   The extents of baronies in the late 1470s appear in BL, Royal MS 18C, XIV, ff 105-5v, 107v. For a discussion and dating of these, see Ellis 1979: app. iii. Various slightly later extents of Meath baronies were copied into Christopher Cusack's commonplace book: TCD, MS 594, ff 2-3v, 5v, 11, 14-15, 18v-22, 38-40v. See also Quinn 1935: 234-9, which prints extracts from this MS.

[34]   TCD, MS 594, ff. 5v, 18v-19v, 21v-22; BL, Royal MS 18C, XIV, ff 108v, 109.

cating an assessment of 344 ploughlands, exceeding even that of 1413 (TNA, SP 65/1, no. 2). These figures, therefore, are a strong indication of increased political stability and prosperity, at least within the Pale maghery. Indeed, the parish of Laracor and the erstwhile border town of Kells, which two decades earlier had both been described as lying in the frontier of the marches, were by 1488 just within the bounds of the maghery (Quinn 1941b: 84; McNeill 1950: 250-51).

Valuations of Duke Richard's former estates in Meath, the lordship of Trim, present a similar picture. In 1322-7 they had been worth around £300 a year; but in 1495, inquiries by the king's undertreasurer showed that the best value of the lordship's eleven manors in recent years was no more than £230 13s. 4d.[35] After 1534, however, when the manors were almost all in the king's hand again, their best value was estimated at £426 8s. 11d.[36]

By the 1530s, therefore, the king's peace stretched further and English rule was effective over a much wider area of Meath than had been the case in the 1460s. After the earl of Kildare's estates had been confiscated following the Kildare rebellion, the receipts for his Meath lands included significant sums from the quondam manors beyond the south-western baronies – from the earl's manors in Fartullagh, in Maghirquirke (now Kilkenny West), and in Kineleagh, amounting to over £75 a year in all, plus rents from lands near Loughsewdy (now in Rathconrath) – all in Meath. Physically, too, Fartullagh had since been integrated into the Pale's frontier defences: a ditch had been erected, extending through Farbill, Carbury, and into Meath as far as the Boyne. The 1541 surveys of crown lands likewise described these estates as lying "in partibus Westmidie" (in the parts of Westmeath), or "in partibus de Fortullagh infra comitatem Midie ubi tamen breve domini Regis non currit" (in the parts of Fartullagh within the county of Meath where, however, the writ of the lord king does not run).[37] And when the diocese of Meath was assessed for first fruits and twentieths by the king's commissioners c.1539, this new taxation included the deanery of Loughsewdy where, for instance, the

---

[35]   BL, Royal MS 18C, XIV, ff 106, 110, 111, 112, 148v (summarized in Conway 1932: 172, 188); Frame 1982: 65. See also TNA, E.101/248, no. 17 (account of the Irish revenue 1485, printed in Quinn 1941a: 17-27).

[36]   TNA, SP 65/1, no. 2; Mac Niocaill 1992: 52-75, 105-23. This figure includes £13 6s. 8d. for the manor of Diamor and Derver "in ffrontura marchiarum", its value in 1495: BL, Royal MS 18C, XIV, f. 106. It was granted to Lord James Butler for life in 1529: Curtis 1932-43), iv, no. 130.

[37]   TNA, SP 65/1, no. 2 (*LP*, xii (ii), no. 1318); Mac Niocaill 1992: 126, 127, 211.

rectory of Loughsewdy was taxed at £16 per annum, the rectory of Newton in Fartullagh at £2 3s. 4d., and the rectory of Rathconnartie at £13 15s. 0d.[38]

In the early Tudor period, however, these districts lay outside the shire's formal baronial structure, so that the king's writs and process could not be executed there. The rectification of this anomaly was one of the aims of the *Act for the division of Meath* passed in 1542. This statute noted that because Meath was "great and large in circuit, and the west part thereof laid about and beset with diverse of the king's rebels", the king's writs and laws were disobeyed in several parts there "for lack of [ad]ministration of justice" and the sheriff was "not able to execute the king's process and precepts [commands]" throughout the shire, particularly "in diverse places of the west part" where the inhabitants had formerly been obedient. Accordingly, the shire was now to be divided into two shires, Meath and Westmeath. Upon the creation of Westmeath as a separate shire, four new baronies were established in the far west of the county on the lands of the English marcher lineages: Dalton's country became the barony of Rathcomyrte (now Rathconrath); Delamare's country, Moybreckry, was made the barony of Rossaughe (later Moycashel); Tyrrell's country became the barony of Fartullagh; and Dillon's country, Maghirquirke, was now the barony of Kilkenny West. The new shire thus had eleven baronies since, besides the existing baronies of Delvin, Moyashel, Magheradernon, Corkaree, Farbill and Moygoish, the large barony of Fore was now divided: the half-barony of Fore in Westmeath became an entire barony, to which was also added another tract of land named Moylagaghe. Significantly, too, the new shire town was Mullingar, which, eighty years earlier, had been a beleaguered outpost in the extreme west periodically burned by the Irish.[39] Robert Dillon was appointed first sheriff of Westmeath, as the statute took effect. Within ten years, too, the head of one of the English marcher lineages, Thomas Tyrrell, chief captain of Tyrrell's country, had been knighted and appointed to the peace commission: Tyrrell, the English rebel, had become Sir Thomas Tyrrell, JP.[40] Why, then,

---

[38]   *Valor Beneficiorum Ecclesiasticorum in Hibernia* (Dublin, 1741), pp. 3-5; TCD, MS 567, ff 3-4.

[39]   Statute roll, 34 Henry VIII, session 1, c. 1 (*The statutes at large passed in the parliaments held in Ireland* (20 vols., Dublin, 1786-1801), i, 232-5); Cosgrove 1987: 571-2; Freeman 1944: 524-5.

[40]   *The Irish fiants of the Tudor sovereigns* (4 vols, Dublin, 1994), I (1521-1558), *Edw. VI*, nos. 1100, 1147; Memoranda roll, 3 & 4 Philip & Mary mm 1, 2 (NAI, Ferguson collection, v, ff 6-6v, 35-7); Memoranda roll, 3, 4, 5, 6 Elizabeth (NAI, Ferguson coll., v, ff 6v-7); Morrin 1861, 284, 368.

did Poynings' officials rechristen 'the four shires' in 1495 as 'the English Pale'? Describing the Pale as 'English' was deliberate. Englishness had a cultural quality, reflected in the region's social structures and market towns. The extension of tillage there had also reinforced its English character: tillage was high on any checklist by English officials of the attributes of English civility. Above all, the English Pale was by 1495 no longer an extended march but a distinct region, with a clearly delineated, defensive frontier, like Calais.

The creation of the shire of Westmeath within what the statute establishing it now described as 'the English Pale' thus crowned the success of this policy of erecting a frontier to defend English ground, and also rendered obsolete the region's earlier designation as 'the four shires'. It had, of course, been in the interests of the king's officers to claim that the English Pale was shrinking and English order and rule collapsing, so as to induce the king to come to the rescue with money and men. But the alacrity with which historians have accepted such *ex parte* statements perhaps tells us more about attitudes to Ireland's modern partition than about the reality of the late medieval frontier. The English Pale remained a frontier of contact, with substantial ties between English and Irish, but it was increasingly also a frontier of separation which allowed the Tudor regime more easily to regulate these relations between native and settler. The erection of a fortified frontier to defend English ground and the English nation from foreigners was also not a new idea: it was a proven strategy, long used against the Scots. It is a mistake, too, to overlook the political terminology in which the conflict was described. The English rhetoric of difference was of course no more than rhetoric – though even this is revealing of English attitudes to the Irish – but terms like 'frontier', 'march', and 'pale' had different nuances, and historians need to pay close attention to when they were used, and in what circumstances. As for the practice of describing two categories of Irishmen, 'Anglo-Irish' and 'Gaelic Irish', this smacks more of modern theories of 'one nation' and shows little appreciation of medieval English concepts of citizenship. The fact is that late medieval Ireland still had two nations, Irish and English; and those who were subjects of the English crown, whether born in Ireland or England, were Englishmen, enjoying the same rights. So to speak of 'two-nation theory' is anachronistic: a more accurate description of this late medieval English strategy for Ireland would be 'two-nation *policy*'.

# Bibliography

### i) Manuscript Sources

British Library, London, Royal MS 18C, XIV.

Marquess of Salisbury's MSS, Hatfield House, CP144.

National Archives of Ireland, EX 3/1, Ferguson collection vol. V.

National Library of Ireland, Dublin, MS 2507.

The National Archives, Kew, E.30/1548, E 101/248 nos. 17, 21, SP 60/1, SP 60/5, SP 65/1 no. 2.

Trinity College Dublin, MSS 567, 569, 594.

### ii) Printed Sources

Berry, H.F. (ed.). (1907). *Statutes and ordinances, and acts of the parliament of Ireland. King John to Henry V*. Dublin: His Majesty's Stationery Office.

Berry, H.F. (ed.). (1910). *Statute rolls of the parliament of Ireland, reign of King Henry the Sixth*. Dublin: His Majesty's Stationery Office.

Berry, H.F. (ed.). (1914). *Statute rolls of the parliament of Ireland, first to the twelfth years of the reign of King Edward IV*. Dublin: His Majesty's Stationery Office. (1897)

*Calendar of the patent rolls preserved in the Public Record Office, 1461-1467*. London: Her Majesty's Stationery Office.

Curtis, E. (ed.). (1932-43). *Calendar of Ormond deeds*. Dublin: Irish Manuscripts Commission.

Freeman, A.M. (ed.). (1944). *Annála Connacht: the Annals of Connacht*. Dublin: Dublin Institute for Advanced Studies.

Harris, W. (ed.). (1747). *Hibernica: or some ancient pieces relating to Ireland*. 1st ed., Dublin.

(1862-1932) *Letters & Papers, foreign and domestic, of the reign of Henry VIII*. 21 vols., London: Her/His Majesty's Stationery Office.

Mac Niocaill, G. (ed.). (1992). *Crown surveys of lands 1540-41, with the Kildare rental begun in 1518*. Dublin: Irish Manuscripts Commission.

McNeill, C. (ed.). (1950). *Calendar of Archbishop Alen's register, c.1172-1534*. Dublin: Royal Society of Antiquaries of Ireland.

Morrin, J. (ed.). (1861). *Calendar of patent and close rolls of chancery in Ireland, Henry VIII to 18th Elizabeth*. Dublin: Her Majesty's Stationery Office.

Morrissey, J.F. (ed.). (1939). *Statute rolls of the parliament of Ireland, twelfth and thirteenth to the twenty-first and twenty-second years of the reign of King Edward IV*. Dublin: The Stationery Office.

Nicholls, K. (1994). *The Irish fiants of the Tudor sovereigns*. 4 vols, Dublin.

O'Donovan, J. (ed.). (1851). *Annála ríoghachta Éireann: annals of the kingdom of Ireland by the Four Masters from the earliest period to the year 1616.* 7 vols., Dublin.

Quinn, D.B. (1941a). Guide to English financial records for Irish history 1461-1558. *Analecta Hibernica*, 10, 1-69.

Quinn, D.B. (1941b). The bills and statutes of the Irish parliaments of Henry VII and Henry VIII. *Analecta Hibernica*, 10, 71-169.

Simington, R.C. (ed.). (1961). *The Civil Survey 1654-6. Vol. X Miscellanea.* Dublin: Irish Manuscripts Commission.

(1786-1801), *The statutes at large passed in the parliaments held in Ireland.* 20 vols., Dublin.

(1741), *Valor Beneficiorum Ecclesiasticorum in Hibernia.* Dublin.

### iii) Secondary literature

Barry, T., Frame, R. & Simms, K. (eds.). (1995). *Colony and frontier in medieval Ireland: essays presented to J.F. Lydon.* Dublin: Four Courts Press.

Conway, A. (1932). *Henry VII's relations with Scotland and Ireland, 1485-98.* Cambridge: Cambridge University Press.

Cosgrove, A. (1987). "The emergence of the Pale, 1399-1447" in: Cosgrove, A. (ed.). *A new history of Ireland. II.* Oxford: Oxford University Press, ch. 18.

Cosgrove, A. (ed.). (1987). *A new history of Ireland II Medieval Ireland 1169-1534.* Oxford: Oxford University Press.

Crooks, P. (2008). "Government, war and society in English Ireland, 1171-1541: a guide to recent work" in: Crooks, P. (ed.). *Government, war and society in medieval Ireland*, 371-3.

Crooks, P. (ed.). (2008). *Government, war and society in medieval Ireland: essays by Edmund Curtis, A.J. Otway-Ruthven and James Lydon.* Dublin: Four Courts Press.

Davies, R.R. (2000). *The first English empire: power and identities in the British Isles 1093-1343.* Oxford: Oxford University Press.

Duffy, P.J., Edwards, D. & Fitzpatrick, E. (2001). "Introduction: recovering Gaelic Ireland, c.1250-c.1650" in: Duffy, P.J., Edwards, D. & Fitzpatrick, E. (eds.). *Gaelic Ireland: land, lordship and settlement c.1250-c.1650.* Dublin: Four Courts Press.

Ellis, S.G. (1977). "Taxation and defence in late medieval Ireland: the survival of scutage". *Journal of the Royal Society of Antiquaries of Ireland*, 107, 5-28.

Ellis, S.G. (1979). *The administration of the lordship of Ireland under the early Tudors* (unpublished PhD thesis, Queen's University Belfast).

Ellis, S.G. (1981). "The destruction of the liberties: some further evidence". *Bulletin of the Institute of Historical Research*, 54, 150-61.

Ellis, S.G. (1986). *Reform and revival: English government in Ireland, 1470-1534.* London: The Royal Historical Society.

Ellis, S.G. (1995). *Tudor frontiers and noble power: the making of the British state.* Oxford: Oxford University Press.

Ellis, S.G. (1998). *Ireland in the age of the Tudors 1447-1603: English expansion and the end of Gaelic rule*. London: Longman.

Ellis, S.G. (1999). "The English state and its frontiers in the British Isles" in: Power & Standen (eds.). *Frontiers in question*, 153-81.

Ellis, S.G. (2007). "Civilizing the natives: state formation and the Tudor monarchy, c.1400-1603" in: Ellis, S.G. & Klusáková, L. (eds.). *Imagining frontiers: contesting identities*. Pisa: Edizioni Plus Pisa University Press, 77-92.

Frame, R. (1977). "Power and society in the lordship of Ireland, 1272-1377". *Past & Present*, no. 76, 3-33.

Frame, R. (1982). *English lordship in Ireland 1318-1361*. Oxford: Oxford University Press.

Khodarkovsky, M. (1992). "From frontier to empire: the concept of the frontier in Russia, sixteenth-eighteenth centuries". *Russian history*, 19, 115-28.

Lydon, J. (1967). "The problem of the frontier in medieval Ireland". *Topic: A Journal of the Liberal Arts*, 13, 5-22; reprinted in: Crooks (ed.). *Government, war and society in medieval Ireland*, 317-31.

Maginn, C. (2010). "Gaelic Ireland's English frontiers in the late middle ages". *Proceedings of the Royal Irish Academy*, 110, 173-90.

Manzano Moreno, E. (1999). "The creation of a medieval frontier: Islam and Christianity in the Iberian peninsula, eighth to eleventh centuries" in: Power & Standen (ed.). *Frontiers in question*, 32-54.

Nicholls, K. (1999). Worlds apart? The Ellis two-nation theory on late medieval Ireland. *History Ireland*, 8 (2), 22-6.

Otway-Ruthven, A.J. (1968). *A history of medieval Ireland*. London: Ernest Benn Ltd.

Power, G. (2008). The nobility of the English Pale in Tudor Ireland, 1496-1566 (unpublished PhD thesis; National University of Ireland, Galway).

Power, D. & Standen, N. (1999). "Introduction" in: Power, D. & Standen, N. (ed.). *Frontiers in question*, 1-31.

Power, D. & Standen, N. (ed.) (1999). *Frontiers in question: Eurasian borderlands, 700-1700*. Basingstoke: Macmillan Press Ltd.

Quinn, D.B. (1935). "The Irish parliamentary subsidy in the fifteenth and sixteenth centuries". *Proceedings of the Royal Irish Academy*, 42, sect. C, 219-46.

Richardson, H.G. & Sayles, G.O. (1952). *The Irish parliament in the middle ages*. Philadelphia: University of Pennsylvania Press.

Rowell, S.C. (1999). "The Lithuano-Prussian forest frontier, c.1422-1600" in: Power & Standen (eds.). *Frontiers in question*, 182-208.

Smith, B. (1997). "Keeping the peace" in: Lydon J. (ed.). *Law and disorder in thirteenth century Ireland: the Dublin parliament of 1297*. Dublin: Four Courts Press, 57-65.

# Russian History and European Ideas:
# The Historical Vision of Vasilii Kliuchevskii

*Kåre Johan Mjør*

To the general public, Vasilii Osipovich Kliuchevskii (1841-1911) is above all known for his *Course in Russian History* (*Kurs russkoi istorii*), which he began reading at the University of Moscow in the 1880s and which was published for the first time two decades later.[1] Since then, his history of Russia has been republished several times; in the late 1980s, a new nine-volume edition of his works even became a best-seller. Kliuchevskii has had tremendous impact on Russian historical self-awareness. His skills as a historian, his appealing schemes and his eloquent style are all factors that have contributed to his canonical position. As the Russian émigré historian Georgii Fedotov (1886-1951) wrote in 1932, Kliuchevskii's history

> is not just one among many – it is the Russian History on which two generations of Russians have been brought up. Specialists may have voiced their objections, but whenever any of us think of historical Russia, what comes to mind is the Russia Kliuchevskii visualized (Fedotov 1986: 204).

Kliuchevskii's idea of Russia also involves an idea of Europe. According to Charles Halperin,

> even when Kliuchevskii emphasized the distinctiveness of Russian historical evolution compared to West-European, West-European history remained the standard by which the past of Russia – or anywhere else – would be judged (Halperin 2000: 404).

It is not difficult to find quotations from his history that testify to this tendency; a typical formulation of Kliuchevskii is "let us now have a look at Moscow's location in relationship to the *other* European states [at the

---

[1]    For Kliuchevskii's biography, see Byrnes (1995).

end of the sixteenth century, KJM]" (2: 397, italics added).[2] His numerous comparisons, by implication, do not primarily aim to maintain an antithetic relationship; rather, they implicitly inform the readers that Russia forms a part of Europe.

> There is not one people in Europe that is capable of such intensive work for a short period as the Great Russian is, but nowhere in Europe, apparently, would you also find a person that is so unaccustomed to regular, moderate and measured, continual work as in Great Russia (1: 314).

It has been argued that this way of comparing Russia to Europe has been highly characteristic of Russian identity discourses, to which historians too have contributed in their works on Russian history. In modern Russia, more specifically, the "idea of Europe" or the "West" has been "the 'other' in relation to which the idea of Russia is defined" (Neumann 1996: 1) or even "the main constituent other, against which [educated Russians] tried to construct a new Russian identity" (Tolz 2001: 1). From the 1840s onwards, both Slavophiles and Westernisers, to mention the most famous example, evaluated Russia in relation to or against an idea of Europe.[3]

However widespread it may seem to have been in Russian intellectual history, the comparison of Russia with the West is still not inevitable. According to Vera Tolz,

> these constant attempts to compare and contrast Russia and the West provided a powerful creative stimulus for Russian cultural figures, but proved dysfunctional as a tool of political analysis of Russia's development (Tolz 2001: 1).

---

[2]    I have taken the opportunity to simplify the references to my primary source (Kliuchevskii's *Course*), i.e. omitted "Kliuchevskii 1956-1959" here and below. Hence the numbers preceding and succeeding the colon refer to volumes of this edition and pages respectively. All translations from Russian are my own.

[3]    In my view, however, there is a marked difference between the Russia of the Slavophiles, which was formulated by way of a rejection of West-European culture, and the Westernisers' view of Russia as basically European (or eventually European) and, by implication, non-Asian. In the writings of Belinskii or Kavelin, to whom I shall return below, the "main constituent other" is not Europe, as far as I can see, but Asia. Tolz's formulation in particular ("against which") – when applied to the Westernisers – appears therefore to be slightly exaggerated.

And while a notion of Europe is clearly present in Kliuchevskii's history of Russia, his main project is not to measure Russia against Europe but rather to represent Russian history as unique and possessing its own logic. In contrast to the two principal positions among Russian intellectuals of the mid-19th century, Kliuchevskii's Russia is neither the Slavophile antithesis to Western Europe nor a belated version of Europe, as most Westernisers would have it. Kliuchevskii conceptualises Russia differently, as I intend to show. But precisely because he shied away from the traditional positions, he was able to reformulate the problem of Russia and Europe in a new and compelling way. It seems to be Kliuchevskii's view that Russia becomes European not through an adaptation but through a rejection of Eurocentric and hegemonic models of historical development.

## Progress and Retardation

While situated on the fringes of Europe geographically, Russia is, Kliuchevskii maintains early in his course, connected with Europe culturally.

> Historically, Russia is of course not Asia, but geographically it is not entirely Europe either. It is an intermediary land (*perekhodnaia strana*), the mediator (*posrednitsa*) between two worlds. Culture has inseparably linked it to Europe, but nature has contributed with features and influences that always attracted Russia to Asia, or Asia to Russia (1: 47).

Kliuchevskii does not make explicit exactly which cultural aspects have tied Russia to Western Europe. One would expect religion to be a factor worth mentioning here; but as Fedotov (1986) has observed, there is a conspicuous omission of Orthodoxy in Kliuchevskii's history, which in turn might suggest that there are other European connections in Russian history which were at least equally important to him but which are not elaborated. What the European character of Russian history consists of must therefore be sought in the way in which his narrative unfolds.

In claiming that Russia is part of Europe, Kliuchevskii remains in agreement with many previous professional Russian historians of the 19th century, most of whom were Westernisers. The term refers to a heterogeneous group of thinkers (not only historians) who in one way or another claimed that Russia was part of Europe, or at least that it would or should become part of Europe. Politically, the Westernisers comprised Hegelians, liberals and utopian socialists, and to most of them Western Europe represented a model for Russian development

(Offord 1985: 1-43). Variations of this view were formulated in response to the Slavophiles, who claimed that Russia formed a civilisation different from that of Western Europe above all because of its deep roots in Orthodox Christianity. Between Eastern and Western Christianity, the Slavophiles believed, there was not only an abyss; Western Christianity even represented an apostasy. Hence they saw Russian culture as fundamentally different from – as well as superior to – European culture. Differences mattered more to them than similarities.

In contrast, Russian thinkers oriented towards the West held that Russia would develop along the same lines as the West-European countries, i.e. that it would go through the same historical phases. A well-known Westerniser of the 1840s was the literary critic Vissarion Belinskii (1811-1848), who in a seminal article of 1842, "Russia before Peter the Great" (Belinskii 1954: 91-152), celebrated the opening up of Russia to Western impact through the reforms of Peter the Great in the early 18th century. According to Belinskii, this event represented the transition from the level of "people" (*narod*) to "nation" (*natsiia*). To Belinskii, "nation" represented a more complex formation than "people", and as to what separated the two he paid particular attention to the introduction of a modern nobility (*dvorianstvo*).[4] Equally important, however, was the "historical process" that this shift itself had inaugurated, whereby Russia came to abandon its "Asianness" and become European.

Similarly, the professional Russian historians of this age too operated in their writings with a universal unilinear scheme for historical development, a notion of world history common to all "historical nations", which they subsequently tried to adapt to Russian history. The most obvious example is Sergei Solov'ev (1820-1879), who was Kliuchevskii's teacher and the most influential Russian historian of the mid-19th century, thanks not least to his twenty-nine volume *History of Russia from the Earliest Times*, which he began publishing in 1851. Defining the historical discipline as the study of national self-awareness, Solov'ev described Russian history as a variation of a threefold universal pattern, which he deliberately adapted from Hegel and the French historian of civilisations François Guizot. According to Solov'ev, the primary stage is made up of the clan (*rod*) and clan life (*rodovoi byt*), and is in turn succeeded by the emergence of a militia (*druzhina*), which challenges the

---

4    Belinskii is thus an interesting counterexample of what Tolz (2001: 15) claims to have been a predominant tendency in Russian nineteenth-century thought: the exclusion of the upper classes from the concept of the Russian "nation" or "people" (*narod*). Indeed, many Russian thinkers have operated with an exclusive concept of nationality, but not Belinskii.

dominance of the clan. The third phase is the creation of a state or "a state principle" (*pravitel'stvennoe nachalo*) (Siljak 1999: 224ff). According to Solov'ev, Russian history begins with the passing from the first stage to the next. On the first page of his history we read that

> Russian history begins with the situation that some tribes, unable to find the way out of the isolated clan life, invite the princes of foreign clan, invite a unified common rule that unites the clans in a whole, provides them with order ... (Solov'ev 1959-1966, 1: 55).

Solov'ev was a prominent representative of what is often labelled the "state school" of Russian historiography, whose interest was centred on the gradual emergence of the Russian state (Hamburg 1999). And he held that the "invitation" of a foreign clan referred to above initiated this process. His history is founded on a firm belief in progress, which was coupled with the fundamental conviction that Russia was an integral part of Europe, of Christian Western civilisation (Siljak 1999; Bassin 1993: 482f).

In historiography, the nineteenth century was the age of historicism. In contrast to the didactic interpretation characteristic of Enlightenment historiography, a historicist representation of the past, according to Friedrich Meinecke's classic definition, implied an emphasis on individuality and development, i.e. on faculties projected from human beings onto collectives (states, nations, cultures).[5] Edward Thaden has suggested that the state school of Solov'ev and others represents the Russian equivalent of West-European historicism (Thaden 1999). In Russia, however, where most historians believed in the existence of a common universal history of progress, development became a more fundamental category than individuality. In Terence Emmons's precise observation:

> In Russia, the classic Enlightenment belief that the story of mankind has a single plot, and that men are everywhere basically the same, survived the challenge of Romanticism in the second quarter of the nineteenth century intact and was still something like an article of faith among professional historians of the late nineteenth century. For the Westernizing intelligentsia as a whole, liberal and radical, reformist and revolutionary, the belief in prog-

---

5   "Der Kern des Historismus besteht in der Ersetzung einer generalisierenden Betrachtung geschichtlich-menschlicher Kräfte durch eine individualisierende Betrachtung. ... Im Wesen der Individualität, der des Einzelmenschen wie der ideellen und realen Kollektivgebilde, liegt es, daß sie sich nur durch Entwicklung offenbart" (Meinecke 1959: 3, 5).

ress and Russia's European destiny, their rejection of the idea of Russian "exceptionalism," depended on an idea of universal history (Emmons 2003: 98).

Another Westerniser, Konstantin Kavelin (1818-1885), characteristically insisted that the presence of development in its history was the main factor that distinguished Russia from the cultures of the East (Asia) and brought it closer to Europe. Just as Belinskii saw development itself as a token of European-ness, defined by its *dynamic* nature (Belinskii 1954: 105), so did Kavelin. As he wrote in his 1847 study on the "Juridical Life of Ancient Russia", "we are a European people, capable of perfection, of development; we do not like to repeat ourselves or to stand on the same spot for an endless number of centuries" (Kavelin 1989: 13).

At the same time, most Westernisers shared a belief that Russia had developed at a slower pace than the remaining civilised world. The shift from "people" to "nation", Belinskii insinuated, had taken place relatively late in Russia. The same held true for the emergence of a Russian state, according to Solov'ev's history. So the differences that clearly existed between Russia and Europe were a result of a *retardation* of the universal historical process on Russian soil. Russia had been held back at a preliminary stage. And the main task for historians became to explain this alleged backwardness.

I would like to suggest, however, that Kliuchevskii's approach to Russian history represents an alternative to this view. He reformulated the relationship of Russia to Europe by suggesting that Russia was European because of their common cultural origin, not their common historical goal. To Kliuchevskii, the universal historical process, of which Russia is part, is one of a gradual diversification.[6] Hence the primary purpose of Russia has not been to imitate the West. In his narrative of Russian history, Kliuchevskii abandons, by implication, the model of unilinear progress and retardation developed by his teacher Solov'ev. Instead, his historiography emerges as more in keeping with both historicist principles – development and individuality – as foreshadowed in the second lecture of his course:

---

[6]   Interestingly, this way of perceiving the universal historical process may be found in other parts of the European "periphery" at this time as well: The Norwegian historian Ernst Sars (1835-1917, i.e. contemporary to Kliuchevskii) shared a similar "myth of origin" in that he conceived of national differentiation and national independence as the most important *result* of the universal historical process (Fulsås 1999: 139).

And if you are able to acquire from my presentation, however full of deficiencies, if only the most general features of the image of the Russian people (*obraz russkogo naroda*) as a historical personality (*istoricheskaia lichnost'*), I will consider the purpose of my course achieved (1: 41).

A people's "personality", Kliuchevskii continues, is the main theme (*osnovnoi predmet*) when studying its history. And in keeping with the human metaphor, he goes on to claim that a people with a personality, such as the Russian, has a calling (*prizvanie*) of accomplishing a set of tasks emerging from its capabilities. Kliuchevskii's historical thinking is permeated by the romantic idea going back at least to Johann Gottfried von Herder (1744-1803) of peoples and nations being individuals, and that peoples possess properties belonging to human beings.

By conceiving of the history of the Russian people in terms of a human personality, Kliuchevskii opens up for individualising the historical development to a greater extent than his predecessors. Despite the tendency in much late 19th century historiography to appeal to models of biological processes in nature in particular in order to assert its scientific character, the past as it appears here, as argued by Narve Fulsås, is above all a scene of *dramatic reversals*: the rise and decline, strength and weakness, perfection and failure of nations, states, or cultures – i.e. a development typical of dramas and narratives about human fate (Fulsås 1999: 135ff). By the same token, Kliuchevskii's history is ultimately the dramatic history of the Russian people (*russkii narod*), of its growth, withering, and possible future recovery.

## The Russian People and the Russian Land

One of Kliuchevskii's most famous statements about Russian history is given early in the second lecture of his *Course*: "The history of Russia is the history of a land that colonises itself (*kolonizuetsia*)" (1: 31).[7] The formulation was

---

[7]  Technically, "is being colonised" is more accurate, since the subject of this sentence is an inanimate one, but this translation has gained foothold in English, as seen most recently in a study by Alexander Etkind (2011: 61-71). In keeping with Etkind, "colonises itself" may be said to be an appropriate solution *hermeneutically* since Kliuchevskii (and Solov'ev) conceived of Russian colonisation as "self-colonisation," i.e. colonisation of one's "own" land. This land not only becomes Russia through (Russian) colonisation; it comes into being. Hence "Russia has constituted itself through the process of colonization" (Etkind 2011: 67f). See also below.

not invented by Kliuchevskii; it was his teacher Solov'ev who first argued that "ancient Russian history is the history of a land that colonises itself" (Solov'ev 1959-1966, 2: 648). But what may this notion of "self-colonisation" have meant?

As it appears in Solov'ev's history, the phrase corresponds to his environmentalism. As Mark Bassin has shown, there is a striking parallel between Solov'ev's vision of Russian history and Frederick Jackson Turner's "frontier hypothesis" about American colonisation. In a famous lecture read in 1893, Turner declared that "the existence of an area of free land, its continuous recession, and the resulting advance of American settlement westward, explain American development" (cited in Bassin 1993: 481). In the writings of Turner and Solov'ev,

> The United States and Russia both represented the product of European expansion into geographical realms that either were not European, in the case of the former, or were only dubiously so, in the case of Russia. ... The two characterized and evaluated their own native society and culture precisely in terms of divergences from what they saw as the "model" of the European Old World (Bassin 1993: 485).

In the case of Solov'ev, and in contrast to Turner, however, the "Russian frontier" assumed a highly ambiguous role. Solov'ev described Russia's natural milieu as an "evil stepmother" (*machekha*) that was assumed to have had a negative impact on its historical progress. The open and sparsely populated spaces of the East-European plain, the "existence of free land" (Turner), represented to Solov'ev first and foremost unfavourable conditions. By implication, the colonisation process turned out to have *retarded* the development and temporarily separated Russia from the West, since it had forced the population of early Russia to continually migrate and thus remain on a quasi-sedentary, half-nomadic level for longer periods than the West-European peoples (Bassin 1993: 502f).

Since Kliuchevskii in general avoids universal schemes as interpretative tools in his historiography,[8] colonisation also assumes a function different from that which it had in Solov'ev. Colonisation to him was not the process in which Russia both adapted to and deviated from universal schemes. Rather

---

[8]   This is not to say that they are entirely absent; in the first lecture he introduces a "scheme of the social-historical process", which operates with the succeeding stages of family, clan, tribe, people, state. In Kliuchevskii's history, however, this scheme cannot be said to represent a major structuring principle comparable to the threefold one of Solov'ev.

than relating it to the development of the Russian state, he sees colonisation as the fundamental vehicle of early Russian history that has testified to the unique character or "personality" of the Russian people.

Kliuchevskii's history of Russian colonisation is not what we today would think of as Russia's colonial, i.e. imperial, history, which began with the eastward expansion into non-Slavic territories in the 1550s, and which was rapidly followed by the conquest of Siberia in the early 17th century. These events do not belong to Kliuchevskii's history of Russian colonisation, and are mainly referred to instead as "conquest" (*zavoevanie*). Few periods in Kliuchevskii's course are described in such detail as the reign of Ivan the Terrible, when this eastward expansion began. However, the Muscovite conquest of the East is only mentioned in passing, and plays in general a marginal role in Kliuchevskii's history; his main interest lies instead in the continual East Slavic resettlement on the East-European plain, in "European Russia", which had been the enterprise of the Russian people in previous epochs. In contrast, Azov and the Baltic areas under Peter the Great, Crimea under Catherine the Great and the Caucasus and Central Asia in the 19th century were all *conquered* by the *state*.[9]

Kliuchevskii's history of Russia, by implication, is not imperial history but national history. He clearly downplays its imperial character by exploring the Russian national core as distinguished from the non-Russian peripheries, thereby drawing implicitly the line between national and imperial spaces. Kliuchevskii might be accused of having ignored the multi-ethnic character of the Russian empire; but the essential point here, in my view, is that he is not interested in Russia as an empire with colonies, such as Siberia. His main project is instead to imagine a "Russian land" and its history, i.e. to appropriate a certain part of the empire as Russian national territory.

Notions of an "interior Russia", "native Russia" or "central Russia" became widespread in the Russian public of the 19th century, in particular among liberal nationalists (Miller 2005; Gorizontov 2008). We should note, however, that

---

[9]   Subsequently, imperial conquest may have led to "colonisation", for instance in parts of Siberia (3: 125; 5: 137). The same goes for "New Russia", i.e. the north coast of the Black Sea conquered in the late 18th century. Although this area seems to be included in his concept of the "Russian land", colonisation here, which was preceded by state conquest, also plays a marginal role in Kliuchevskii's narrative as compared to colonisation before the 16th century. Etkind is thus correct in observing that the historian extended the concept of (self-) colonisation "well into the modern age" (2011: 67), but he does not distinguish between colonisation and conquest (or colonisation proper and colonisation upon conquest), as Kliuchevskii, in my view, did.

Kliuchevskii achieves his national history by means of the imperial distinction between centre and periphery, i.e. the distinction put forward in the early 18th century in the aftermath of the proclamation of the Russian empire, when the Urals was symbolically defined as the border between Europe and Asia, between European and Asian Russia, and thus between metropolis and colony of the empire. Kliuchevskii's history of the Russian *nation* takes place in this European centre. In other words, he creates a national history of Russia on the basis of the imperial imaginary geography of Russia as European.

Hence Kliuchevskii's concept of colonisation is confined to the "Russian land" (*russkaia zemlia*), i.e. the land that is assumed to have been "colonised" by the Russian people, in contrast to the land conquered by the Russian state later. Kliuchevskii's concept of colonisation is far more positive than that of Solov'ev; it comes, in fact, closer to Turner's concept of the frontier as an area of continual expansion – also because it is seen as part of European expansion. As an example, we may quote Kliuchevskii's summary of Early Russian relationship to the Asiatic, nomadic neighbours in the southeast:

> Russia's (*Rus*) nearly two-hundred years of struggle with the Polovtsians is significant to European history. At the same time as West-European crusaders undertook an offensive struggle in the Asian East, and a similar campaign against the Moors began on the Pyrenean peninsula, Russia covered the left flank of the European offensive through its struggle on the steppes (1: 281f).

The scene of Russian colonisation is the East-European plain (*ravnina*), frequently also referred to as the "Russian plain" and even "our plain" (*nasha ravnina*). Tolz (2001: 159) has suggested that Kliuchevskii sees Russia as having possessed a "manifest destiny" in colonising these areas. The "ancient issue (*staroe delo*) of territorial and national unification of the Russian land", Kliuchevskii writes in the opening of his 82nd lecture, is finally accomplished in the early 19th century:

> The Russian state territory in Europe reaches its natural geographical borders – comprises the entire East-European plain and at some places even crosses its boundaries; the Russian people, correspondingly, is politically unified, with one single exception (5: 186f).[10]

---

[10]    The "exception" to which Kliuchevskii refers here is probably the areas that today make up Western Ukraine, which was part of the Habsburg Empire until the First World War.

Although geography is systematically and technically discussed in the initial lectures, it gradually assumes a symbolic character through this "Russification".

The concept of the "Russian land" might appear to be a translation of the East Slavic term *ruskaia zemlia*, the "Land of the Rus", which occurs frequently in East Slavic medieval texts and refers primarily to areas ruled over by princes of the Riurik dynasty, which in the earliest texts was also named "Rus". However, Kliuchevskii's concept is not so much a translation as a modern reinterpretation, in which a medieval dynastic concept is reified as a 19th century nationalist conception of Russia (Halperin 2000: 390, n. 24). To Kliuchevskii the Russian land is first and foremost the land of the Russian people. His concept is ethnic and geographical, not dynastic.

Ukraine ("Little Russia") is also part of Kliuchevskii's "Russian land", a claim that has contributed to the opinion that he represents the empire as a nation-state (Plokhy 2008: 19). Indeed, Kliuchevskii did share the widespread view of his age that Ukraine (Kiev and Left-bank Ukraine) became "reunited" with the remaining part of Russia in the mid-17th century. While his opinion of Ukraine may be called "imperial", however, this does not mean that he treats the entire empire in the same way. In contrast to the panslavist Nikolai Danilevskii, who in his famous book *Russia and Europe* of 1869 conceived of the entire empire as one "natural region" (*estestvennaia oblast'*, Danilevskii 1995: 19), the distinction between the Russian and non-Russian lands is if not explicitly pronounced then clearly felt through the way in which Kliuchevskii's narrative proceeds.[11]

---

[11] I thus share Tolz's view that Kliuchevskii and other Russian liberals "downplayed the imperial nature of the Russian state", but not because he "upheld the view that the Russian empire was a Russian nation state" (Tolz 2001: 172). Kliuchevskii, in my view, was simply not concerned with the entire empire when composing his history. More generally, Tolz argues that the "vision of the Russian empire as a Russian nation-state" (2001: 155) was *the* commonly held perspective in Imperial Russia. This has later been questioned by Aleksei Miller (2005), who claims that Ernest Gellner's theory of nationalism as a quest for congruence between the national and political unit (1983: 1) does not apply very well to late Imperial Russia, where it was possible to be nationalist and imperialist at the same time, i.e. to defend the existence of the empire while at the same time imagining a truly "Russian land" within it. Russian nationalism in this sense may have been expansionist, in the case of Ukraine or the Volga district, but refrained more often than not from encompassing the entire empire. See also Bassin (2006), who operates with a three-fold scheme of Russian imperial visions: "Russia as a European empire", "Russia as an anti-European empire" and "Russia as a national empire".

## The Rise and Decline of Russian Nationhood

Kliuchevskii's narrative of Russian history begins in the Carpathian Mountains (the seventh lecture), in the "common nest of the Slavs" (*obshcheslavianskoe gnezdo*). After a "five-century long Slavic sojourn (*stoianka*) in the Carpathians", some tribes departed to the south and the west, while Kliuchevskii follows the tribe which headed eastwards.

> Our history begins with the entering of the Eastern branch of Slavdom, which later developed into the Russian people, onto the Russian plain from one of its corners, from the southwest, from the slopes of the Carpathian Mountains. … Conditioned by its historical life and the geographical factor the Slavic population spread out on the plain not gradually by means of a growing population, not by settling apart but by resettling (*ne rasseliaias' a pereseliaias'*) – it was carried away like migrating birds (*perenosilos' ptich'imi pereletami*) from one district to another, leaving fertilised places behind and settling on new ones (1: 30f).

It is this event, and not the first state-like formation as in Solov'ev's history, which also took place far later, that marks the beginning of Russian history according to Kliuchevskii. This history begins with resettlement, with "colonisation". In his dynamic narrative, Kliuchevskii visualises this process by means of an imagery in which a halt (*stoianka, perestanovka*) is always followed by further resettlement (*rasselenie, pereselenie*). This resettlement is repeatedly described in terms of a "stream from" (*otliv*) or "stream into" (*priliv*). In the 7th and 8th centuries, he writes, the Eastern branch of the Slavs "gradually poured out towards (*malo-pomalu otlivala na*) the east and northeast" (1: 114) As we see in the above quotations, East Slavic resettlement is also conceptualised with help from similes of nests and birds.

This first settlement on the East-European plain also marks the opening of what Kliuchevskii distinguishes as the "first period" of Russian history, the "Dnepr period" of urban commerce. Of the towns that appeared on the banks of the Dnepr for commercial reasons, Kiev became the most important – in time it became the central principality of the Eastern Slavs, which in turn meant the "first Russian state" (1: 147). While the creation of this state-like formation may have been enforced by an immediate need for defending commercial centres such as Kiev, the fundamental, underlying cause for its emergence was still the resettlement of the Eastern Slavs. Thus we may see how Kliuchevskii's concept of Russian history differs from that of the state school representatives. While Solov'ev saw an overall continuity in the gradual evolution of state formations, Kliuchevskii focuses on the Russian people and their colonisation of the Russian land. For Kliuchevskii, colonisation *is* Russian history, not a factor obstructing it.

Furthermore, the Kievan principality did *not* evolve into a more complex state. In the mid-11th century, it disintegrated instead into several minor principalities. In addition, this process was paralleled with further Slavic migration to the northeast. These shifts mark the second period of Kliuchevskii's scheme. Here, agriculture replaces commerce as the most important economic factor. The disintegration of the Kievan principality was due to a complex hereditary system, according to which the land was subdivided by a ruler and bequeathed equally among his sons. According to Kliuchevskii, this system had two consequences:

It 1) ruined the political wholeness, the state unity of the Russian land (*gosudarstvennoe edinstvo Russkoi zemli*), with which, apparently, the first Russian princes were so successfully concerned, and it 2) contributed to the awakening in Russian society (*russkoe obshchestvo*) of a feeling for the unity of the land (*chuvstvo zemskogo edinstva*), to the birth of Russian nationhood (*russkaia narodnost*). [...] The awakening in the entire society of the idea of the Russian land (*mysl' o Russkoi zemle*) as something complete, of the common land-related cause (*ob obshchem zemskom dele*) as an unavoidable, obligatory cause for each and everyone, all this made up the most fundamental, deepest fact of this period. ... The historical epoch, in whose issues the entire people took part and through participation in which it experienced itself as one people by contributing to a common cause, has always expressed itself particularly deeply in the memory of the people. ... The Russian land, which was mechanically coupled by the first Kievan princes from a manifold of ethnographic elements into one political whole, now began, while losing this political wholeness, for the first time to experience itself as a complete national or land-related configuration (*narodnyi ili zemskii sostav*) (1: 202ff).

In this idealised description, the main idea is that the *decline* of a centralised state formation makes possible the emergence of Russian nationhood (*russkaia narodnost*), founded on a shared "feeling for a common land" (*obshchezemskoe chuvstvo*). Loss of political unity brings about an imaginary community and even a "civil society" (*grazhdanskoe obshchestvo*), as he terms it. "Of course, this fact cannot be proved by means of quotations from the historical sources, but it glimmers everywhere, in each expression of spirit or mood of the period" (1: 204).

While Kliuchevskii on the one hand breaks down Russian history into four different periods, i.e. emphasises diachronicity to an extent that results in synchronicity as to the individual periods (Ankersmit 1995, 153), he recreates on the other an overall coherence by means of a "narrative substance" (Ankersmit), in which the "principal mass of the Russian population (*glavnaia massa russkogo naseleniia*)" becomes the main agent of his narrative.[12] It is his idea of the Russian people and its continual resettlement on the Russian land that provides his history, while divided into separate periods that are isolated and treated as unique phases, with coherence.[13] Kliuchevskii creates a continuity in Russian history on the basis of an "imaginary migration of Russians from the area around Kiev to the northeast" (Ostrowski 2009: 73), i.e. by claiming that it was the *same* people that first lived in the Dnepr region – which was subsequently "emptied", a commonplace among Russian 19th century historians – and later settled in the Upper Volga region.

> The Suzdal region, which in the early twelfth century was still a remote corner in the north-eastern part of the Russian land, is in the early thirteenth century a principality that resolutely rules over the remaining Rus. The political pivot has clearly moved from the banks of Middle Dnepr to the banks of Kliazma. This movement (*peredvizhenie*) was the result of the Russian forces streaming from (*otliv russkikh sil iz*) the banks of the Middle Dnepr to the Upper Volga region (1: 331f).

This quotation shows how Kliuchevskii conceives of colonisation as the major, shaping force of early Russian history, testifying to the free initiative of the people itself. The establishment of the new political centre is a consequence of migration; political formations are set up afterwards. "The appanage order itself

---

[12] Solov'ev, in contrast, claimed that one should "not divide, not split Russian history up into singular parts, periods, but look mainly for the connection of phenomena, for the immediate succession of forms" (Solov'ev 1959-1966, 1: 55). By the same token, I do not find Robert Byrnes's analysis of Kliuchevskii's "flow of Russian History" (Byrnes 1995: 163-166), while insightful in its parts, to be sufficiently to the point. His one-sided emphasis on Kliuchevskii's history as one of a "constant, slow change" fails to identify the historian's idea of a hidden continuity in an otherwise discontinuous past, subdivided into discrete periods. According to Ankersmit and his narrativist approach to historicism (1995), this combination of synchronicity and diacronicity is a defining feature of historicist thinking and writing.

[13] This analysis goes in a direction different from that which sees Kliuchevskii as a founder of "historical sociology" in Russia (Bohn 1997). Without denying these innovatory aspects in his work, it is my view that Kliuchevskii's emphasis on economic factors and social forms (*obshchezhitie*) in favour of the state did not imply a replacement of narrative representation by positivist "explanation," as Bohn seems to suggest (Bohn 1997: 368). Bohn's approach tends to ignore the importance of his grand narrative.

... was one of the political results of the Russian colonisation of Upper Volga with help from the nature of the region (*pri uchastii prirody kraia*)" (1: 353).

In the third period, however, this relationship is gradually reversed. Having described Russian nationhood as the result of a dissolving political unity, Kliuchevskii proceeds to the rise and expansion of Moscow, i.e. the re-emergence of a new state.

> In Moscow one felt that a great, long-standing project was accomplished, which mattered deeply to the inner structure of the life of the land (*zemskaia zhizn*). ... The Chronicles describe the great prince Vasilii III as the last gatherer (*sobiratel'*) of Rus. ... If you imagine the new borders of the Muscovite principality, the result of numerous territorial acquisitions, you will see that it incorporated an entire nation (*narodnost*) (2: 113).

Kliuchevskii, by implication, would have disagreed with Ernest Gellner's well-known thesis that it is "nationalism which engenders nations, and not the other way round" (Gellner 1983, 55). To Kliuchevskii, the splitting up of "Russian land", the nation, fosters Russian nationhood, a nationalist sentiment, which in turn makes possible a "striving for political unity on a popular basis (*na narodnom osnove*)" (2: 115). Only in the third period, then, does Russian nationhood become embodied in a Great Russian State.

The rise of Moscow was both inevitable and desirable; in Kliuchevskii's history, this "unification of Russia" is the expression, as suggested by Lawrence Langer, of the "historical *primum mobile*" (Langer 1986: 257). However, what initially appears to be a very positive as well as necessary process – a solid state ensuring a vulnerable nationhood – turns out to have an ambiguous character, not least for Russian nationhood itself. Kliuchevskii's description of the Muscovite period of Russian history is concentrated on the gradual disappearance of independent spheres of freedom as a process complementary to the centralisation of the state. The boyars lose power and influence; the peasants are "fastened to the land" (*prikreplenie krestian k zemle*) and the small, independent monasteries that once contributed in expanding the Russian land to the north are replaced by mighty monasteries loyal to the tsar. The colonisation by the Russian people yields to the consolidation of the Russian state, which subsequently begins to conquer non-Slavic areas.

The splitting up of the Russian land, a seemingly negative event, carries within itself a positive consequence: the emergence of nationhood. The subsequent "gathering of the Russian land", in turn, led to the disappearance of both a pre-modern civil society and of free and unlimited migration by the Russian people – all factors that made Russian nationhood possible. The Russian people, which has so far been the dominant force in Russian history, is replaced by the state as its main agent and disappears from the scene. Colonisation is replaced by serfdom. This is the tragic logic of Kliuchevskii's history of Russia.

## Restoring the Balance

This process comes to a climax in the fourth period, the "All-Russian period" from the early seventeenth century onwards, in which huge territorial expansion and increasing productivity were "reversely proportional" to the evolution of the people's freedom and creativity.

> The popular forces (*narodnye sily*) in their development fell behind the tasks that were raised before the state as the result of its rapid external growth; the spiritual work of the people could not keep up with the material activity of the state. The state grew fat (*pukhlo*) and the people grew lean (*khirel*) (3: 12).

The final stroke in this respect becomes the abolition of obligatory service for the nobility in 1762, an event that completely isolated it from its people, whom it was supposed to serve. The year of 1762 may be said to mark the end of Kliuchevskii's populist history.[14] In the 81st lecture, the Westerner Kliuchevskii describes the introduction of West-European norms, institutions, habits etc. with great suspicion and irony, and he sees the aristocratic culture of this new nobility as superficial and even pathological. This Europeanisation represented, according to Kliuchevskii, an anomaly in the course of Russian history in that it imposed Enlightenment thoughts and ideals that were alien to, as he consistently terms it in this context, "Eastern Europe", i.e. to nations that had not taken part in the feudal and Catholic traditions that formed the background for these imported ideas.

On this basis, Wolfgang Kissel has suggested that Kliuchevskii's history terminates in a satirical mode, a feature that makes it comparable to Jakob Burckhardt's works as Hayden White has interpreted them. I agree that there is much satire and irony towards the end of his history, but if I were to adopt

---

[14]    The remaining five lectures on the eighteenth and nineteenth centuries have, when compared to the preceding ones, a rather summarising character. The populist tendency in Kliuchevskii, i.e. that he was "deeply interested in and sympathetic to the life of the lower classes (the peasantry)", is discussed by Fedotov (1986: 207).

White's framework, i.e. the fourfold genre typology of Northrop Frye, I would rather claim that the overall plot structure of his history is that of a tragedy, since it describes the development "from happiness to misery" (Aristotle) – seen from a populist point of view. In addition, Kliuchevskii's history encourages its addressees to *learn* from history, an invitation that is difficult to combine with a consistent satirical approach. Tragedy has a therapeutic purpose; it aims to "prepare men to assume responsibility for their own destinies by the construction of institutions and laws adequate to the cultivation of their noblest capacities" (White 1973: 204).

Such a practical purpose is fully compatible with the scientific programme for the study of history, Kliuchevskii maintains in his opening lectures. And it is in agreement with the general tendency in European nineteenth-century historicism. Although Leopold Ranke's oft-quoted "as it really was" (which was part of his critique of the didactic historiography of the Enlightenment) might indicate otherwise when read in isolation, the study of the past should indeed be related to the political and social tasks at present. The aim of history as understood at that time was to understand not only the past but also the present and even the future in order to serve a society's interests and need for orientation, as well as contributing to its identity formation (Jaeger & Rüsen 1992: 42). And the kind of historical identity that historicism above all maintained was national identity. "The compelling literary expression Kliuchevskii gave his insights helped to shape the "Russianness" of his compatriots; by bringing to life Russia's past he contributed to his readers' sense of historical identity" (Raeff 1986: 202).

In keeping with the imagery of the people as a "historical personality" with a particular calling, Kliuchevskii conceptualises the past as the educational process, the "historical education" (*istoricheskoe vospitanie*) of this people.

> Only through a historical study is the course of this education supervised. The history of the people, rendered on the basis of research, becomes an account book, in which the deficiencies and excesses (*nedochety i perederzhki*) of its past are added up. The sincere task for the nearest future is to reduce the inflations and replenish the arrears, to restore the balance of national tasks and means (1: 42).

In the Russian past, the "lack of balance" consists above all in the emergent discrepancy between a mighty, successful state and its downtrodden people who have not been able to make use of its potential for the benefit of the Russian nation. As a result, the Russian people "still does not stand in the front line among the other European peoples" (1: 43).

What Russia lacks more specifically, Kliuchevskii suggests, is a well-developed *civil society*, a concept that for liberals in late Imperial Russia "exercised a strong symbolic influence independent of its practical realization" (Engelstein 2000: 25). This "dream of a civil society" is also shared by Kliuchevskii; his work is founded on the belief in history as being capable of fostering civic participation and social solidarity (Bohn 1997: 365; Wendland 2008: 417), all issues that had become urgent to the Russian intelligentsia after the abolition of serfdom in 1861. "Each of us ought to be at least a little historian, in order to become a consciously and honestly active citizen (*grazhdanin*)" (1: 44). This potential Russian historian-citizen is the main addressee of Kliuchevskii's course, which draws the listeners' and readers' attention to the lost paths of history: the pre-modern civil society and its common feeling for a common land. By visualising an indigenous, alternative way Kliuchevskii aims to restore the continuity of Russian history from the Medieval period up to the present.

## Russia, Europe and Kliuchevskii

Kliuchevskii's historical vision is enabled by contemporary European ideas, above all historicism and nationalism. It represents a continuation of Herder's critique of Eurocentrism and defence of cultural pluralism, i.e. the "equal validity of incommensurable cultures" (Berlin 1976: 209). Kliuchevskii's adaptation of European ideas, in other words, has made it possible for him to reject hegemonic notions of Europe. His historicism, furthermore, resumes the ideas of Herder and the early Wilhelm von Humboldt, who denied that the state was the ultimate goal of history, as Ranke and Humboldt himself later would say, and focused instead on humanity and civil society respectively (Iggers 1968: 41).

Kliuchevskii's critique of modern, Europeanised Russia might suggest a Slavophile tendency in his work; but as I hopefully have shown, he is in general very far from such a position. First and foremost, he wanted Russia to be on equal terms with the remaining parts of Europe – on its own terms. Eastward Slavic migration starting from a common cultural origin appears to the Kliuchevskii's basis for claiming that Russia is Europe. Although he may be said to idealise the past, above all early Russian colonisation, his past is founded not on the antithesis of Russia and Europe, but rather on an open and inclusive notion of the latter. To Kliuchevskii, Europe was not a neutral concept, as we saw above; Russia should aim to be ranked among the other European nations. However, Western Europe does not represent the benchmark for the Eastern "peripheries". Kliuchevskii rejects the idea of a unilinear advance in history common to all nations.

By implication, Kliuchevskii's Russia also presents us with an alternative to the dichotomisation so characteristic of the debates on national identity in 19th century Russia. His historiography, I would claim, was an attempt to conceptualise Russia outside the Hegelian framework, according to which the essential question was whether Russia was a "historical nation" or not. While both Slavophiles and Westernisers had viewed Russia as "poised on the border between two worlds, fated to choose one and leave the other entirely behind" (Siljak 2001: 357), Kliuchevskii refrained from seeing this as an either/or question. Russia was already European and should not attempt to adapt further to West-European cultural models.

## Bibliography

Ankersmit, F.R. (1995). "Historicism: An Attempt at Synthesis". *History and Theory*, 34 (3), 143-161.

Bassin, M. (1993). "Turner, Solov'ev, and the 'Frontier Hypothesis': The Nationalist Signification of Open Spaces". *The Journal of Modern History*, 65 (3), 473-511.

Bassin, M. (2006). "Geographies of Imperial Identity" in: Lieven, D. (ed.). *The Cambridge History of Russia*, vol. 2: *Imperial Russia 1689-1917*. Cambridge: Cambridge University Press.

Belinskii, V.G. (1954). *Polnoe sobranie sochinenii*, vol. 5: *Stat'i i rezentsii 1841-1844*. Moscow: Izdatel'stvo Akademii nauk SSSR.

Berlin, I. (1976). *Vico and Herder: Two Studies in the History of Ideas*. London: The Hogarth Press.

Bohn, T.M. (1997). "Historische Soziologie im vorrevolutionären Rußland". *Historisches Zeitschrift*, 265, 343-372.

Byrnes, R.F. (1995). *V.O. Kliuchevskii, Historian of Russia*. Bloomington: Indiana University Press.

Danilevskii, N.Ia. (1995). *Rossiia i Evropa: Vzgliad na kul'turnye i politicheskie otnosheniia slavianskogo mira k germano-romanskomu*. St Petersburg: Glagol.

Emmons, T. (2003). "The Problem of 'Russia and the West' in Russian Historiography (with Special Reference to M.I. Rostovtsev and P.N. Miliukov)" in: Evtuhov, C. & Kotkin, S. (eds.). *The Cultural Gradient: The Transmission of Ideas in Europe, 1789-1991*. Lanham: Rowman & Littlefield.

Engelstein, L. (2000). "The Dream of Civil Society in Tsarist Russia: Law, State, and Religion" in: Bermeo, N. & Nord, P. (eds.). *Civil Society before Democracy: Lessons from Nineteenth-Century Europe*. Lanham: Rowman & Littlefield.

Etkind, A. (2011). *Internal Colonization: Russia's Imperial Experience*. Cambridge: Polity.

Fedotov, G.P. (1986). "Kliuchevskii's Russia" in: Raeff, M. (ed.). *Kliuchevskii's Russia: Critical Studies* (=*Canadian-American Slavic Studies*, 20 (3-4), 203-221).

Fulsås, N. (1999). *Historie og nasjon: Ernst Sars og striden om norsk kultur*. Oslo: Universitetsforlaget.

Gellner, E. (1983). *Nations and Nationalism*. Oxford: Basil Blackwell.

Gorizontov, L. (2008). "The 'Great Circle' of Interior Russia: Representations of the Imperial Center in the Nineteenth and Early Twentieth Centuries" in: Burbank, J., Hagen, M.v. & Remnev, A. (eds.). *Russian Empire: Space, People, Power, 1700-1930*. Bloomington: Indiana University Press.

Halperin, C.J. (2000). "Kliuchevskii and the Tatar Yoke". *Canadian-American Slavic Studies* 34 (4), 385-408.

Hamburg, G.M. (1999). "Inventing the "State School" of Historians, 1840-1995" in: Sanders, T. (ed.). *Historiography of Imperial Russia: The Profession and Writing of History in a Multinational State*. Armonk & London: M.E. Sharpe.

Iggers, G.G. (1968). *The German Conception of History: The National Tradition of Historical Thought from Herder to the Present*. Middletown: Wesleyan University Press.

Jaeger, F. & Rüsen, J. (1992). *Geschichte des Historismus: Eine Einführung*. Munich: C.H. Beck.

Kavelin, K.D. (1989). *Nash umstvennyi stroi: Stat'i po filosofii russkoi istorii i kul'tury*. Moscow: Pravda.

Kissel, W. (1995). "V.O. Ključevskijs Darstellung der postpetrinschen Adelskultur: Das Pathogramm eines Zivilisationsprozesses" in: Ebert, C. (ed.). *Kulturauffassungen in der literarischen Welt Rußlands*. Berlin: Berlin-Verlag A. Spitz.

Kliuchevskii, V.O. (1955-1959). *Sochineniia v vos'mi tomakh*. 8. vols. Moscow: Gosudarstvennoe izdatel'stvo politicheskoi literatury.

Langer, L. (1986). "In the Path of History: The Place of Novgorod and Pskov in Kliuchevskii's History of Russia" in: Raeff, M. (ed.). *Kliuchevskii's Russia: Critical Studies* (=*Canadian-American Slavic Studies*, 20 (3-4), 243-257).

Meinecke, F. (1959). *Werke*, vol. 3: *Die Entstehung des Historismus*. Munich: Koehler.

Miller, A. (2005). "The Empire and the Nation in the Imagination of Russian Nationalism: Notes on the Margins of an Article by A.N. Pypin" in: Miller, A. & Rieber, A.J. (eds.). *Imperial Rule*. Budapest & New York: Central European University Press.

Neumann, I.B. (1996). *Russia and the Idea of Europe: A Study in Identity and International Relations*. London: Routledge.

Offord, D. (1985). *Portraits of Early Russian Liberals: A Study in the Thought of T.N. Granovsky, V.P. Botkin, P.V. Annenkov, A.V. Druzhinin and K.D. Kavelin*. Cambridge: Cambridge University Press.

Ostrowski, D. (2009). "The Mongols and Rus': Eight Paradigms" in: Gleason, A. (ed.). *A Companion to Russian History*. Malden: Wiley-Blackwell.

Plokhy, S. (2008). *Ukraine and Russia: Representations of the Past*. Toronto: University of Toronto Press.

Raeff, M. (1986). "Foreword" in: Raeff, M. (ed.). *Kliuchevskii's Russia: Critical Studies* (=*Canadian-American Slavic Studies*, 20 (3-4), 201-202).

Siljak, A. (1999). "Christianity, Science, and Progress in Sergei M. Solov'ev's *History of Russia*" in: T. Sanders (ed.). *Historiography of Imperial Russia: The Profession of Writing History in a Multinational State*. Armonk & London: M.E. Sharpe.

Siljak, A. (2001). "Between East and West: Hegel and the Origins of the Russian Dilemma". *Journal of the History of Ideas*, 62 (2), 335-358.

Solov'ev, S.M. (1959-1966). *Istoriia Rossii s drevneishikh vremen*. 15 vols. Moscow: Izdatel'stvo sotsial'no-ekonomicheskoi literatury.

Thaden, E.C. (1999). *The Rise of Historicism in Russia*. New York: Peter Lang.

Tolz, V. (2001). *Russia*. London: Arnold.

Wendland, A.V. (2008). "The Russian Empire and its Western Borderlands: National Historiographies and its 'Others' in Russia, the Baltics, and Ukraine" in: Berger, S. & Lorenz, C. (eds.). *The Contested Nation: Ethnicity, Class, Religion and Gender in National Histories*. Basingstroke: Palgrave Macmillan.

White, H. (1973). *Metahistory: The Historical Imagination in Nineteenth-Century Europe*. Baltimore: Johns Hopkins University Press.

# Excluding the West: Nataliia Narochnitskaia's Romantic-Realistic Image of Europe

*Jardar Østbø*

> Russia is indeed the true Europe, without the predominance of gays, without marriages between pederasts, without punk pseudo-culture, without lackeying for America. We are the true Europeans, because we have preserved ourselves, proving our Europeanness again and again in wars with both the crusaders and the Mongols[1]
>
> Dmitrii Rogozin (Russian deputy prime minister).

This chapter is a case study of how the Russian image of Europe is constructed in the hegemonic Russian "romantic realist" foreign policy discourse. It demonstrates how Nataliia Narochnitskaia's efforts to define "Europe" by offering a historical narrative of Russian-European relations are rooted both in romantic nationalism and in a pseudo-realist view of international politics. As the driving force in this narrative is the perceived eternal confrontation of Good and Evil, the image of Europe is drawn in an absolutist manner that leaves no room for dialogue, since discrepant views are dismissed as heretical.

## Introduction: the Romantic Realist Hegemony

"The West" and "Europe" are main reference points for Russian national identity construction. While Russian identity is often defined in *opposition* to "the West", its relationship to Europe is an object of constant debate. And while in the Russian discourse Russia is often referred to as a European nation, this is usually not perceived as entirely straightforward, either by Russians or by (other) Europeans (Morozov 2004: 1).

Since the 18th century, Russian discourse has tended to produce a kind of image of Europe that Russia can identify with, i.e. what Iver Neumann (1996) calls "true Europe". To some extent, this is a projection of what is perceived as

---

[1]   Rogozin & Bondarenko 2004 (Rogozin was appointed in 2011).

Russian values (Morozov 2004: 8f). On the other hand, there is "false Europe", which in its most extreme form is a *negation* of what is perceived as Russian values. Thus, in the Russian discourse on Europe, there is a mechanism of inclusion and exclusion: Russia is assiduously included in "true Europe", while nations that are normally, and especially in their own eyes, seen as European, are entirely or partly denied this status.

This delimitation of true and false Europe arguably occupies an important place in contemporary Russian foreign policy discourse. One example is Russia's relations with the Baltic states. After the dissolution of the Soviet Union, there has been a tendency that to prove their Europeanness, former Soviet republics Estonia, Latvia and Lithuania have been trying to show that Russia is not European, or at least that Russia is far less European than they are. Conversely, it has seemed to be a Russian strategy to frame the Baltic states as the black sheep of Europe (Morozov 2005: 278).

In today's Russian foreign policy discourse, the West's official motivations for political action are habitually not taken seriously. Instead, numerous "hidden motives" are suggested. For instance, the official rationale for the 1999 Nato bombing of Yugoslavia, i.e. to prevent genocide in Kosovo, was almost unequivocally rejected. According to Foreign Minister Igor' Ivanov, the bombing was instead motivated by a desire to colonize the Balkans, and Vladimir Kruzhkov of the Foreign Ministry claimed that the real reason was the wish to prevent a flow of refugees. However, such "realist" arguments rarely stand on their own feet, since they most often cannot explain fully how rational self-interest makes it necessary to, for instance, conduct an expensive military campaign that actually did cause a flow of refugees. The "realist" arguments are therefore often, implicitly or explicitly, supported by a set of essentialist assumptions about the "nature" of certain nations, such as the "violent character" of Romance and Germanic nations. This is why Viatcheslav Morozov has coined the term *romantic realism* to designate the hegemonic Russian foreign policy discourse (Morozov 2002: 409-413).[2]

---

[2]   This is not to say that realist theory of international relations excludes the idealist "organic" notion of state and/or nation. Quite the opposite: realist theory is itself rooted in this understanding of the state (Palan & Blair 1993). Morozov is well aware of this and refers to Palan and Blair, but he rightly argues that the romantic nationalist element is particularly strong in the Russian discourse (2002: 413).

# Nataliia Narochnitskaia – a Child of the Cold War

Politician, historian and public intellectual Nataliia Narochnitskaia (b. 1948) is a typical and influential exponent of this romantic realism. A self-professed Neo-Slavophile, she has also been called a Panslavist and Europeanist (Sidorov 2006: 333). Narochnitskaia is a pivotal figure in several Kremlin-supported or -initiated "soft-power" projects, such as the Foundation for Historical Perspective (FHP), a national-conservative think-tank that aims to provide analysis from the perspective of Russian interests and values (as opposed to the Carnegie Endowment and the Heritage Foundation, which FHP regards as enterprises that merely represent US interests) (cf. its website "O fonde"); the Institute for Democracy and Cooperation, which intends to study the U.S. and French political systems and "recommend improvements" (Osborn 2008); as well as the Presidential Commission to Counter Attempts to Falsify History to the Detriment of Russia's Interests.

By family background, education and profession, Narochnitskaia was clearly part of the Soviet elite. Her father, party member and distinguished historian Aleksei Narochnitskii, earned a Stalin prize for his work, but later he suffered obstacles to his career due to his excessively patriotic views (Khevrolina 2007: 246ff). A graduate of the prestigious Moscow Institute of International Relations, Narochnitskaia worked for the Soviet representation to the UN in New York in the 1980s. Unsurprisingly, at that time she was a member of the Communist party, although she claims in retrospect that that in no way meant that she was an unabashed supporter of the regime (Narochnitskaia 2008a). However, the demise of the Soviet Union was a truly devastating experience for her, especially what she perceived as the new elite's rejection of most of Russian history (Prokhanov & Narochnitskaia 2003). She has described how, on the day of the dissolution of the Soviet Union, she lay on the couch, weeping (V den', kogda ...).

This apparently sparked her political engagement, and in the 1990s and early 2000s Narochnitskaia was a leading activist in various (mostly short-lived) patriotic parties and organisations. From 2003 to 2007, she was a deputy of the State Duma for the Motherland Bloc and a member of the Russian delegation to the Parliamentary Assembly of the Council of Europe. Narochnitskaia is also involved in Orthodox political organisations, most prominently as one of the founders of the World Russian Council, an international organisation under the auspices of the Russian Orthodox Church.[3]

---

3    (VRS). In 1995, moderate members broke out and formed the World Russian People's Council, which, contrary to VRS, is still active (Pribylovskii 2009).

Although she has published several books and many articles, Narochnits-kaia's fundamental work is *Russia and the Russians in World History* (2003). It was first printed in 1996 by the prestigious publishing house Mezhdunarodnye otnosheniia, with a relatively large (for a 500-page history book) print run of 5,000 copies (Nowak 2009). Since then it has been reprinted five times. In this book, Narochnitskaia expresses her views on the history of Russia's international relations, mainly with Europe, and, later, with the USA. In *Russia and the Russians* one finds the very foundation of Narochnitskaia's ideology. Given her social position and her views on key topics, the book can be seen as an elaboration on the Russian hegemonic discourse on Europe in the form of a historical narrative.

## Narochnitskaia's *Weltanschauung*

Narochnitskaia's arguably most important weapon in her verbal crusade against the West and her efforts to exclude it from the notion of Europe is the change of focus. Studying the history of Russia's international relations through Western categories will inevitably make Russia inferior. Instead, having acquired the freedom to discard historical materialism (but far from rejecting the entire corpus of Soviet historiography) and access to formerly secret archives, Narochnitskaia proposes to study the history of Russia's international relations from the point of view of religion.

From the very beginning of the book, Narochnitskaia accuses most Western, but also some Russian historians (both liberal and Marxist) of reductionism. For her, the driving forces in history lie in the spiritual, not in the material and economic domain. The secular paradigm in Western and in Soviet Marxist history writing has led historians to ignore religion as a motivating force among, for instance, Russian rulers such as Ivan the Terrible, and this has led to false views of Russian history. It is also one of Narochnitskaia's main objections against (mainly Western) historians who, in her opinion, fail to understand the importance of religion. By using her approach, she writes, a lacuna will be filled, since no substantial effort has been made to conduct such a study (2003: introduction).

> The study of religious/philosophical roots of foreign policy doctrines and ideologies together with concrete events and turns of history helps us to understand the formation of stereotypes in public consciousness, which in their turn influence politics. Such an approach makes

it possible to see that during the entire 20th century, the same geopolitical constants have been manifesting themselves ... (ibid.).

Thus, while very preoccupied with geopolitics Narochnitskaia takes a "soft" stance as compared to, for example, "classic geopoliticians", who were often prone to geographical determinism. Narochnitskaia is more preoccupied with *ideas*, which in her view are crucial to the course of history. And the most fundamental mindset is religion (cf. 2003: 13). For her, present or past ideologies or political doctrines of even the most secularised countries of the West can be explained by tracing their religious roots (ibid.: 16).

At the risk of oversimplification, I will maintain that her main theses may be boiled down to three:

- The countries of the West, especially the Anglo-Saxons, have through history been, and are at present, heretical or godless, and their policy towards Russia is generally guided by hostility, fear and the desire to conquer and annihilate Russia.
- Russia, although with numerous flaws and wrong-doings, was a protector of the true faith up to the 1917 revolution, and its policies have historically been far more justifiable morally than the West's. The Russian state's expansion beyond "Russian (*russkii*) soil" was for the most part in self-defence and/or can be justified by international law.[4]
- The dominating image of Russia in the West (as barbaric, inherently expansionist and anti-democratic) is stereotypical and essentially false, partly because the most important research on Russia is not objective. It is rooted in heretical and inhuman thought and misunderstandings and is closely related to geopolitics, i.e. to the desire to conquer and annihilate Russia.

This list could be made even shorter, since the last claim derives from the other two. I chose to formulate it separately, since, as we will see, it is important for this article. But in fact, I will argue that almost all of Narochnitskaia's other theses can be seen as being derived from these contentions. Thanks to the consistency of her views, her works appear as one long argument to substanti-

---

4    The Russian language has, since Peter the Great's proclamation of the Empire (1721), two words for Russian. *Russkii* bears ethnic and cultural connotations, whereas *rossiiskii* is a legal and geographical term.

ate them. In a sense, they function both as the starting point and the goal of virtually all her texts.

## The Religious Dimension: A Moral View of History

The two (three) main theses identified above imply the opposition "Russia vs the West". As her main point, this dichotomy deserves further explanation. Already in the publisher's introduction to *Russia and the Russians*, the reader is informed that Narochnitskaia regards Russia's historical international relations as a "permanent conflict between Orthodox Russia and the West", and most of her writings are rife with rabid anti-Western statements. But how does she define "the West"?

Narochnitskaia characterises the relations between Russia and Europe in the Middle Ages as a unity grounded on Christian values (2003: 26). The Christian faith is for Narochnitskaia the very essence of Europe. In a TV debate in 2007, she denied that the concept of Europe had anything to do with liberal democracy:

> And Europe – that is first of all "The Lord's Prayer". That is what unites us. … And the Sermon on the Mount. The real worth of man does not follow from 20th century civil society, but from Christian doctrine (Narochnitskaia 2007a).

This unity was destroyed when more human-centred religious thought emerged in the West. In its turn, Renaissance humanism laid the ground for the rationalism of Descartes. Unintentionally, Narochnitskaia continues, his philosophy made God superfluous in Western epistemology, whereas in Byzantine Christianity the religious world-view was preserved. In the West, the Western development is largely regarded as positive, leading to scientific and technological progress, wealth and freedom of the individual. But in Narochnitskaia's Orthodox perspective, it was catastrophic, because it made man alien to God. In Narochnitskaia's opinion, the Western apostasy led to present-day nihilism, with Europe, deprived of all values, essentially being just a "gigantic corporation serving to fill the carnal needs of individuals" (2007b: 122).

Hence, for Narochnitskaia, Russia is not part of the post-Renaissance Western European civilization, whose philosophical basis consists of Descartes' rationalist philosophy, the intellectual barrage of the French Revolution and the Protestant ethics of labour and wealth (2003: 19).

Narochnitskaia is opposed to Hobbesian contract theory, which she regards as one of the constituent parts of the Western, secular concept of the state. She distinguishes sharply between, on the one hand, the "Romance-Germanic", Catholic Enlightenment, which she characterises as a largely positive development, and on the other, the Anglo-Saxon Enlightenment, about which she is highly negative. Narochnitskaia regards Thomas Hobbes, John Locke and Adam Ferguson as direct descendants of Calvinist thought, a theology which for her is sheer heresy. These philosophers further developed the embryonic individualism (that followed from Calvin's dogma of predestination) into the view that individuals are fully autonomous,

> … not connected, either by spirit, world-view, historical experience, or by common notions of sin and virtue, all of which, according to Christian, especially Orthodox, judgment, make a nation out of a population (2003: 80).

As will have become clear by now, Narochnitskaia's approach is far from, for instance, Max Weber's sociology of religion. The division between Russia and the West is not merely one of theological disagreements and social and cultural consequences thereof, but one of morals, with Russia being superior and the West being inferior. Narochnitskaia's value system is firm, consistent and bipolar, even manichean. Normative moral considerations permeate her writings. In her judgments of historic events and policies, there is a sharp, clear delineation between good and evil. In a sense, claiming the double authority of a historian and a literate Orthodox believer, Narochnitskaia elevates herself to the status of a moral judge. Her moral absolutism, it can be argued, relates to historical events and historians alike. The starting point of Orthodoxy as the sole true faith thus makes possible the arguably strongest possible condemnation of one's opponents: denouncing them as heretics.

As we can see, this is not merely a way of judging Russia on its own terms rather than on Western ones. It is also a way of judging Western Europe on Russia's terms, making Russia the superior part. To some extent, it can even be interpreted as a universalist claim, a claim to be the possessor of the higher values and the right to define Europe. In the first chapters of the book, Narochnitskaia focuses on the common roots of Eastern and Western Christianity, and thereby the common roots of Russia and Western Europe. But she regards post-Renaissance Western Europe as an apostate from true Christianity, and, *consequently*, from Europe. According to Narochnitskaia, after the Middle Ages, the Europe of Latin Christianity simply ceased being Europe.

## The Geopolitical Dimension: "The Eastern Question"

Throughout history, the antagonism between the two has according to Narochnitskaia materialized in geopolitical rivalry over the "Eastern question". While "the Eastern question" in European history writing usually refers to the problem of the decaying Ottoman Empire in the 19th and 20th centuries, Narochnitskaia uses it in a wider sense, both geographically and temporally, for what she perceives as the ever-continuing struggle for control over the space between the Baltic and the Black Seas. She attributes enormous importance to this region, regarding it as the main battlefield of the eternal confrontation between "false Europe" and "true Europe" (to borrow Neumann's terms). For the outside observer, this nearly obsessive preoccupation might be difficult to grasp. For Narochnitskaia, on the other hand, the Eastern Question is far more than just a problem of disputed territory. Its importance relies on a set of interwoven factors.

According to Narochnitskaia, the foreign policy ideology of Great Britain, and later the USA, rests firmly on Puritanism. For instance, Cecil Rhodes' British imperialist ideology and the American messianist idea of "Manifest Destiny" are to be understood as direct offshoots of Puritan thought.[5] She regards contemporary US foreign policy as a result of an amalgam of the Monroe doctrine, the Calvinist doctrine of predestination and the belief in universal progress. Narochnitskaia does not see liberal democracy as a universal value, but as an American concept which she connects directly to the belief in Manifest Destiny (2003: 80ff). The democratisation of the former communist countries in Eastern Europe since the dissolution of the Warsaw Pact is thus to be regarded not as some kind of liberation or progress for the nations involved, but simply as a materialisation of Anglo-Saxon desires to control this region.

British geopolitician Sir Halford Mackinder is criticized by Narochnitskaia for a kind of geographical determinism that is rooted in Puritanism (Narochnitskaia 2003: 147ff). Nonetheless, she grants Mackinder significant influence in the sense that she regards him as one of the main ideologists of Anglo-Saxon foreign policy up to this day. And he paid special attention to the region between the Baltic and the Black Seas, control over which he proclaimed (in a famous passage) was a prerequisite to control the so-called

---

5    Here Narochnitskaia actually refers to Weber and his sociology of religion (Narochnitskaia 2003: 66-69).

Eurasian "Heartland", which in its turn was necessary to "command" the world (Mackinder 1996: 106).

But the strategic importance of the post-Byzantine space also has a more objective explanation, according to Narochnitskaia. Here she refers to the Russian geographer Veniamin Semenov-Tian-Shanskii (1870-1942),[6] who studied how influence over territory has been achieved through history. Semenov-Tian-Shanskii identified a certain belt around the globe, from the Equator to 45 degrees North, where climatic, topographical and biological conditions were especially favourable for cultural development. The geographer held that this belt around "the three mediterraneans" (The European Mediterranean and the Black Sea, the China Seas plus the Sea of Japan and the Yellow Sea, and the Caribbean including the Mexican Gulf) have fostered the most original and strong civilizations and states. And the people that was able to conquer one of these regions, was, due to the limited geographical imagination of earlier times, regarded as the "master of the world". And this has not changed, Semenov-Tian-Shanskii maintains; the "master of the world" is the people that is the master of one or more of these "mediterraneans" and the surrounding land (2008).

The panslavist Nikolai Danilevskii is known for, among other things, his theory of "cultural-historical types" and his view of the relations between Russia and "Romano-Germanic Europe" as an irreconcilable conflict. The origins of this antagonism, Danilevskii explains, are cultural and religious differences, as well as Great Britain's aim to conquer the Asian continent (2009). Narochnitskaia and Danilevskii share the view that the geographical centre of this antagonism "in the most remarkable way is entangled in one knot in the Bosphorus, the Dardanelles and in Constantinople" (Narochnitskaia 2003: 151; Danilevskii 2009).

In this way, the West's thirst for the post-Byzantine space is framed as unquenchable. It is explained by providing it with two "inner" or subjective, and two "objective" motivations. Of the subjective motivations, there is one religious-psychological (the Puritan conviction of being destined to rule the world) and one geographical-psychological (the Anglo-Saxon conviction that the post-Byzantine space is the key to world dominance). The "objective" motivations pertain to the natural sciences (Semenov-Tian-Shanskii's geographical explanation) as well as the humanities (Danilevskii's theory of

---

6    Not to be confused with his father, the better-known geographer Petr Semenov-Tian-Shanskii (1827-1914).

"cultural-historical types"). Thus, the post-Byzantine space stands out as very important, "objectively" speaking, and *extremely* important to the West. If one agrees with these premises in Narochnitskaia's account, the West *inevitably* becomes expansionist. Nevertheless, this cocktail of arguments underpinning the seemingly already postulated "inherent expansionism" of the West ("false Europe") reveals the circularity of Narochnitskaia's romantic realist logic.

## The Historiographic Dimension: Ahistorical Historiography

Narochnitskaia accuses Western historians and writers (Richard Pipes, above all) of being unwilling or unable to study ideas and political acts in their original context, to find out "how it really was". She presents them as either victims or perpetrators of *ideologization* in the sense that they project their own (hegemonic) convictions onto Russia (cf. Narochnitskaia 2003: 120). In the same way, they are also accused of the historian's cardinal sin – anachronism. By studying their motivation and the roots of their convictions, Narochnitskaia intends to expose the falsehood of their theses, framing them as *unscholarly*.

Though not concealing the author's political motives and polemical stance, *Russia and the Russians* is presented as a work of scholarship (*nauchnyi trud*), and on the publisher's website it is listed under the headline "history" (Istoria. *Izdatel'stvo…*). But as indicated in the introduction to this chapter, her perspective is far from that of a disinterested historian. According to Narochnitskaia, the West has been at odds with Russia at least since the Great Schism (1054). The notion of this conflict has the clear earmarks of a dogma that guides Narochnitskaia's interpretation and representation of all historical events. It seems to be an *idée fixe* that Russia's problems are the results of Western hostility, due to cultural and above all religious differences as well as the West's expansionism.

The clearest indications of this are Narochnitskaia's often strained historical parallels, whose far-fetched nature is only mitigated by the fact that they are fully consistent with the "inner logic" of Narochnitskaia's romantic realist view of international relations. A blatant illustration is the direct line she draws between Rome's offer to Aleksandr Nevskii in the mid-13th century and Nato's ultimatum to Yugoslavia in 1999:

> In 1248, and then in 1251, … Rome … offered St. Aleksandr Nevskii, under the condition that he adopt Catholicism, its patronage and help against the Mongols, the selfsame horsemen from whom the pious prince had just liberated Russian soil. Many historical

instances of this kind of temptation can be mentioned, including blackmail on the eve of the Nato aggression against the Serbs, in which Catholic (now liberal) Europe took part. *Like Satan, the tempter, it said to decrepit Byzantium: "Look at this Kingdom, bow down and worship me, and it will all be yours"*[7] (Narochnitskaia 2003: 115, italics added).

The italicized passage is particularly telling. It is apparently one of Narochnitskaia's favourite lines, since she has used it several times, for instance after the death of Slobodan Milošević and in an anti-globalization context (Narochnitskaia 2006a, 2006b and 2006c). The quotation ("Look at …") has a biblical tone and is apparently a reference to the temptations of Christ in Matthew 4, 8-9 and Luke 4, 6-7. However, the preceding sentence (as well as the following) reveals that it is copied, without reference, from Danilevskii's 1871 panslavist treatise *Russia and Europe*. The latter relates the Biblical quote to the attempted union between the Eastern and Western Churches in 1439 and the efforts to enlist Byzantium against the Ottomans (Danilevskii 2008: 382). As we see, Narochnitskaia applies the analogy freely to several other historical situations. The *leitmotif* of *Russia and the Russians*, i.e. the confrontation between the West and Russia, is given an extra dimension when the West is directly likened to Satan and Russia is seen as Christ.

The unwillingness to distinguish between Great Britain of the early colonial period and USA in the 21st century, repeatedly calling both Anglo-Saxon, is also descriptive of Narochnitskaia's romantic realism. Such questionable historical parallels and the use of more or less obsolete terms to denote (arguably) recent phenomena help to *minimize or even erase the differences between historical situations and events*. Paradoxically enough for a "history book", this may be the very aim: to show that although the world may seem to have changed, it has not in fact done so. In *Russia and the Russians* then, the conflict between Russia and the West appears to be an unavoidable fact.

Narochnitskaia leans heavily on her authority as a professional historian, while doing her best to deprive Western historians of theirs. Nevertheless, she uses history to construct an image of an enemy that in essence is unchangeable, even transhistorical. Narochnitskaia's largely chronological account notwithstanding: on a higher, perhaps semiotic level, historical events and phenomena stand out as historical manifestations of certain *eternal* traits. To take one example, in her world-view expansionism becomes an inherent quality of the

---

[7]  The Russian original: "Как сатана-соблазнитель говорила она одряхлевшей Византии: 'Видишь царство сие, пади и поклонись мне и все будет твое'".

West. In this way, it becomes impossible to separate history and historiography. Narochnitskaia presents not only history but even historiography as a manichean struggle in which if one takes her views to their logical extreme, she is rightful and her opponents are heretics.

## Conclusion: Impossible Invitation

Like the adherents of the realist school of international relations, Narochnitskaia implies a view of (groups of) nations/states as organic wholes similar to persons pursuing their "rational" interests. However, as the romantic nationalist she arguably is, she ascribes, at least implicitly, certain inherent qualities to these (groups of) nations. Her general approach, i.e. a rather political notion of Russian Orthodoxy, makes her definition of Europe rigid and absolutist.

Throughout Narochnitskaia's works, the West, whether it be represented by the Holy Roman Emperor, the Pope, Nato, or contemporary historians, is framed as an embodiment of vices or even Evil. This can be illustrated by the following dichotomies:

| | | |
|---|---|---|
| Good | – | Evil |
| True Europe | – | False Europe |
| Russia/(Eastern) Slavs | – | Anglo-Saxons |
| Eastern Christianity | – | Western Christianity/liberalism |
| Orthodoxy | – | Heresy |
| Orthodoxy (metaphorical) | – | Heresy (metaphorical) |
| Truth | – | Lies |
| History | – | Myth |
| Religious perspective | – | Secular reductionist perspective |
| Morality | – | Immorality |
| Virtue | – | Vice |

On such a background, her repeated "invitations", perhaps most notably at the Sorbonne in 2008, to "constructively unite the historical heritage and accomplishments of all ethnic, confessional and cultural parts of Europe; Germanic, Romance and Slavic; Latin and Orthodox Europe" (Narochnitskaia 2008b) sound absurd.[8] The irreconcilable Russian-Western conflict represented by

---

8    This passage is also rendered elsewhere. See e.g. Narochnitskaia 2007b: 223.

the dichotomies above is not only the *outcome* of Narochnitskaia's historical inquiry. It is the very lens through which she sees. This unavoidably casts her image of Europe in absolutist categories, making dialogue impossible.

## Bibliography

Danilevskii, N. (2008). *Rossiia i Evropa*. Moscow: Institut russkoi tsivilizatsii.

Danilevskii, N. (2009). "Gore pobediteliam!". *Khronos*. http://www.hrono.ru/libris/lib_d/gore1.html. Accessed 2009-07-03.

Istoria. *Izdatel'stvo Mezhdunarodnye otnosheniia*. http://www.inter-rel.ru/history.php. Accessed 2010-06-11.

Khevrolina, V.M. (2007). "Istoriia byla ego prizvaniem. K 100-letiiu so dnia rozhdeniia akademika A.L. Narochnitskogo". *Vestnik Rossiiskoi Akademii Nauk,* 77 (3), 245-249.

Mackinder, H.J. (1996). *Democratic Ideals and Reality. A Study in the Politics of Reconstruction*. Washington D.C.: National Defence University Press.

Morozov, V. (2002). "Resisting Entropy, Discarding Human Rights. Romantic Realism and Securitization of Identity in Russia". *Cooperation and Conflict,* 37 (4), 409-429.

Morozov, V. (2004). "Inside/Outside: Europe and the Boundaries of Russian Political Community". *PONARS Working Paper*.

Morozov, V. (2005). "The Baltic States in the New Europe: a Neo-Gramscian Perspective on the Global and the Local" in: Smith, D.J. (ed.). *The Baltic States and their Region: New Europe or Old?* Amsterdam: Rodopi.

Narochnitskaia, N. (2003). *Rossia i russkie v mirovoi istorii*. Moscow: Mezhdunarodnye otnosheniia.

Narochnitskaia, N. (2006a). "On ne khotel torgovat' Serbiei". *Pamiati Slobodana Miloshevicha*. http://www.slobodan-memoria.narod.ru/st/otkliki1.htm. Accessed 2009-07-03.

Narochnitskaia, N. (2006b). "Kogda zhe pridet nastoiashchii den'?". *pravos.org*. http://www.pravos.org/docs/doc285.htm. Accessed 2010-06-11.

Narochnitskaia, N. (2006c). "Rossiia i slaviane v epokhu peremen". *Zolotoi lev* (75-76). http://www.zlev.ru/75_198.htm. Accessed 2009-06-15.

Narochnitskaia, N. (2007a). "Vremena": "Pochemu Rossiia ne Evropa" (04.03.07). Stenogramma. *narochnitskaia.ru*. http://www.narochnitskaia.ru/cgi-bin/main.cgi?item=1r400r070306184751. Accessed 2009-07-01.

Narochnitskaia, N. (2007b). *Velikie voiny XX stoletiia*. Moscow: AJRIS-press.

Narochnitskaia, N. (2008a). "SShA ochen' boleznenno otnosiatsia k vosstanovleniiu Rossiei svoei voli". *Inosmi.ru*. http://www.inosmi.ru/world/20080731/242942.html. Accessed 2009-05-05.

Narochnitskaia, N. (2008b). "Budushchee Rossii – eto budushchee Evropy. Lektsiia, prochitannaia v Sorbonne". *pravoslavie.ru*. http://pravoslavie.ru/smi/845.htm. Accessed 2010-06-15.

Nataliia Narochnitskaia. "V den', kogda raspalsia SSSR, ia rydala". *Russkaia liniia*. http://www.rusk.ru/newsdata.php?idar=726511. Accessed 2008-05-12.

Neumann, I.B. (1996). *Russia and the Idea of Europe: a Study in Identity and International Relations*. London: Routledge.

Nowak, A. (2009). *History as an Apology for Totalitarianism* http://www.obta.uw.edu.pl/~zoja/NowakHistoryas.pdf. Accessed 2009-02-21.

O fonde. *Stoletie.* http://stoletie.ru/fip/. Accessed 2009-05-08.

Osborn, A. (2008). "Russia-Backed Think Tank to Study Western Democracy". *The Wall Street Journal.* 2008-01-18.

Palan, R.P. & Blair, B.M. (1993). "On the Idealist Origins of the Realist Theory of International Relations". *Review of International Studies,* 19 (4), 385-399.

Pribylovskii, V. (2009). "Vsemirnyi Russkii Narodnyi Sobor". *anticompromat.ru*. http://www.anticompromat.ru/vrns/spr_vrns.html. Accessed 2009-05-08.

Prokhanov, A. & Narochnitskaia, N. (2003). "Rossiia – vsegda imperiia". *Zavtra,* 26. http://www.zavtra.ru/cgi/veil/data/zavtra/03/501/21.html. Accessed 2009-07-10.

Rogozin, D. & Bondarenko, V. (2004). "My i est' nastoiashchaia Evropa" (Beseda s Vladimirom Bondarenko). *Zavtra,* 89. http://www.zavtra.ru/denlit/089/131.html. Accessed 2009-04-20.

Semenov-Tian-Shanskii, V. (2008). "O mogushchestvennom territorial'nom vladenii primenitel'no k Rossii: ocherk po politicheskoi geografii". *Russkii obozrevatel'.* http://www.rus-obr.ru/library/913. Accessed 2009-07-02.

Sidorov, D. (2006). "Post-Imperial Third Romes: Resurrections of a Russian Orthodox Geopolitical Metaphor". *Geopolitics,* 11 (2), 317-347.

# The Text-Catena in the Frescoes in the Sanctuary of S. Maria Antiqua in Rome (705-707 A.D.): An Index of Cultural Cross-Over in 7th-8th century Rome?[1]

*Per Olav Folgerø*

## Preamble

The aim of this article is to present some main lines in the investigation on the iconography of the early 8th c. frescoes in the church of S. Maria Antiqua in Rome, lines that will be elaborated in a forthcoming book which, in fact, contains a discussion – from two different viewpoints – of the iconographical system by my colleague professor Per Jonas Nordhagen and myself. The problems that are raised in this work, which bears the title *Byzantine Iconography. The First Phase*, are not solely restricted to a detailed analysis of the iconography *per se*; our aim is to use the *rather unique* pictorial material in S. Maria Antiqua as a *"tracer"* of lines in the *development* of iconographical systems. Our study implies an investigation of *migration* routes of *political* as well as *theological* ideas, that is: the *spread* of culture within the large Mediterranean basin in this particular period of the early Middle Ages: what role was played by the capital of the Byzantine Empire, the city of *Constantinople*, as compared with the influences emanating from other centres in mere peripheral areas of the Empire such as *Jerusalem* and *Rome*?

## The frescoes of John VII in the church of S. Maria Antiqua

Since its re-discovery and excavation in the year 1900, the church of S. Maria Antiqua, which is located on the *Forum Romanum*, at the slope of the Palatine

---

[1]    The main lines presented in this article have been published previously in: Folgerø 2009a; Folgerø 2009b; Folgerø 2009c.

Hill, has been subjected to extensive investigation, and has proved to be an almost inexhaustible source of information concerning the use of pictures in the Early Middle Ages.[2] In this article, I will focus in particular on the text-*catena* written in Greek letters, consisting mainly of Old Testament sayings, which is part of the vast "Adoration of the Crucified" scene located on the *upper zone* of the triumphal arch. The frescoes on this arch are (with the exception of the so-called Palimpsest wall on the r. side of the apse) all dated to the Pontificate of John VII, which means that they were executed in the years A.D. 705-707.[3]

The main iconographical programme on the triumphal arch consists of two separate zones. The upper zone – an "Adoration of the Crucified" – is separated from the lower zone by a broad dark border. In this "Adoration scene", then, are displayed, in two separate registers, crowds of adoring Angels, Seraphim, Cherubim in the upper register and Men in the lower.

The Greek text-*catena*, the main subject of this article, is inserted between the two registers.

On the same fresco layer, on the lower zone of the arch, four popes and four church fathers are organized symmetrically in two superimposed zones on each side of the apse.[4] Pope John VII's programme for the apse is *completely lost*. As to what can have been depicted there, it is generally assumed that it can have been nothing but a representation of Mary, enthroned or standing with the Child in her arms, in accordance with John VII's deep devotion to the Virgin.

Significant for the iconographical interpretation of the sanctuary programme is the fact that the pope to the far left, depicted with a square blue halo, is John VII, who commissioned these paintings; while the pope farthest

---

[2]  For the history of the research on this monument, with bibliographical notes, see Osborne, Brandt & Morganti 2004.

[3]  For a detailed description of the figures in the Adoration of the Crucified scene, cf Nordhagen 1968: 47ff.

[4]  Their presence in the programme of John VII seems, more or less, to reiterate the programme of Martin I; as demonstrated by G.M. Rushforth and F.E. Brightman, the appearance of the Church Fathers *in Martin's layer* on the lower zone of the so-called Palimpsest wall, carrying scrolls quoting from their works (texts that were cited by the Orthodox faction at the *Lateran Synod* 649 A.D.), tells us that given the circumstances of time and place, we can hardly doubt that they have been selected because they were quoted as witness to the Orthodox Faith at the Lateran Synod of 649 A.D., which condemned the Monothelete heresy: see Rushforth 1902: 73.

*Fig. 1. S. Maria Antiqua. Triumphal arch and apse. The programme of John VII's Adoration of the Crucified (705-707 A.D.) is located in the upper zone. The popes and the church fathers are located in the lower zone. The two zones are separated by a dark border. The apse illustration postdates John VII's programme. The illustration is a computer reconstruction (by Alf Andresen at the University of Bergen in Norway) based on two watercolours after Wilpert 1917 and a drawing by Antonio Petrignani, Soprintendenza Foro Romano e Palatino, c. 1900.*

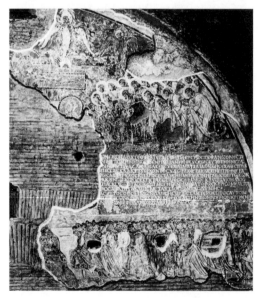

*Fig. 2. The Adoration of the Crucified. After Wilpert 1917.*

to the right is Martin I. This means that John VII and Martin I appear *in a strict symmetrical pattern*, on the far left and right side of the arch respectively: surely a demonstration of John VII's tribute to Martin, the pope who called the strongly *anti-Monotheletic*[5] Lateran Synod in Rome in the year 649 (cf. n. 4), a synod in which Palestinian theologians played a central part (see below).

The enigmatic character of the Adoration of the Crucified scene, described by the German specialist Christa Ihm as "wholly unique" (Ihm 1992: 93), is no less striking today than it was when the excavator Giovanni Boni brought the frescoes to light in 1900/1901. Over the years, many scholars have speculated on this visual enigma. The different ways of probing deeper into what may be called an "iconographical labyrinth" will be at the centre of the forthcoming book written by Nordhagen and myself. It arises out of our theoretical conviction that any single-minded as well as one-dimensional interpretation will fail to grasp the wealth of sub-themes that may occur in a given display of motifs.[6] Hence, several avenues of examination should be pursued. A central point in our discourse includes the question of *provenance* of the S. Maria Antiqua iconography. While Nordhagen argues for what he calls *"The Constantinopolitan thesis"*, I will stress that the presence of some *Palestinian* leads in the Greek text-*catena* on the triumphal arch underlines that there is also a *"Palestinian connection"* in this extraordinary painting. We will return to these Palestinian leads after a presentation of some main lines in Nordhagen's "Constantinopolitan thesis".

## The Constantinopolitan Thesis

As to "The Constantinopolitan Thesis", Nordhagen and other scholars have repeatedly stressed that the material under discussion has to be regarded as a product of the Byzantine cultural hegemony in Italy in the centuries before A.D. 800. Still, uncertainty long ruled as to its classification. An important

---

5   The heresy of Monotheletism maintained that Christ had only one *will* (thelema) and one *energy*, not a separate *human will* and *energy* in addition to the *divine will* and the *divine energy*. From an Orthodox position, this is a serious *underrating* of the meaning of the *human nature of Christ* for the salvation of Man.

6   According to K. Moxey, another danger lies in scholars being unconscious of the distance in time that separates them from the objects they study, and thereby also from the *context* from which they spring; this fact, he asserts, invalidates even the most serious attempts at interpretation. For his reflections see Moxey 1993: 30.

step was E. Kitzinger's study of 1934 on the style and date of the monuments in Rome of the seventh to the ninth century. In discussing the frescoes of the early eighth century in the S. Maria Antiqua church, he noticed their striking iconographic affinities with later Byzantine art (Kitzinger 1934: 19).

In 1958, then, Kitzinger published his work on art in the time between Emperor Justinian the Great and Iconoclasm, which means from the mid-6th c. until the first decennia of the 8th c. Here, he ascribed the "Hellenism" visible in the material from S. Maria Antiqua to a milieu saturated with reminiscences of classical painting, a school that could hardly have existed elsewhere than in the great and still prosperous Christian capital of Constantinople (Kitzinger 1958). Kitzinger's thesis is also central in Nordhagen's ascription of the iconography under discussion to Constantinople.

As to the interpretation on a deeper level of the "Adoration of the Crucified" scene in S. Maria Antiqua, the Italian art historian E. Tea, in her work published in 1937, was the first to link this rare specimen of a Crucifixion to a specific historical act, namely that of the promulgation of the famous Eighty-Second Canon voted by the Quinisext Council, also called the Council in Trullo, which took place in Constantinople in A.D. 692 (Tea 1937: 66 ff.).

This council had been summoned by the Emperor Justinian II to bring to conclusion the deliberations of the foregoing ecumenical assembly, The Sixth Ecumenical Council, and its acts include a number of regulations destined to uproot unwanted religious practices. The 82nd Canon, the most notorious of these, *forbade the use of the Lamb* as a symbol of Christ and decreed that, from now on, the Saviour should be depicted in human form only.

According to Tea, then, the large scene figuring the crucified Christ worshipped by the heavenly hosts *must* have been an invention to celebrate and promulgate this important decree. Tea's intuition made her aware of the connection that may have existed between Pope John VII's picture in S. Maria Antiqua and the ban on the Lamb introduced by the will of his great contemporary, Emperor Justinian II.

Her thesis linking the "Adoration of the Crucified" to the 82nd Canon and its Lamb-banishing formula fits, *in fact*, well with an observation made some thirty years earlier by G.M. Rushforth, the director of the British School of Rome, who was the first to publish the material from the church after its excavation in the year 1900. It was Rushforth who was the very first to observe that this many-faceted scene, comprising the Multitude of the Blessed below and the choirs of Angels and Seraphims flanking the Cross above, seems broadly to mirror representations of the Adoration of the Lamb of the kind found in manuscripts illustrating the Book of Revelations (Rushforth 1902: 61).

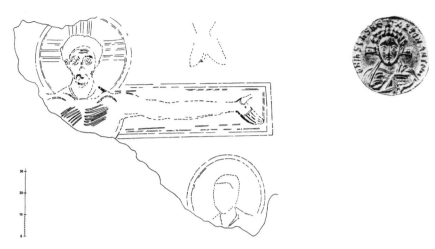

*Fig. 3a. Adoration of the Cross. Detail, tracing. After Nordhagen 1968.*
*Fig. 3b. Head of Christ, Type B. From of the coins of Emperor Justinian II (705-711). After Breckenridge 1959.*

An important step towards a deeper understanding of the Adoration of the Crucified scene in *apocalyptical terms* was Nordhagen's discovery that the physiognomic traits of Christ actually link Him directly with Justinian II's coinage, where Christ is represented with a *short beard* and with *curly hair.*

The foremost expert on Justinian II's numismatic iconography, J.D. Breckenridge, gave his full support to Nordhagen's identification of the physiognomic type of Christ found on the S. Maria Antiqua fresco, the so-called Type B in Breckenridge's system, and the type found on the coins of Justinan II. Breckenridge's discussion, for the details of which we must refer to his study, thus adds considerable weight to the assumption, so central in Nordhagen's thesis, that the emblem which was set up on the arch in the Forum church is a transformed Adoration of the Lamb, based on the 82nd Trullan Canon, and the Book of Revelations.[7] This so-called "inverted Lamb adoration" is, according to Nordhagen, a foremost illustration of the text of Revelations 9,

---

7   Breckenridge 1959: 78-90 & PL. I. Breckenridge endorsed Nordhagen's 1968 reading (Breckenrige 1972). Later it has been underwritten by A.D. Kartsonis, (Kartsonis 1994: 178ff.) U. Nilgen's learned and balanced critique is a major contribution to the discussion (Nilgen 2004). She fails, however, to include in her discussion the Type B head of the Crucified, a feature which posits the image in the highest religio-political sphere, where it draws on practices alien to those of Rome.

7 which states that: *a great multitude, which no man could number, of all nations … stood before the throne, and before the Lamb, clothed with white robes, and [with] palms in their hands.* Nordhagen's conclusions, then, as they were spelled out in his illuminating publication of 1968, can be summarized as follows (Nordhagen 1968: 50 ff.): The Crucifixion scene set in its centre, with Christ on the Cross flanked by Mary and John, has been incorporated into a pictorial scenario that is probably inspired by *apocalyptic iconography*. This means that the Adoration of the Crucified is an *inverted Adoration of the Lamb*. Hence, the Lamb is replaced by the Crucified, and the whole composition is an illustration of the Lamb adoration as it is described in the Book of Revelations. As to the discovery of the physiognomic traits of Christ *Type B* in this fresco, Nordhagen stresses that "…the adherence to the new official Christ image of Justinian II in respect to the hair and beard produces a type of the Crucified Christ which is as unique as the composition whose centre it occupies. We may not be wrong in concluding that if the composition as a whole was dictated by the Eighty-Second Canon, its use of the Christ of Type B may also be linked in some way to the ideas expressed in this Canon" (Nordhagen 1968: 53). This means that both the iconography and the style (cf. Kitzinger above) point towards *Constantinople* as the centre from which this unique scenery has its origin. We will, briefly, return to the 'Constantinopolitan Thesis' in the concluding section of the present article. In the succeeding paragraph, I will now present my own thesis about a Palestinian connection, grounded on an analysis of the selection of Biblical texts in the Greek text-*catena* on the triumphal arch.

## The Palestinian Connection. Palestinian influence on the Old Testament text-*catena* on the Triumphal Arch: A Hypothesis

### An ambiguity explored

The right half of the inscription on the triumphal arch is preserved almost in its entirety (See Fig. 2), while only a small fragment of *intonaco*, containing a few letters *in situ*, is preserved at the extreme l. side of the wall. The beautifully calligraphed white letters on a red ground seem to emulate such luxury purple manuscripts as the Rossano Gospels; also, according to G. Cavallo, the letter forms in this inscription draw on the Constantinopolitan Imperial ambience (Cavallo 1988: 486). However, we must carefully record the certain ambiguity as to the origin of this exquisite epigraphy that is perceptible in Cavallo's study: the purple manuscripts from which he draws his best clues may, as Cavallo himself has stressed, all belong to the Egypt-Palestine-Syria axis (Cavallo 1988: 492). Are there also, in the selection and organization of the Old Testament texts that make up this *catena*, indications regarding the liturgical traditions on which they draw? And is it possible to extract from this collection of Biblical quotes some further leads as to what content the vast iconographic display on the arch was meant to transmit?

First transcribed by Rushforth (Rushforth 1902: 60; cf. Nordhagen 1968: 48ff.), the *catena* has preserved, on the fragment of its l. part, what must be the very first letters in this series of Biblical excerpts. However, the content of this part of the *catena* is wholly lost. The fragment is illustrated in a watercolour in J. Wilpert's corpus (1917) on the Roman paintings and mosaics (Wilpert 1917: Pl. 156, I (plates in vol. IV).

The text on the preserved right side of the *catena* has the following composition:

Lines:  1-3     Canticles 3, 11
        3-6     a) Zechariah 9, 11
                b) Zechariah 14, 6&7
        6-8     Amos 8, 9&10
        9       Baruch 3, 36 (in the *catena* presented under the name of Ιερεμίας.
        10      a) John 19, 37[8]
        10-11   b) Deuteronomy 28, 66

Following its first transcription by Rushforth (Rushforth 1902: 60), the text was recorded by W. de Grüneisen in a "tracing" and a photograph,[9] and later given in a new and exact tracing and corrected transcription by Nordhagen with a new reading by the Norwegian theologian E. Molland (Nordhagen 1968: 44, 122).

---

[8]   As demonstrated by Einar Molland (in Nordhagen, 1968: 122), the text quotes Zech 12, 10 in a version *different* from the LXX (cf. Rahlfs 1921).

[9]   de Grüneisen 1911. On the *catena* see: V. Federici (in de Grüneisen 1911), *L'épigraphie de l'église Sainte-Marie-Antique* (399-447) with a special *Album épigraphique* also by Federici: v. *Album épigraphique*, Pl. XIII.

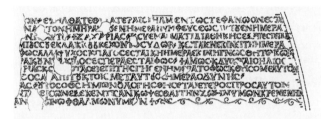

Fig. 4. S. Maria Antiqua. Large inscription. Transcription: Rushforth/Nordhagen. After Nordhagen 1968.

[σελαμ]ιωΝ ℘ΕΞΗΑΘΑΤΕ Θ[υγ]ΑΤΕΡΑΙC ΙΗΑΜ ΕΝ ΤΩ CΤΕΦΑΝΩ ΟΝ ΕCΤΕ    (i)  Canticles iii. 11.
[φάνωσε]Ν Α[ὐ]ΤΟΝ Η ΜΗΡ ΑΥ[τ]ΟΥ ΕΝ ΗΜΕΡΑ ΝΥΜΦΕΥCΕΩC ΑΥΤΟΥ ΕΝ ΗΜΕΡΑ
[εὐφροσύ]ΝΗ[ς] ΑΥΤΟΥ ℘ ✠ ΖΑΧΑΡΙΑC ℘ κ̣ CΥ ΕΝ ΑΙΜΑΤΙ ΔΙΑΘΗΚΗC ΕΞΑΠΕCΤΕΙΛΑC    (ii)  a. Zacharias ix. 11.
[ἕσο]ΜΙΟΥC COΥ ΕΚ ΛΑΚ℘ΟΥ ΟΥΚ ΕΧΟΝΤΟC ΥΔΩΡ ℘ κ̣ ΕCΤΑΙ ΕΝ ΕΚΙΝΕΙ ΤΗ ΗΜΕΡΑ    b. xiv. 6, 7.
[οὐκ ἔσται]ΦΩC ΑΛΛΑ Ψ̇ΥΧΟC κ̣ ΠΑΓΟC ΕCΤΑΙ κ̣ Η ΗΜΕΡΑ ΕΚΙΝΗ ΓΝΩCΘΗ ΤΩ Κ̅Ω̅ κ̣
[οὐχ ἥμ]ΕΡΑ κ̣ ΟΥ ΝΥΞ κ̣ ΠΡΟC ΕCΠΕΡΑ ΕCΤΑΙ ΦΩC ℘ ✠ ΑΜΩC·κ̣ ΑΥCΕΤΑΙ Ο ΗΛΙΟC    (iii)  Amos viii. 9. 10.
[μεσημβ]ΡΙΑC κ̣ CΥ[σκ]ΟΤΑCΕΙ ΕΠΙ ΤΗC ΓΗC ΕΝ ΗΜΕΡΑ ΤΟ ΦΩC κ̣ ΘΗCΟΜΕ ΑΥΤΟΝ
[ὡς πέν]ΘΟC ΑΙ[γ]ΑΠ[ι]ΤΟΥ κ̣ ΤΟΙC ΜΕΤ ΑΥΤΟΥ ΟC ΗΜΕΡΑ ΟΔΥΝΗC ℘
[Ιερεμί]ΑC ℘ ΟΥΤΟC Ο Θ̅C̅ ΗΜΩΝ ΟΥ ΛΟΓΗCΘΗ CΕΤΑΙ ΕΤΕΡΟC ΠΡΟC ΑΥΤΟΝ    (iv)  Baruch iii. 36.
[καὶ ὄψε]ΝΤΑ[ι] ΕΙC ΩΝ ΕΞΕΚΕΝΤΙCΑΝ κ̣ ω̣ ♱ΕCΘΑΙ ΤΗΝ ΖΩΗΝ ΥΜΩΝ ΚΡΕΜΕΝΗΝ    (v)  a. John xix. 37.
[ἀπέν]ΑΝ[τι τ]ΩΝ ω̣ΦΘΑΛΜΩΝ ΥΜΩΝ ✠ ℘    b. Deuteronomy xxviii. 66.

Inscription on the triumphal arch (cf. p. 47). After Rushforth, with corrections.

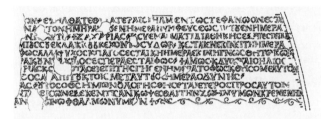

Fig. 5. The catena. Tracing by Nordhagem. After Nordhagen 1968.

It has been commented upon by several authors, most thoroughly by B. Brenk (1971), who, referring to patristic sources, found that the text is typologically related to the Passion.[10] W. Tronzo (1985) was the first to notice that the verses deriving from Zechariah 14, 6-7, Amos 8, 9-10 and John 19, 37 were constituents of the Jerusalem Good Friday rite of the 7th century (Tronzo: 1985: 100). No less important is A.D. Kartsonis' observation (1994) that "the surviving selection of biblical quotes parallels the ones chosen by Cyril of Jerusalem in his Catechetical Lecture 13", that which has the title *On 'who was crucified and buried'* (Kartsonis 1994: 170). I will now add some further remarks to this Palestinian and Cyrillian stamp in the *catena*. Crucial for the comments which follow is the important *comparative* study by S. Janeras (1988) on the Good Friday Liturgy in the Eastern tradition. In this he demonstrates how the original practice followed in the liturgy of Jerusalem can be reconstructed with the help of Armenian and Georgian lectionaries.[11] The same liturgical practice has also left its imprint in certain areas in the West. As pointed out by A. Jacob

---

[10]    B. Brenk, in a review of Nordhagen, *The Frescoes of John VII*, in *Byzantinische Zeitschrift* 1971: 392-396; on the *catena*: 394ff.

[11]    For the following descriptions of the Byzantine and Palestinian traditions, cf. Janeras 1988.

(1976), the migration of Syrian and Palestinian Christians to Italy, caused by the Persian and Arabian assaults on the Holy Land and North Africa, must account for the strong Palestinian element visible in liturgical manuscripts from South Italy. Such alien components are contained even in manuscripts that in other respects fully adhere to the Constantinopolitan *Byzantine* rite (Jacob 1976: 29-64).

## Table according to S. Janeras

According to the study by S. Janeras of the Good Friday rite in the Eastern tradition, the leads in our *catena* pointing to Palestine can be further substantiated. In the table which we – following Janeras[12] – present below, we list, firstly, the Good Friday lections found in manuscripts of the Georgian [LG] and Armenian [LA] tradition, which reflect the Palestinian liturgy in its most ancient form (LA + LG in Janers 1988: 412). The succeeding columns record the development of the liturgy. This development can be followed through the Sabaite tradition, named so because of manuscripts that can be traced to the scriptoria of the Monastery of San Saba on the outskirts of Jerusalem.

The table shows the list of lectures before [*Vat. gr. 771*; *Typicon of Anastasis*[13] and *Sin. gr. 1096* (TA)] and *after* (third and fourth column) the fusion of Palestinian and Byzantine elements took place.[14] This fusion affected the Palestinian as well as the Byzantine liturgy, here represented by the Slavonic Triodion and what Janeras designated as diverse Byzantine manuscripts (Janeras, 1988: 214ff.). In the fifth column, then, one finds the Constantinopolitan tradition in its original form, i.e. before the later fusion with Palestinian elements. In Constantinople, at this early date, all verses are centred on the celebration of the Third to Sixth Hour: the τριτοέκτη.[15] Finally, in the sixth column, are listed the paragraphs in the Catechesis of Cyril of Jerusalem that contains Biblical verses corresponding exactly to those found in our *catena*.

---

12  The present table is a synthesis of those in Janeras 1988: 212-217 & 412.

13  The *Typicon of Anastasis* probably records the Jerusalem Liturgy of the 10th century; Janeras 1988: 40.

14  On the fusion of the Palestinian and the Constantinopolitan rite, which took place in the 9th-10th/11th centuries, see Taft 1990: 22-23.

15  The τριτοέκτη (the Third-Sixth Hour) consists of: Troparion; Prokeimon (Ps 69 (70): 2, 3a, 3b); Lecture (Zac 11, 10-13); Prokeimon (Ps 11 (12): 8, 2, 3).

TABLE 1: *LECTIONS IN THE EASTERN GOOD FRIDAY RITE*

The lections marked in **bold face** are included in the *catena* on the triumphal arch of S. Maria Antiqua.

| LA/LG | Sabait:Vat.gr.771/ TA* | Slav. Triod. | Div.Byz. m.s. | Constantinople | Cyril. Cat. |
|---|---|---|---|---|---|
| | **Cant 3, 11:** At vespers | | | | **Cant 3, 11:** Cat 13, 17 |
| | | | | | **Zech 9, 11:** Cat 12, 10/ Cat 13, 34 |
| Zech 11, 11-14 | Zech 13, 4-9 | Zech 11, 10-13 | Zech 11, 10-13 | Zech 11,11-14: Τριτοέκτη.** | |
| Gal 6, 14-18 | Gal 6, 14-18 | Gal 6, 14-18 | Gal 6, 14-18 | | |
| Is 3, 9b-15 | Is 3, 9b-15 | | | | |
| Phil 2, 5-11 | Phil 2, 5-11 | | | | |
| | Mt 27, 1-56 | Mt 27, 3-56 | Mt 27, 3-56 | | |
| Is 50, 4-9 | Is 50, 4-8 | Is 50, 4-11 | Is 50, 4-11 | | |
| Rom 5, 6-11 | Rom 5, 6-11 | Rom 5, 6-10 | Rom 5, 6-10 | | |
| **Amos 8, 9-12** | **Amos 8, 9-11** | | | | **Amos 8, 9-10:** Cat 13, 25 |
| I Cor 1, 18-31 | I Cor 1, 18-31 | | | | |
| | Mk 15, 1-32 | Mk 15, 16-41 | Mk 15, 16-41 | | |
| Is 52, 13-53, 12 | Is 52, 13-53, 12 | Is 52, 13-54, 1 | Is 52, 13-54, 1 | | |
| Hebr 2, 11-18 Mt 27, 3-56 | Hebr 2, 11-18 | Hebr 2, 11-18 | Hebr 2, 11-18 | | |
| Is 63, 1-6 | Is 63, 1-6 | | | | |
| Hebr 9, 11-28 Mk 15, 16-41 | Hebr 9, 11-28 | | | | |
| | Lc 22, 66-23, 49 | Lc 22, 66-23, 49 | Lc 23, 32-49 | | |
| Jer 11, 18-20 | Jer 11, 18-20 | Jer 11, 18-12, 15 | Jer 11, 18-12, 15 | | |
| Hebr 10, 19-31 Lc 23, 32-49 | Hebr 10, 19-31 | Hebr 10, 19-31 | Hebr 10, 19-31 | | |
| **Zech 14, 5-11** | **Zech 14, 5-11** | | | | **Zech 14, 6-7:** Cat 13, 24 |
| I Tim 6, 13-16 | I Tim 6, 13-16 | | | | |
| | | | | | **Bar 3, 36** Cat 11, 15 |
| **Jn19, 25-37** | **Jn 18, 28-19, 37** | **Jn 18, 28-19, 37** | Jn 19, 23-37 | | **Jn 19, 37/ Zech 12, 10** Cat 13, 41 |
| | | | | | **Dt 28, 66** Cat 13, 19 |

Table 1: Readings for Good Friday in the Georgian and Armenian tradition [LA + LG], in the Sabaite Tradition [Vat. gr. 771; TA: Typicon of Anastasis-Sin.gr. 1096], in the Byzantine tradition after the fusion with the Palestinian tradition [Slavonic Triodion; diverse Byzantine manuscripts], and in the ancient Constantinopolitan tradition centred in the τριτοέκτη. Apud: Janeras 1988: 212/215/217/412.

* The readings listed in the TA [*Typicon* of Anastasis and *Sin. gr. 1096*] and in the *Vat. gr. 771* are almost identical. The minor differences are restricted to the following texts, which [in the Typicon of Anastasis] are: Mt 27, 1-32; Amos 8, 9-12; I Cor 1, 18 – 2, 2; Zech 14, 5 – 12b.

** Cf. n. 15.

The table demonstrates that:

(1) Until the Byzantine liturgy was influenced by Palestinian formulas in the 9th-10th centuries, the Constantinopolitan lectionaries for Good Friday had only one reading in common with the Palestinian tradition: Zech 11, 11-14/10-13 (cf. column 5). This reading took place at the τριτοέκτη (cf. above, n. 15). The preserved remains of the *catena* in S. Maria Antiqua, however, show no trace of this particular quotation from Zechariah.

(2) When the later Constantinopolitan lectionaries, i.e. those that originated *after* the fusion had taken place between the Byzantine and the Palestinian tradition (cf., for instance, the Slavonic *triodion* and the diverse Byzantine manuscripts in the table above), are compared with our *catena*, it appears that there is only one text shared by all: John 19, 37. This text, however, is not found in the early lectionaries in Constantinople and may therefore, presumably, stem from the Palestinian rite.

(3) As the table shows, it is, then, only the Armenian and Georgian lectionaries and the lectionaries of the Sabaitic tradition that have: Zech 14, 6-7, Amos 8, 9-10, and John 19, 37.[16] The fact that John 19, 37 also appears in the later Byzantine tradition should not confuse us: it is the result of a general assimilation of Palestinian lectures into the Constantinopolitan rite (Cf. n. 14). One manuscript, the *Vat. gr. 771*, an important document in the Greek-Italian tradition and with strong elements of Sabaitic liturgy (Cf. Janeras 1988: 46, n. 56), has *four* readings in common with the *catena*: Zech 14, 6-7, Amos 8, 9-10, John 19, 37, and Cant 3, 11 (included among the readings at Vespers). This manuscript lacks, however, the passages from Zech 9, 11 and Baruch 3, 36 as well as Deut 28, 66, and neither are they found in lectionaries of the Byzantine liturgy for the Holy Friday. On the other hand, both Zech 9, 11 and Deut 28, 66 are found in Cyril of Jerusalem's 13th Catechesis On 'who was crucified and buried' (cf. Kartsonis *above*). This evidence shows that parts of our *catena*, unquestionably, are to be traced to Palestine, which, spelled out more specifically, would mean the Sabaite tradition of Jerusalem.

---

[16]   As already stated, in the Armenian and Georgian lectionaries the Palestinian tradition is reflected in its most ancient form; such manuscripts as the *Typicon of Anastasis* and *Vat. gr. 771* represent a later stage in the development of this Hageopolite tradition. Nevertheless, all of these manuscripts include the readings from Amos 8, 9-10, Zech 14, 6-7 and Jn 19, 37, as in the *catena* of S. Maria Antiqua.

As stated above, the question of why, in this *catena*, these particular verses from the Old Testament have been selected and linked in the manner we find them here, holds an ambiguity that waits for further investigation. What can be said, however, is that the inclusion, in the concluding sequence of the *catena*, of John 19, 37 reminds us of the place this same text has in the liturgies of Good Friday. The linking of Zechariah 14, 6-7 and Amos 8, 9-10 parallels the way they are coupled in Cyril of Jerusalem's *Catechesis* 13, XXIV-XXV, where the texts refer to the occlusion of the sun that lasted from the sixth to the ninth hour.

It may also be assumed that a *catena* consisting of readings from the Cyrillian Catechesis may have been selected for the reason that this theologian consistently links the prophetic witnesses of God's presence, their visions of His glory, to the earthly epiphany of God. Hence, one function of these texts may have been to stress the unity in Christ of the divine nature, as described by the prophets, and the human nature revealed through His theophany on earth. The position of the *catena* within the panel of which it is a part, i.e. between the Heavenly and Earthly beings in adoration on the arch, seems to sustain such a hypothesis. Actually, the concluding sequence, the linking of Baruch 3, 36, John 19, 37/Zech 12, 10 and Deut 28, 36, may point in the same direction: as underlined by Cyril (*Cat.* 11, XV, *PG* 33, 710 AB), the statement in Baruch reading "He is our God, no other will be numbered beside him" proves that *the one Incarnated is God*. Since, in our *catena*, this is linked to the verse stating that "they shall look on him whom they pierced" (John 19, 37/Zech 12, 10), the same sentence seems to stress the *Divine supremacy* and the *human vulnerability* and suffering, hence, the two natures in Christ. Finally, the concluding quotation from Deuteronomy about "*life* hanging", linked by Cyril to the narration in Num 21, 9 about the brazen serpent (*Cat.* 13, XIX-XX; *PG* 33, 797A-B), seems to mean *life everlasting* through Christ crucified.

## *The eschatological level: Cyril's 15th Catechesis*

Considering the iconography of the sanctuary arch, this Crucifixion which includes Seraphim, Cherubim, and Angels as well as the Multitude of Men in adoration of the Crucified, is *not a historical* representation of the Golgotha scene. The motif has *eschatological* as well as *liturgical* overtones. As we have seen, Nordhagen, in his 1968 publication on the frescoes of John VII, sets forth the thesis that the motif is an *inverted Lamb adoration* in apocalyptical terms (Nordhagen 1968: 50ff.). While I do not by any means exclude this possibility, the Palestinian leads in the *catena* may open an alternative path for probing the eschatological levels of meaning in this programme: Cyril of Jerusalem opens his 15th Catechesis *"On The Second Adventus of Christ"*, with a quotation from Dan 7, 10-13 (*PG* 33, 870). The *thousand times a thousand* in v. 10 are here interpreted in terms of *angels* and *human beings*:

> Thus you see, O Mortal, before what a *multitude of witnesses* you shall enter into judgment. The *whole human race will be present there.* Try to imagine all those who have existed since the time of Adam to the present day. That is a great crowd, but still it is little. The *angels are more numerous.* They are the ninety nine sheep, whereas humanity is the one sheep. After all, it is written that His ministers are a *thousand times a thousand* [Χίλιαι χιλιάδες], not that this figure sets a limit to their multitude, but rather because the prophet could not express a larger number (*Catechesis* 15, XXIV, *PG* 33, 904B) (Quoted from: Danielou 1957: 109ff.).

Can we exclude the idea that Daniel's vision, as well as Cyril's interpretation of it, may be a lead in our search for the essential meaning behind the adoration scene on the arch?

I am aware of the obstacles concerned with an excessively liberal use of quotations from the Church Fathers as "proof" of a particular reading. Still, I am tempted to quote Cyril of Jerusalem from another passage in his 15th Baptismal Catechesis; here he posits the Crucified into an *eschatological* setting:

> In His first coming he endured a cross, despising shame (Heb. 12, 2); in His second He will come in glory, attended by a host of angels.[17]

As I will argue, this strongly brings to mind our "Adoration of the Crucified" scene in S. Maria Antiqua. It is therefore even more interesting that one detail in this vast iconographical constellation seems to point towards an *eschatological* meaning of this scene.

## *Triumphal arch, lower zone: "The Resurrection of the Dead"?*

There is one area which, up to this point, has not been included in this discussion of the iconography, namely the zone immediately *below* that of the

---

17    Cyril of Jerusalem, *Cat.* 15. I; in a translation by McCauley and Stephenson 1970 (vol.1): 53.

*Fig. 6. Santa Maria Antiqua. Detail of a 'photo-mosaic' of the triumphal arch compiled by Werner Schmid and Kirsti Gulowsen (2006-07; printed with their permission) showing the slanting object.*

Multitude of Men assembled at the foot of the Cross. What remains of this zone, which originally must have spanned the entire width of the arch, but was found nearly obliterated when the church was excavated in 1900/1901, is described in detail by Nordhagen (1968)[18]: "The height of the zone is 93 cm … An area to the extreme right end [… is preserved] in its full height, showing a dark background divided into two zones, the lower green, the upper blue. Against this background … is the slanting right side of a yellow object" (Nordhagen 1968: 50). Delineated by straight black contours, the yellow object seen at the point where the painted plaster breaks off is clearly tilted to the right, angled about 60 degrees.

In a *note* in the Journal of the Warburg and Courtauld Institutes (2009), to which I refer for a detailed discussion of the archaeological as well as the theological evidence, I argue for the thesis that the "yellow slanting object" seen against the blue and green background, the square form of which proved by its straight contours, and which is located in a zone immediately below the large Crucifixion scene, can be nothing but a part of a *sarcophagus* or, possibly, *the raised lid of a sarcophagus*, such as those seen in scenes with the Dead rising from their Graves (Folgerø 2009b: 207-219). Hence, it might be suggested that the lost zone once held a *scene of resurrection* viz. the resurrection of the "saints which slept in their graves" and which took place at the moment of the Death of Christ on Golgotha according to Matthew 27, 52, and which will take place also at the moment of His glorious Second Adventus, such as can be seen in numerous representations of The Last Judgment in Eastern as

---

[18]    This part of the fresco was already destroyed in 1702: cf. Nordhagen 1968: Pl. XLI.

well as Western depictions (On the development of the Last Judgment scene, see Brenk 1966).

## Rome as a melting pot of cultural migration

In the concluding sequence of this article, the S. Maria Antiqua iconography will be investigated for information "labelling" the complexity of the multi-cultural state of Papal Rome in the 7th-8th centuries.

The postulate presented above, about a "Palestinian connection" in the art of John VII, also draws its cues from that signal element of his decoration, the "portrait" he set up on the triumphal arch of his predecessor Martin I. Martin's imago is irrefutable proof of John's veneration of the pope who called the *anti-Monotheletic* (i.e. *pro-Orthodox*) Lateran Synod which took place in Rome in the year 649. As shown abundantly by the sources, Eastern immigrants to Rome played their part at this synod, including the following Palestinian presbyters:

> *Johannes abba presbyter monasterii… sancta Sabbae* and
> *Theodorus … abba presbyter monasterii labrae sancti Sabbae* (Sansterre 1980: 11).

As stressed by J.-M. Sansterre (1980), this is a strong and incontestable argument in favour of the thesis that it was a close contact between Rome and the important Palestinian Great Lavra of San Saba, which was located in the Kidron Valley on the outskirts of Jerusalem (Sansterre 1980: 25ff).

As also pointed out by Sansterre, the aggression against the Holy Land, which started with the Persian massacres in the year 614, and was followed by the Arab raids that culminated with the conquest of Jerusalem in the year 638, did primarily strike the *anti-Monotheletic* churches. Emigrants from the Great Lavra of San Saba in the Kidron Valley now fled to the upper tip of Africa, where they lived temporarily in a monastic community together with some other refugees, Nestorian monks from the Nisibian monastery. The severe Arab raid taking place in the years 647 and 648, then, led to their *immigration* to Rome.

Among the monks settling in Rome was Maximus the Confessor (Sansterre 1980: 25ff.), who was *in fact* the very "soul" of the Lateran Synod of A.D. 649 (Schulz 1986: 45), in whose teachings the crucial tenets of Pope Leo the Great, and the so-called *Chalcedonianism* – the Christology that stresses the meaning of the *two natures* of Christ for the salvation of Man – stood centrally.

Sansterre refers to a Syrian text recording the life of St. Maximus the Confessor, which suggests that this saint and his disciple Anastasios lived temporarily in the above-mentioned monastery in North Africa before they travelled to Rome. This source tells us, in addition, that the refugees, on their arrival in Rome, were received by Pope Martin I – the one depicted on the triumphal arch of S. Maria Antiqua – who donated a monastery called *Cellae novae* to these monks (Sansterre 1980: 26). As demonstrated by Sansterre, this monastery seems to be identical with the San Saba located on the Little Aventine,[19] consecrated in the name of the great Palestinian monk Sabbas, the one who had established the Great Lavra in the Kidron Valley.[20]

My main point is that the presence of immigrants from Palestine may, through the traditions which they brought with them, have altered the liturgical practices of Rome, particularly in churches presumably served by Greek ecclesiastics such as S. Maria Antiqua.

As a whole, the appearance in the *catena* of some of the prophetic texts that are also found in the Palestinian lectionaries for Good Friday, deriving ultimately, as we have seen, from the 13th Baptismal Catechesis of St. Cyril of Jerusalem (cf. Kartsonis, above), goes well with what we know of the Palestinian presence in Early Medieval Rome (See e.g. Krautheimer 1980: 89-108). On the other hand, given the late-Hellenistic *Byzantinizing* style and the frequency of Byzantinizing iconographic matter in John VII's frescoes to which Nordhagen *and* Kitzinger have repeatedly pointed, the Palestinian imprint which can be perceived in the crowning picture in this ensemble may seem rather baffling (Kitzinger 1934: 19; Kitzinger 1958; Nordhagen 1968: 106-114). One of the questions to which we have just pointed is still unanswered: *where* can this striking *confluence* of heterogeneous *theological* and *iconographical* matter have taken place?

One reasonable explanation [the Constantinopolitan thesis] could be that this merger may have occurred in Constantinople, the great Byzantine capital itself, due to the presence there of a Palestinian faction possibly driven to the city by the upheavals of the time. This explanation cannot by any means be

---

[19] Sansterre convincingly argues that the *terminus post quem* for the foundation of the *Cellae novae/San Saba* is A.D. 647, co-temporal with the great sack of North Africa by the Arabs, and that the *terminus ante quem* is 653, the year when pope Martin I was deposed and arrested by the Byzantines: cf. Sansterre 1980: 28ff.

[20] "… Saint-Saba sur le petit Aventin [Rome] était … occupé par quelques nestorien de Nisibe et *sourtout par les moines de la Grande Laure du Cèdron*" (my italics), Sansterre 1980: 31.

excluded, given a situation like the one outlined here, that the creation of a religio-political programme in pictures like that seen in S. Maria Antiqua could have happened with the consent and under the control of the Emperor and the Constantinopolitan church hierarchy. From here, then, it could have been brought into outlying Byzantine areas like Rome.

Another possible explanation [the Palestinian connection] for the Cyrillian and Palestinian imprint on the *catena* selection of texts is that it is a corollary of a general *cultural* and *theological* cross-over in the wake of the 7th century *immigration* from Palestine to Rome. The fact that our text-*catena* includes the passages of Amos 8, 9-10, Zech 14, 6-7 and Cant 3, 11, which are only documented in the Palestinian tradition, while they appear to be wholly *absent* in the Constantinopolitan texts for that same day, may indicate an influence that came *directly* to Rome from Palestine; such an influence seems to be well documented by the liturgical studies to which I have referred, such as those of A. Jacob and S. Janeras.

Perorating or pulling the threads together, one concession shared by professor Nordhagen and myself has to do with what we may call the *geocultural* context. This regards the source, or sources, of the iconography or iconographies involved. Despite our insistence on locating the fountainhead of the iconographical idiosyncrasies that we have studied in widely different parts of the Mediterranean basin, a third possibility appears: that of an independent *Roman school* either of innovation or hybridization, or both.

Following this path of reasoning, the extraordinary *blending* of theologically charged imagery in the frescoes of John VII may have taken place on *Roman soil* by command of the papal authorities, based on widely different iconographical traditions and models. Pope John VII, being the noble son of a Byzantine official in Rome, is a possible candidate for the role of chief ideologist in this matter. A reasonable suggestion will be that the programme executed for him in S. Maria Antiqua may have been based on pictorial conventions already established in Rome before his time, conventions being brought about *partly* by the Byzantine domination there during this period, and *partly* by a *Palestinian presence* that had not abated since the mid-seventh century *immigrations*. As stressed by Sansterre, the fact that two of the popes succeeding John VII, Sisinnius (708) and Constantine (708-715), were Syrians, as was also Gregory III in the 730s (731-741), the Syrian-Palestinian and Egyptian *immigration* continued to be important also in the first decennia of the 8th c., as a result of Muslim persecution of Christians (Sansterre 1980: 39ff.).

The evidence we perceive in the S. Maria Antiqua is many-facetted, and the final answer is not given. But one thing is clear: any attempt to identify the individual who composed this programme will have to take into account that he lived and worked in what could best be described as *a cultural and theological melting pot*, the Rome of the 7th-8th centuries, in which several reciprocally contrasting traditions lived side by side and could hybridize.

## Bibliography

Breckenridge, J.D. (1959). *The Numismatic Iconography*. New York: The American Numismatic Society.

Breckenridge, J.D. (1972). "Evidence for the Nature of Relations between Pope John VII and the Byzantine Emperor Justinian II". *Byzantinische Zeitschrift*, 65, 364-373.

Brenk, B. (1966). *Tradition und Neuerung in der christlichen Kunst des ersten Jahrtausends. Studien zur Geschichte des Weltgerichtsbildes* in *Wiener byzantinistische Studien*, Band III. Wien: Österreichische Akademie der Wissenschaften.

Brenk, B. (1971). "P.J. Nordhagen. The frescoes of John VII in S. Maria Antiqua in Rome". *Byzantinische Zeitschrift*, 64, 392-396.

Cavallo, G. (1988). "Le tipologie della cultura nel riflesso delle testimonianze scritte" in: *Bisanzio, Roma e l'Italia nell'alto Medioevo*. Settimane di studio del centro italiano di studi sull'alto medioevo XXXIV 3-9 april 1986. Spoleto: Centro italiano di studi sull'alto Medioevo in Spoleto.

Danielou, J. (1957) *The Angels and their Mission. According to the Fathers of the Church*. Allen, Texas: Christian Classics. A division of Thomas More Publishing.

de Grüneisen, W. (1911). *Sainte Marie Antique*. Rome: Max Bretschneider.

Folgerø, P.O. (2009a). *"Tekst-katena na freskakh v tserkvi Santa-Maria Antikva v Rime (705-707): Palestinkoe vliianie ili raznoobrazie kul'turnykh traditsii v Rime 7-8 veka"* (The Text-catena in the Frescoes in the Sanctuary of S. Maria Antiqua in Rome (705-707 A.D.). A 'Tracing' of Palestinian Influence and an Index of Cultural Cross-over in 7th-8th c. Rome?) in: *Khristianskoe iskusstvo*, 42-55.

Folgerø, P.O. (2009b). "The Text-*catena* in the Frescoes in the Sanctuary of S. Maria Antiqua in Rome (705-707 A.D.). A Note on its Links to the Catechetical Lectures of Cyril of Jerusalem", *Bollettino della Badia Greca di Grottaferrata*, III serie, 6, 45-66.

Folgerø, P.O. (2009c). "The Lowest, Lost Zone in the *Adoration of the Crucified* Scene in S. Maria Antiqua in Rome: A New Conjecture". *Journal of the Warburg and Courtauld Institutes*, Vol. LXXII, 207-219.

Ihm, C. (1992). *Die Programme der christlichen Apsismalerei vom 4. Jahrhundert bis zur Mitte des 8. Jahrhunderts*. Stuttgart: Franz Steiner Verlag.

Jacob, A. (1976). "Deux formules d'immixtion syro-palestiniennes et leur utilisation dans le rite byzantine de l'Italie mèridionale". *Vetera Christianorum 13*, 29-64.

Janeras, S. (1988). *Le Vendredi-Saint dans la tradition liturgique byzantine. Structure et historie de ses offices* in *Studia Anselmiana 99. Analecta Liturgica*, 13. Rome.

Kartsonis, A.D. (1994). "The Emancipation of the Crucifixion" in: Guillou, A. and Durand J. (eds.), *Byzance et les images,* Paris.

Kitzinger, E. (1934). *Römische Malerei vom Beginn des 7. bis zur Mitte des 8. Jahrhunderts.* Munich: R. Warth & Co.

Kitzinger, E. (1958). "Byzantine Art in the Period between Justinian the Great and Iconoclasm". *Berichte zum XI. Internationalen Byzantinisten-Kongress.* Munich.

Krautheimer, R. (1980). *Rome. Profile of a City, 312-1308.* New Jersey: Princeton University Press.

McCauley, L.P. & Stephenson, A.A. (1970). *The Works of Saint Cyril of Jerusalem.* The Fathers of the Church. Washington D.C.: Catholic University of America.

Moxey, K. (1993). "The Politics of Iconology" in: Cassidy, B. (ed.). *Iconography at the Crossroads. Papers from the Colloquium sponsored by the Index of Christian Art, Princeton University 23-24 March 1990.* Princeton.

Nilgen, U. (2004). "The Adoration of the Crucified Christ at Santa Maria Antiqua and the Tradition of Triumphal Arch Decoration in Rome" in: *Santa Maria Antiqua al Foro Romano cento anni dopo. Atti del colloquio internazionale Roma 5-6 maggio 2000*, 129-135. Rome: Campisano.

Nordhagen, P.J. (1968). "*The Frescoes of John VII (705-707 A.D.) in S. Maria Antiqua in Rome*" in: *Acta ad Archaeologiam et Historiam Artium Pertinentia*, III. Rome: "L'Erma" di Bretschneider.

Osborne, J., Brandt, J.R. & Morganti, G. (eds.). (2004). *Santa Maria Antiqua al Foro Romano cento anni dopo. Atti del colloquio internazionale Roma 5-6 maggio 2000.* Rome: Campisano.

Rahlfs, A. (1921). "Über Theodotion-Lesarten im Neuen Testament und Aquila-Lesarten bei Justin". *Zeitschrift f. d. neutestamentliche Wissenschaft*, 20 (1921), 182-199.

Rushforth, G.M. (1902). *The Church of S. Maria Antiqua*, in *Papers of the British School at Rome*, I. Rome.

Sansterre, J.-M. (1980). *Les moines grecs et orientaux à Rome aux époques byzantine et carolingienne (milieu du VIe s.– fin du IXe s.).* I. Brussels: Académie Royale de Belgique.

Schulz, H.-J. (1986). *The Byzantine Liturgy. Symbolic Structure and Faith Expression.* New York: Pueblo Pub. Co.

Taft, R. (1990). "A Tale of Two Cities. The Byzantine Holy Week Triduum as a Paradigm of Liturgical History" in: Neil Alexander, J. (ed.). *Time and Community. In Honour of Thomas Julian Talley (NPM Studies in Church Music and Liturgy).*Washington D.C.: The Pastoral Press.

Tea, E. (1937). *La basilica di Santa Maria Antiqua.* Milan: Società Editrice "Vita e Pensiero".

Tronzo, W. (1985). "The Prestige of Saint Peter's: Observations on the Function of Monumental Narrative Cycles in Italy". *Studies in the History of Art* 16, 93-112.

Wilpert, J. (1917). *Die römischen Mosaiken und Malereien der kirchlichen Bauten vom IV. bis XIII. Jahrhundert*, II. Freiburg.

# A Metaphorical View on Cultural Dialogues: Struve's Meridian Arc and Reflections on Memories in Eastern and Northern Borderlands

*Knut Ove Arntzen*

Nature and culture often interact in artistic interpretations, for instance in landscape paintings from the Romantic period. Northern borderlands were initially depicted in artistic representations through the artistic work of members of great scientific expeditions, who helped to mould the way in which the Northern areas were represented in the arts. This representation was characterized by landscapes of tundra, taiga as well as naked coastal landscapes in the borderlands of Northern Scandinavia and Russia. In this chapter I will give some examples of artistic expression in a borderline situation. In doing so I will try to define a dialogic space, which is created by way of a literal measuring of landscapes, which results in the establishment of a meridian reflecting images of the landscape by transference.

One of the first scientific expeditions contributing to defining arctic landscapes by means of visual art was the French *La recherche* expedition to Northern Scandinavia, to Finnmark and Svalbard, in the 1830s. By creating images of the Northern areas these French artists, who had been hired for the purpose of scientific documentation,

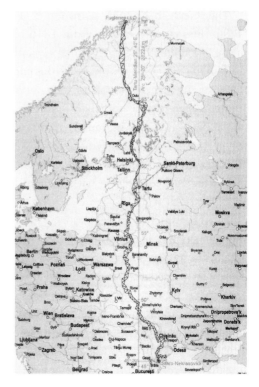

*Fig. 1.*

came to inspire Norwegian painters to develop a fascination for the Northern areas and their landscape and geography. Landscapes can be seen in the perspective of visual art, and it is obvious how it is being reflected in a dramatic manner in paintings as well as in drama and performance.

Dialogic space is a concept used to describe communication between two or more partners in an exchange situation. In this chapter I will focus on dialogic spaces for communication by referring to the triangle as a symbol of cultural and political border exchange. This can be exemplified with regard to the way in which an abstract figure can be transformed into a metaphorical model for the way in which memories and meetings are reflected on in arts and cultural communication.

I want to do this by making a metaphorical transference of the image of the triangle as a three-sided communication model of cultural exchange. Of the triangle's three basic triangular lines, one reflects the political dimension, one the vernacular dimension and one the spiritual dimension. The metaphorical transference is then made by referring to the triangle as a geometrical tool as applied in land-measuring processes, by which an instrumental basis is created for the geodetic land measuring of the 19th century with the aim of establishing meridians. I shall give some further explanations.

The German-Russian astronomer Friedrich Georg Wilhelm Struve (1793-1864) took 39 years, from 1816 to 1855, to complete the project of measuring the meridian arc, which is named after him, from the Black Sea to the Barents Sea. The monument to this endeavour in Hammerfest, Finnmark, is one of the few memorials to have survived the destruction of the Second World War in this, the northernmost city of the world. Struve's meridian reflected Norway's entry into international cooperation, and from a geo-cultural perspective this meridian symbolized the border in Europe between East and West, extending from the Black Sea, through Ukraine, White Russia and Lithuania, and connecting with Finland and the Nordic Countries, ending up in the polar region.

In trigonometric land measuring, the figure of the triangle is based on triangular points in the landscape, putting the meridian arc as a middle line in relation to the points. My point of view is that if we inscribe a triangle in a circle, it will relate to a space, which we can define metaphorically as dialogic space, by the way triangular lines intersect as in a web. As mentioned above, I propose to refer to the basic triangular lines reflecting by metaphorical transference of images to political, vernacular and spiritual dimensions in a dialogic space. The middle line of the triangles in the making of Struve's meridian intersects with the geographical space from the Black Sea area up to the Arctic Sea and regions of the pole. In this area there are a wide range of linguistic and political contrasts and reflections of landscapes of borderlands, their history and cultural interaction. This geographical space largely coincides with the post-Soviet area.

The Soviet-Lithuanian philosopher Grigorij Pomerants has spoken about the truth of the dialogue *(dialogens sannhet)* (Pomerants 2000: 151-61).

Pomerants worked as a librarian in the early post-Stalin period, by the 1950s gaining access to the secret books on spiritual philosophy in Moscow. I wish to draw some kind of parallel between Struve's meridian and Pomerants's sense of dialogue in a cultural space. Pomerants worked on the religious dimension towards the Oriental and Shamanistic, which may be connected to ecology, aesthetics and ethics in addition to religion as ways of understanding culture.

One could even speak of some kind of intersection inbetween the aesthetic, the ethical and ecological, relating to spiritual tendencies that had already been expressed in European philosophical thought. There is a long tradition of spiritual thinking in Western philosophy, opposing materialistic understanding in the Aristotelian and Hegelian tradition. Gottfried Leibniz and Ernst Cassirer belong to different periods, but are still simultaneous to each other in a synchronic sense in opposition to the diachronic understanding of history to be fulfilled by making utopian ideas come true.

The German philosopher Gottfried Wilhelm Leibniz (1646-1716) defined our metaphysical reality by describing it as consisting of individual substances that, through their mutual relations, create an abstract universe touching on conceptions of absolute space and absolute time. Leibniz did not see these as absolute space and separate quantities, but rather as dimensions with mutual relations. From this point of view, time and space form a system in which they are determined by each other and expressed by various events. An artist may get into touch with these events and perhaps also express them in his art.

We know these artistic expressions from the descriptions of events of the mythical world, where the legends speak of creatures of fantasy and mythical figures. This is a social and physical space beyond our sense of reality, but it reaches us through symbols and figurative expressions that apparently live their own lives. In our time it is artists who describe metaphysical events and create symbolic pictures. This space has no fixed structure and is only given meaning when we look at events and artwork in relation to each other.

According to the German philosopher Ernst Cassirer (1874-1945), the significance of these events and symbols changes as the space goes from being mythical to being aesthetic. Nevertheless, art must relate to the mythical space and its distinctive atmosphere, while consciousness of form arises through the artistic process. The artist's main priority is form – a form that in this context does not have to relate to certain concepts of reality. Such an imaginary reality may be as real as empirical or concrete reality. The artist has no duty to legitimize himself like the scientist must. He may be en route in a never-ending process that continues of its own accord (Cassirer 1985).

In the visual arts, the concept of landscapes and interiors reflects the individual's gaze and standpoint. Such landscapes and interiors can be metaphoric expressions and reflections of the dialogue between man and nature. The ability to use the gaze in a metaphorical way can be used in art and science as a means to apprehend cultural and personal identities as expressions of personal context and experience.

The theatrical gaze is a gaze from the outside, which looks and conceptualizes from a personal vantage point. Construction of meaning, both in the absolute and utopian sense, has proved insufficient for comprehension in both the artistic and the scientific senses. Since the symbolism of the early 20th century this experience of re-ritualized art inspired by movements of mysticism and spiritualism has found recurrent expression both in visual arts and in theatre

I would claim that it is against the background of this tradition that we recognize that the viewer or audience member has to adopt a personal stance with regard to an artist's picture or a scenographic installation in the theatre. The gaze has, so to speak, been absolved from having to master meaning on the basis of established criteria for judgements of taste.

Landscapes and interiors, through the memories that are attached to them, are expressions of open structures that can only be given meaning by the spectator. Metaphors are the tools by means of which the gaze defines what is perceived by the gaze. So it is also possible to conceive of new paradigms in art. The diversity of landscapes and interiors create complex structures. They have to be viewed in connection with the insight that meaning can no longer be inferred from conventional notions of what artistic expression should or should not convey. Like the philosopher, the artist can work with dynamic and plastic concepts of metaphorical origin. The artistic gaze both recognizes the complexity of context, is motivated to seek this complexity by perception and experience, and expresses itself through metaphors.

Contextual factors influence the development of art and theatre in a way that transforms them into an expression marked by a decentralized and nomadic comprehension. The various elements in such processes can be recycled.

In other words, concepts, icons and plastic elements tend to be redeployed or duplicated, thereby acquiring a character of their own that is independent of human presence.

The great innovator of modern theatre and scenography, Edward Gordon Craig, envisioned a form of theatre in which living actors would be replaced by a kind of super marionette (*Übermarionette*). Forms expressed through the effects of light and shadow would convey a kind of spirituality that could not be achieved by means of material, physical presence. Thus Craig represents a spiritual and meditative approach to art that accorded considerable freedom to the use of varied styles and forms of expression. Giving life to puppets or marionettes by performers can be seen as a process of animation that is reflected in traditions of vernacular puppetry.

Visual art, as well as dramatic expression, is a matter of various personal approaches creating a break with what we could call mainstream thought or the mainstream orientation. This kind of break can result in what I have dubbed an artistic *post-mainstream* (Arntzen 1998). This is in turn an expression to indicate how the arts are liberated from the centralized thinking of the mainstream, thus becoming capable of accommodating marginalities of the vernacular, the spiritual and the political.

The dissolution of centralized thinking is an outcome that allows the gaze to wander freely through the metaphoric landscape, almost like in a virtual world, where one door after another is opened at every touch of the computer keyboard. Personal, cultural and contextual premises are relentlessly gaining greater ground. In this connection, works of art that assume a closed aesthetic are becoming steadily more obsolete.

Hybrids that merge various artistic genres or various historically distinct artistic periods contribute to an experience of art that is more open than we could hitherto have imagined. Landscapes of hybrids and borderlands are marked by the intersection of cultural lines, creating new images or interiors in the vernacular, spiritual and political sense. Artistic expressions based on these intersections become meaningful as loci of exposed materiality, free of or including human individuals.

The materiality of human life, in the sense of a materiality cultivated for its own sake, has been criticized by the tradition we associate with symbolism and mysticism. Landscapes and interiors can reveal an awareness of a method for investigating emptiness as such. In much the same way as Craig dispensed with human presence through his notion of the Übermarionette, it would appear that he was motivated in this by the notion of a zero point, comparable to certain ideas in Buddhist and Hindu philosophy. A similar notion of a zero point is expressed in art and literary theory in Roland Barthes's famous essay on the "zero degree of writing" (Barthes 1953).

One can view this resetting to zero as a meditative process – a way of breaking with and opposing human materiality. Antonin Artaud (1896-1948) sought to place theatre's visual and aural means of expression on an equal footing with the dramatic text, and in the 1950s and 60s, influenced by meditation and esoteric systems of philosophy, awareness developed of what is called the actor's third eye. This was the notion of an intuition that corrects and overrides the eyes with which we usually look on the world, the idea that through meditation we can attain an awareness of the third way.

I believe that there is a third way that lies between what we call deconstruction and reconstruction, and that in a postmodern perspective this third way makes it possible to reconstruct and assemble new images from the fragments that remain after the devastating critique of materiality and conventional truths. A new consciousness of context, identity and difference is more and more reflecting the vernacular, the spiritual and the political – especially in borderland areas of collapse and reconstruction. A desire has arisen to reintroduce a metaphysical seriousness to replace the collapse of values brought about by the 20th century's chaos of wars and upheavals.

Polish theatre director Jerzy Grotowski (1933-1999), who was a borderliner between east and west, claimed a zero point position by emphasizing the poverty of theatre, through the will to dispense with exteriority and spectacular technical means of expression. Antonin Artaud had already asked for a theatre based less on language or speech and more on physical expression and situation.

A certain influence also came about from the Russian purveyor of mysticism Georg Ivanovitsj Gurdjieff (1872-1949), who referred to the actor's third eye, something I have come across in conversations with actors. Perhaps there is a third way between deconstruction and reconstruction opening up to new images and ways of understanding the dialogue between the artist, nature and landscapes. Thus a new consciousness about context and identities would come about, as well as a new understanding of how one can deal with the fragments and the bits and pieces after the moral collapse of political systems like the Soviet Union. Metaphorically speaking one could say that the gaze may be redefined and purged.

What is the situation with regard to a more spiritual way of understanding in the arts and science in the area of the former Soviet Union? To what extent would the spiritual be visible in communist society after materialist thinking had vanished? I have already mentioned Grigorij Pomerants, who was appointed "librarian of the secret books", the books that were not meant to be read by the general – books on spiritual philosophy, Zen Buddhism, yoga and so on. Books on spiritual movements had also been widely researched and studied by earlier Soviet Russian anthropologists and folklorists as well as historians of religion. I need only mention Mikhail Bakhtin and Wladimir Propp, alongside, for instance, the theatre and film director Sergej Eisenstein, who undertook a trip to Mexico to film the landscapes of snakes and mescaline before Artaud went there.

In the following I will refer to a few more examples from the area more or less touched upon by Struve's meridian. First of all by reminding myself of a meeting with the Ukrainian philosopher Michael Blumenkrants in 2001, together with the Norwegian theatre company Verdensteatret in Odessa. We organized a debate in a hotel room. This debate focused on the way in which the bits and pieces of an exploded postmodern world could be put together again – like a mosaic. Verdensteatret was about collecting visual and auditive materials for their production of *Tsalal*, collected during a trip from Kiev to Odessa, and from Odessa to Istanbul.

It was also clear to me that Turkish dervish dances and SUFI culture had been a strong source of inspiration for the Soviet Russian theatre and film creators of the 1920s and 1930s, in a period when many Turkish theatre people went to Russia to study. This was also the case for the mentor of Turkish theatre director Ulusoy, who French theatre researchers have studied with a view to finding some common roots in the area of the Black Sea. One of these French theatre researchers was Béatrice Picon-Vallin (Picon-Vallin 2008: 123-135).

*The Wanderer* was a production by the Finnish performance group Houkka Brothers in 2005, directed by the contemporary Finnish stage director Kristian Smeds in cooperation with the performance artist Juha Valkeapää and the visual artist Tero Nauha. This production was based on a 19th-century story taken from holy books, and here is a quotation taken from it:

> Thanks to the grace of the lord I am a Christian man, through my proper actions I am a great sinner, and by my vocation I am a homeless person carrying my goods around in a knapsack. That is everything.

This spiritual wanderer was a Russian pilgrim from the classical Russian-Orthodox stories of humility and searching for final salvation. The spiritual wanderer also passed by the famous Valamo Monastary at the Ladoga Sea towards Karelia. The story continues by explaining that the spiritual man had

*Fig. 2. Image of the meridian stone column at Fuglenes in Hammerfest commemorating Struve's meridian arc. Hammerfest municipality, photo by Bjørn Geirr Harsson.*

to pray thousands of times in one day, and that this goal would be difficult to achieve.

Kristian Smeds is well known for the spiritual orientation of his artistic work. He wanted to use theatre for research into spiritual realism, also staging well-known dramatists like Anton Chekov in a spiritual way, which in fact corresponds to Russian symbolism. The old pump station in Helsinki, where he staged *Uncle Vanja* with his Teatteri Takomo in 1998, provided an architectural experience because it was transferred virtually into a cathedral with tall, narrow windows, as pointed out by the Finnish critic Harru Hanju (Harju 2000: 70-77).

Later on Kristian Smeds also worked as an artistic director at the municipal theatre in Kajani, close to the landscape of Karelia on the Russian side of the borderline. Here he staged a production about the Swedish priest Lars Levi Læstadius, who lived and worked in Northern Finland and Northern Norway in the 19th century. The production's title was "The Voice of One Crying from the Wilderness", and it was about religiosity and the wilderness. With this production from 2001, Smeds became a name in Western European continental theatre, and after this production he visited both Brussels and Düsseldorf.

In a Lithuanian context I would say the performance artist Benas Šarka is a kind of shaman in productions connected to strong physical efforts and risky experimentation. His work is very concrete and more or less advocates a one-to-one relation between man and nature. Some of the re-enactments of historical events in the Baltic countries seem to move in the direction of similar stagings of a ritualistic kind.

In September 2009 the SEAS festival was organized in Tromsø, focusing on the Black Sea to the Arctic Sea in the perspective of cultural exchange. Vilna Scena from Kiev in the Ukraine visited Tromsø at this upper end of Struve's meridian in the polar regions, with their production based on William Shakespeare's *Richard III* directed by Dmytro Bogomazov under the title *Sweet Dreams*. This resembled a multimedia drama, creating the effect of dream-like situations, and it was staged in a green-light atmosphere. Figures were projected and the atmosphere was very dense with sound images to conjure forth a tormented Richard III (Eilertsen 2009: 77).

My conclusion is that by metaphorical reflections of art, according to the three sides of Struve's geodetical triangle, one can understand art in its landscapes and interiors – or in even more concrete terms: in dialogic spaces referring to working on and discovering cultural memory, and thus we can see the appearance of a new context of art in borderlands.

## Bibliography

Arntzen, K.O. (1998). "Post-Mainstream as a geocultural dimension for theatre". *Trans. Internet-Zeitschrift für Kulutrwissenschaft*: http://www.inst.at'/trans/5Nr/arntzen.htm.

Barthes, R. (1953). *Le Degré zéro de l'écriture,* Paris: Editions du Seuil.

Cassirer, E. (1985). *Symbol, Technik, Sprache. Aufsätze aus den Jahren 1927-1933.* Hamburg: Felix Meiner Verlag.

Eilertsen, J.H. (2009). "Richard IIIs søte drømmer". *MARG*, No. 3-2009. Tromsø.

Harju, H. (2000). "Teatteri Takomo and the Art of Transsubtantiation". *Nordic Theatre Studies*, vol. 13, 2000: Theatrical Illusion and the Text, guest. ed. Knut Ove Arntzen, Förenigen Nordiska Teaterforskare.

Picon-Vallin, B. (2008). "Les modalités du récit dans les spectacles-montages de Mehmet Ulusoy" in: Candan, Aysin (ed.). *Formes du narratif dans le théâtre.* Istanbul: Yeditepe University/Groupe de recherche Spectacle vivant.

Pomerants, P. (2000). *Dialogens sannhet.* Oslo: Cappelen.

# Multiple Dimensions and Multiple Borderlines:
# Cultural Work and Borderline Experience

*Gordana Vnuk*

Coming from a small country of the European periphery like Croatia while aspiring to encompass the whole world has made my job as an artistic programmer rather schizophrenic. On the one hand, I encounter a large amount of bias and prejudice at home: in a country whose main job has been to affirm and constitute its national identity, you can never do enough for Croatian artists and artists from abroad are not always welcome, particularly if they question local practices by the quality of their work.

On the other hand, if you do not belong to the European economic and cultural centres but want to be critical of the values established by those same centres, which are taken for granted in an international context, then you have an additional problem. Working in between these borders, geographical and spiritual, I have gathered a range of borderline experiences in multiple dimensions because my theatre work has stretched from the period of Tito's socialism, through the war in ex-Yugoslavia, up to the transition period and Croatia's endless queuing at the door of the European Union.

Today many people, especially the younger generations, are not aware of the unique position Yugoslavia once had or of the original political path it pursued in the era of The Cold War. The so-called Tito's Third Way positioned Yugoslavia between East and West, between communism and capitalism. In foreign policy, Tito (1892-1980), the life-long president of Yugoslavia, was one of the founders of the movement of non-aligned nations which represented an alternative to the East and West blocks. At local level, a political system of "self-management socialism", a milder kind of communism, was developed which allowed a certain amount of private initiative and gave the citizens passports to travel abroad. We were allowed to cross the borders that were forbidden to citizens of other communist countries.

It is important to stress that after the 2nd World War Tito was the only communist leader who opposed Stalin's politics, which led to a major crisis in 1948 when Soviet troops arrived at the Yugoslav border ready to march in. However, this did not happen and Tito continued to resist the Soviet pressure by enforcing, on the domestic level, anti-Stalinism with Stalinistic methods. Tito was not a democrat and he placed obstacles in the path of anyone wishing to introduce democratic changes. His era was a period of harsh imprisonment and the execution of political opponents.

In the 1950s the social and political structure was formed around workers' self-management, with workers' councils playing an important role – although they were always under the surveillance of the guiding hand of the party (the League of Communists or SKJ), which also managed to keep, on a federal basis, different nationalities and ethnicities together in six republics (today independent states). The international reputation of Yugoslavia grew steadily, with Tito serving as a mediator between East and West and playing the role of a *buffer* between the two blocks. The non-aligned movement which he launched together with Nehru and Nasser in the sixties gave hope to the decolonized Third World that alliances were possible outside the big world powers.

This *in-between* position enabled Yugoslavia to be a meeting place of East and West where, especially in the arts, people tried to annihilate the borders and create a united artistic community. In the late sixties it was the only place where Grotowski could find Living Theatre, and the only place where Robert Wilson was a regular guest in the seventies.

During the Cold War Zagreb was (alongside Nancy, Wroclaw, Erlangen and Parma) one of the centres of a very active and political students' theatre movement on the European scale. The legendary International Festival of Students' Theatre (IFSK) enabled Polish, Hungarian or Czech theatre groups to encounter their Italian, English or Spanish colleagues.

What allowed such artistic exchanges was also the fact that citizens from the countries belonging to the communist block, while not being able to travel to the West, could travel to Yugoslavia because Yugoslavia had a special status in this area.

Being aware of how little is known today of these borderline experiences in our region, Kampnagel dramaturgist Branko Brezovec and I conceived and carried out a large and ambitious project on Tito which came out in 2007. It was my last season in Kampnagel, a huge performing arts space in Hamburg of which I was the artistic director for six years.

Why Tito? And why in Germany? What do we have to do with it? These were the questions I was asked by my German team. They had very little knowledge about the East German past either, and did not see any reason why Kampnagel should engage in such a project. I tried to explain that we needed to increase the awareness of German audiences of themes from the European periphery because these themes also reflect the key issues of the recent German past. The

Germans ignored the degree to which Tito's policy influenced Willy Brandt's attitude towards East Germany, but the project also had a totally far-sighted dimension at the time of its execution: it was being conducted in Hamburg, only a few kilometres from Heiligendamm, where the G8 summit was taking place. Anti-globalist protesters under the slogan "Another World is Possible" were influenced by utopian thoughts similar to those which had previously influenced Tito: is there a world order which can exist outside the big world powers? They were advocating political and social alternatives which today, following the collapse of liberal capitalism, make Tito's Third Way more topical than ever.

Throughout his life Tito was a contradictory and controversial person. On the one hand, he was a dictator and supported a centralised government; while on the other he was an internationally recognised politician. But he is not just a biography; he was a programme, maybe even a copy of the programme with a sequence of hasty decisions, a lifestyle and ideology of style with numerous desired and undesired consequences and pressures. Our project wanted to show these controversies, including his responsibility for the demise of Yugoslavia which ended in the cruellest war that Europe had known since the 2nd World War.

The Tito project was a complex and spectacular event with eight performances and a number of accompanying programmes (workshops, films, symposiums, public debates and lectures – one of them with a very controversial title called "How Stalinism saved the humanity of man!" by Slavoj Žižek) which were aimed at providing audiences with access to broader historical, critical and theoretical dimensions. The project involved over one hundred artists and co-producing partners from almost all the countries of ex-Yugoslavia as well as from Germany, Russia, Italy, Egypt and India. We offered these artists a task to open up *titoism* – from the troubles one has with utopian thoughts to abstract, philosophical and dialectic reveries about the number "three". What we got was a series of non-ideological discourses which refused to take a stand *against* or *for*: the performances did not wave red flags, but they did not fall into the trap of irony and cynicism either. They tried to give an artistic view of the theme about which most of the people in ex-Yugoslavia were silent in those days, when the consequences of the war which ended Tito's era were still being strongly felt. Therefore the project was given the name "Tito – The Fourth Way". This fourth, artistic way was concerned with the possibilities of political theatre today – political theatre being responsible for and engaged with society as well as being contemporary in its expression. In this context, one of the aims was to test new artistic forms which would function without ideological pressures.

Today, especially after 11 September, it seems there is no lack of engaged issues that the theatre can speak about; and yet many artists still struggle with the form. The theatre heritage of Bertolt Brecht has been long forgotten (it seems that people do not know what to do with it nowadays), but there are no new strong ideas in sight of how political content can be adequately transformed into a contemporary theatre form which would represent an intellectual and emotional challenge to its audience. In most cases, what can be described today in the western world as *theatre dealing with political issues* is reduced to irony and self-indulgence. It seems as if messages from the stage are not able to affect the audience anyway, so why bother? If real-life images from television cannot do that either, what can be expected from the theatre, which many regard as a weaker and more old-fashioned medium.

Starting from this diagnosis, in our working process in several countries we had the rare privilege of observing the immediate impact of a politically charged theatre project on its surroundings, which were still highly sensitive with regard to the content it dealt with. The reception varied a great deal from one country to the next. As we moved from the south to the north of the region, the reactions changed from being emotionally charged to being colder and more distant, with audiences seeming to prefer oblivion as a point of view.

In Macedonia, where lots of people still believe that they had better lives under Tito, the Macedonian performance (which was part of our project and which followed the stages of Tito's life) caused the biggest controversy. The project was arranged with the left government and its Minister of Culture, but during the rehearsal period there was an election followed by a change of government. The right-wing coalition (an absurd combination of Macedonian and Albanian nationalists) came to power and wanted to ban the performance just before the opening night; but protests by the media and intellectuals were so strong that the new Minster of Culture, an Albanian, had to resign as he proved unable to handle the situation. The premiere took place in Bitola, and a thousand people in the audience experienced, we dare say, a collective catharsis. Ovations and tears, emotions all over the place. For contemporary theatre this was not such a bad result – where else does theatre overthrow ministers and cause government crises?

As we moved the same performance towards the north, reactions softened. Although the controversy about the subject still remained, causing some degree of protest in Croatia, in general the project did not give rise to any great emotions, we can even say that the attitude was expressed by ignoring the event. For the high level of conceptuality which could be seen in eight performances, we did not have the interlocutors. People expected red flags and a lot of shouting (a political theatre cliché), but this is not what we offered. We offered sophisticated conceptual forms in various genres: dance, performance, multimedia and some text-based theatre which did not present a direct message and refused to sell any kind of ideology. While in daily politics people either saw Tito's era as positive or completely denied it, our artists did not take political sides but opted to show this complex theme in all its controversial aspects. For example: in the Italian-Croatian episode entitled "Weddings and Trials", the Croatian director Branko Brezovec juxtaposed a play by Italian author D'Annunzio and a story placed in the partisan environment by the Slovenian communist writer Edvard Kocbek, exposing in this way hidden mechanisms that lie behind struggles for power. The dance piece choreographed by German Felix Ruckert, which used elements from Indian traditional dance, was a playful variation on the number "three": "three" as a number of syntheses on which the world should be constructed (the world cannot be based only on the relationship between thesis and antithesis, that is, on the number "two" which, as an anti-dialectical number, makes every truth relative).

The German multimedia group Schoene Gegend used animated film and performance to speak about an encounter between East and West through an imaginary journey of the beehive keeper Titus through different regions of former Yugoslavia. The Russian group Akhe composed a non-verbal scenic essay full of experiments, from chemical to visual ones, which reflected on the historical position of an unidentified hero. The Egyptian director Ahmed El Attar brought on stage Nasser's speeches (a former Egyptian president, a close ally of Tito, and one of the founders of the non-aligned movement), spoken coldly by an Egyptian actor sitting on a sofa among the performers from Montenegro, whose conceptual playfulness acted counter to the political content of the texts.

The ease with which this project managed to cross borders (geographical, political, artistic, borders between different genres etc.) made it a unique and fascinating experience.

Another example of border crossing with artistic ease thanks to knowledge and talent comes from a generation of theatre directors from ex-Yugoslavia who not only mastered the theatre medium to full extent, but also enriched it with procedures which were both unusual and innovative for the time.

The unique position of Yugoslavia which I have already described also left traces in theatre developments in the region. While being informed of everything that was going on in the West, artists could have added to that knowledge an experience of living in a different political and social system. For several theatre directors who developed a specific aesthetics very different from the *new theatre mainstream* which was governing the western theatre market at that time, these facts helped to create an authentic approach towards local traditions which were incorporated in their entirely contemporary directing methods.

Eurokaz Festvial in its constant search for impulses that change perception habits and push the theatre language forward, offered them an international platform and was their great supporter. So when Eurokaz hosted a plenary meeting of IETM (now the most influential theatre network in Europe) in 1990 – just before the outbreak of the war in former Yugoslavia, the first meeting to be held in one of the so-called East European countries since the organisation's foundation ten years earlier, the foreign guests from Western Europe were confronted for the first time with an organised presentation of the previously unknown theatrical and cultural strategies of a socialist country on the verge of breakdown.

That year's Eurokaz programme brought together representatives of the new generation of Yugoslavian (as they were still called then) directors and their productions, which would go on to have a cult reputation.

The productions of Dragan Živadinov, Branko Brezovec, Vito Taufer and Haris Pašović (joined by Eurokaz's co-production of the Bulgarian Ivan Stanev) testified to the exceptional creative potential of a group of artists who had been trained in the institutions of a rigid theatre system, but who, thanks to a free flow of information and cultural mobility (allowing interesting aesthetic, cultural and multilingual leaps) produced strong concepts and erudition of the highest order comparable to any relevant European "generation" project.

These directors did not belong to the so-called *independent scene* that the *new theatre* productions of Europe were familiar with; instead they directed astoundingly radical productions in big repertory and national theatres, some of which had programming policies that were open towards research and innovation. Here was an infrastructure that a majority of West European directors with an inclination towards experimentation could at that time only dream about. However, that wasn't the only thing that confused our western colleagues who arrived here with very reserved expectations and strong stereotypes, certain that they would be bored with poor, old-fashioned *East European* theatre, smelling of the reiteration of Kantor and Grotowski. What created the most misunderstandings was the so very *determined* theatrical discourse and directorial sway, both quite unknown in the West, and rather peculiar to its taste infused as it was by Flemish orderliness. These directors jumped with superiority and grand gestures through different, sometimes incompatible dramatic levels within one performance, referring to the *ritual* solemnity of Yugoslavian cultural and social memory. This created a contaminated style that stood out against the formalism and hygiene of theatrical languages that burdened the West European market. Traditional forms communicated on an equal level with contemporary directing methods, the theatre of image with ancient ritual, Bosnian Sevdah songs with Robert Wilson, emptied, recycled historical styles with technological schizophrenia.

Theatrical Europe responded in the same confused way to these scenes of authenticity as European politics responded to the changes in Eastern Europe – it filed away these authentic theatrical energies as fast as it could (while buying some along the way), and then, a few years later, it awarded those who stooped to overripe dramaturgical models and imitations of mostly dance languages which had helped Brussels and Amsterdam to win over their new markets.

In this way the new Slovenian theatre, first recognized and forcefully presented in the Eurokaz programme, became a theatrical fact in Europe, but only through its second generation of directors and choreographers whose breakthrough happened due to these aforementioned circumstances: blend into Europe in the safest possible way, a Europe where everyone dances to the same score.

If there is anything left from the meeting in Zagreb, then it is definitely Zagreb's contribution to the surge of multiculturalism in the following years. The programme in Zagreb offered the concept of *vertical multiculturalism* that was to help in the clarification of the multicultural fog that had been hovering over West Europe since the time of Peter Brook.

In opposition to *horizontal multiculturalism*, by which I mean cultural and social activity focused on minorities or the decorative use of traditional forms of mostly non-European cultures (Brook, Barba, Mnouchkine), a *musaka* that, with a little Indian make-up, magnificent Japanese costumes, or screams of a few token black actors, tries to convince us that it is engaged with the rest of the world, while in fact its manner of piling up sensations is intrinsically Western. Contrary to this, to name it properly, *colonial* approach, artists of *vertical multiculturalism*, working at the intersections of different cultures and penetrating the *simultaneity* of different cultural identities by using a kind of *schizo-analytical* approach, build a unique, innovative artistic form. This kind of actor manages to keep together a multitude of different archaic combinations and procedures within his mental habitus. At the same time his *physis* emanates the *gesture* of modern theatre responsible for giving vertiginous dimensions to the inner ritual element and the ritual sense of time. The same can be said about the aforementioned directing procedures.

The problems that appeared in the theatre communication and understanding between East and West, between centre and periphery, were further elaborated, during the war in ex-Yugoslavia, in two symposiums on *post-mainstream*, a notion which was introduced by Knut Ove Arntzen, who was one of the main speakers. In 1994 and 1995 when the symposiums took place, Eurokaz brought together international artists and producers who, dissatisfied with the dictate of aesthetics linked to theatre centres (where economic power had produced a cultural imperialism) such as Brussels, Amsterdam and Frankfurt (it was precisely the River Main that gave the name *to post-Main-stream*), and who wished to establish a different system of values and open perceptions of different cultures and theatre languages. These issues became very fashionable some ten years later, when suddenly everybody started to talk about multiculturalism or interculturalism, and about a "centre-periphery" division, finding in the European periphery (including Eastern Europe and in a wider context non-European cultures) new impulses to refresh the existing uniform and artistically jaded theatre and dance scene.

Unlike the productions of the European *new theatre mainstream*, especially dance productions that are *silent* in the same globally understandable language and do not create perceptual problems, the reception of *post-mainstream* artists requires a diligent approach, a measured reception, sometimes even an ethnological concentration on certain scenic references. Following this path, the Eurokaz programme of the wartime and post-war period abandoned Europe as the unquestionable arbiter of contemporary theatre and opened up towards other cultures where it found impressive traces of *Novum*.

Theatres from Latin America, Asia and Africa appeared in this context at Eurokaz; the mature authenticity of their performances testified that the *new theatre mainstream* was slowly losing its breath. *Post-mainstream* productions dealt with the reinterpretation of tradition, atypical dramaturgical procedures of sequencing (combining theatre of the image with ritual theatre, or high technology with traditional forms, for instance) which was impossible within the concept of postmodern theatre. The relation to the body is not neurotic and narcissistically auto-referential as it is in European theatre and dance, but touches on the collective emotional experience or addresses metaphysical questions. These productions dare to use the elements of spectacle that abolish the typically European concept of individuality and the European notion of experimentation which receded into an intimate and perfectly controlled sphere.

In subsequent festival editions, Eurokaz expanded its *post-mainstream* programme by invitations to African dance companies and directors. The best of

African choreographers, although many of them had been trained in Europe, refused to imitate the *style* of the Western contemporary dance and managed to develop authentic dance languages which cannot be classified by stereotypes such as "a fusion of tradition and modernity", which is today such a common discourse concerning African contemporary dance. On the contrary, African dance traditions, as a part of daily life, are constantly within a status of modernity (that is, in the status of spontaneity) because they have always reacted in a non-figurative way outside the dialectical alternation of forms, that is, outside the tradition as well, so that all such fusions of "modern and traditional" hide an unnecessary logocentric trap.

The issues mentioned above were the main pillars of my work as the artistic director of Kampnagel in Hamburg. Kampnagel is a huge site, a former crane factory turned theatre 30 years ago which today encompasses six stages with seating for audiences of 100-800 people. It was a great challenge – how can the claims of various interest groups, the size of the halls, and the demand for high visitor numbers be combined with the request to promote experimental art, create a home for the free groups in Hamburg and promote emerging artists? And in addition: to remain true to one's self, to engage in the totality of the theatre world, to be active beyond the local scene and to formulate a cross-border artistic statement? Hamburg, a truly global Hanseatic city and a port known for its openness as an intersection of many cultural influences, offered its support for our attempts to introduce a different, responsible discourse in theatre which implies a willingness to take risks, especially if one wants to win over a new audience in this way.

My team and I have attempted to work productively with these contradictions. First of all, we understood Kampnagel as a multifunctional centre with a variety of programmes. In dance, our emphasis was on non-European choreographers who in many cases introduced a different relationship towards dance and the body as exemplified above. However, while artists of the centres have their critics and theoreticians, particularly when post-dramatic theatre is involved, the others are still waiting for a corresponding responsible discourse.

In this sense, the programming strategy endeavoured to build connections and make parallels visible, thereby creating a context in which theatres of various origins can exist and be assessed alongside each other. The Kampnagel Summer Festival Laokoon and the appointment of its non-European curators, the Polyzentral festival presenting theatre and dance from the Middle East, Central Asia, Africa and India, and thematic blocks were intended as platforms for this.

By choosing such an unusual name (Laokoon) for a festival – a name which horrified the Kampnagel marketing department because it felt that nobody would want to visit an event whose name was incomprehensible to and indeed unpronounceable by the general public – we naturally wanted to refer to Lessing's text (but who reads Lessing today, even in Germany?) and to the problem of borders between different art forms. At the time we started this festival in 2001, the term *cross-over theatre* had become very fashionable. The stages were overloaded, and still are, with projections, TV monitors, hi-tech equipment, the directors often came from a visual arts background, and theatre seemed the right place to mix different media and arts. But inside such work, the dramaturgical procedures and the acting were often not very innovative. It looked as if in the medium of theatre itself not much had been done. Of course, the easiest way, if a director has a dramaturgical problem, is to solve it by introducing a film or an image, that is to help himself to other art forms. However, the most difficult task has always been to make a revolution inside one medium itself, which is why the fundamental material of theatre like the actor and the text have most often remained handcuffed to psychology and illustration. No, we were not advocating media purity, we just wanted to open the problem (which is not a simple one). There were many other reasons for the name Laokoon apart from the issue of borders between art forms. Some of them referred to the sculpture itself: the secret of its facial expression and the role of imagination on the part of the spectator, but this is another topic that would need a separate text.

What is more important is that the Laokoon festival programme offered an insight into the theatre and dance of other cultures from the point of view of non-European curators (a Japanese theatre critic Hidenaga Otori for three years, a Columbian choreographer Alvaro Restrepo for one year). In other words, the people involved were not Western programmers travelling around the world in search of sensations and having a very poor knowledge and lots of prejudices about the countries they were visiting, but people belonging to these cultures who were perfectly aware of their contexts and circumstances. They presented us with the *Otherness*, which was sometimes foreign to the European *taste*, but gave a testimony of the richness of artistic expressions which, even if not liked, have to be respected.

Although today we no longer speak so much of the *New* as of the *Other*, theatre astounds us with the fact that within it, the historical eschatological force has still not reached its end. From the appearance of Robert Wilson in Europe in the seventies until today, there is no lack of a *delighted blasphemy* by artists who, playing *va banque*, hit our perceptual habits and revolutionize the language of theatre with a number of informal procedures. Artists who understand how to fill spaces are well known – there are quite a few of them. But those with the potential to shift and modify these spaces are rare. Identifying these artists across borders and supporting them has always been my goal. In this context, research and projects in the countries which Western Europe regards as peripheral have confirmed our claim that artists in all these parts of the world take part in the development of artistic ideas, hence in the history of contemporary theatre, on equal terms with the artists of Western civilisation.

I returned to Croatia in 2008. Ten years of working abroad was enough, and I felt the time had come to apply my experience and knowledge acquired in leading positions in two European theatres to my local context. Eurokaz is not any more the only source of information of theatre trends or the sole place of contemporaneity in Croatia: new festivals have been created which specialize in the fields which were previously covered by Eurokaz, like the Festival of New Circus, Perforations, the Urban Festival, the Festival of World Theatre, etc. Our artists travel, they are well informed, they participate in international workshops and visit artistic schools in all parts of the world. We can say that even repertory theatres, very conservative and old-fashioned for decades, have finally reached the phase of modernity even in the mainstream productions.

In such changed circumstances, Eurokaz has redirected its strategy and turned towards producing in order to work with young generations and to be more influential and active in the local theatre context. In the past four years Eurokaz has produced and co-produced some 20 projects, the majority of which featured Croatian artists and theatres with the emphasis being placed on collaboration with the Theatre Academy and its students. A new generation of theatre directors has emerged who, influenced by Eurokaz aesthetics, have produced innovative projects of great value.

These activities acquired a new meaning when we moved into a new theatre venue called Gorgona, which is part of the Museum of Contemporary Art in Zagreb and where we started in January 2010 to programme monthly. Eurokaz's own projects and international guest performances are shown on a regular basis, while the festival in June represents a culmination of our year-round activities.

Times and borders are currently changing in Europe. After successfully having completed negotiations with the European Union, Croatia will be admitted as a new member state in 2013. This will imply a new border situation for the country and the region. Nevertheless, groups of artists such as Eurokaz promotes will meet the future from their borderline perspective on societies by continuing to work at dissolving borders and attempting to re-establish connections across this region which once constituted a common cultural space.

## Bibliography

Eurokaz (2006): *20 Years of Eurokaz*. Zagreb.

Kampnagel (2007): *Sechs Jahre anders*, Kampnagel 2001-2007. Hamburg.

www.ietm.org.

www.eurokaz.hr.

www.kampnagel.de.

# Second section:
## Constructions of National, Regional and Artistic Identity in Literature and Art

# The Colonizer and the Colonized:
# On the Orientalized Caucasus as Alter and Alternative Ego in Russian Classical Literature

*Lillian Jorunn Helle*

This chapter focuses on the relationship between the colonizer and the colonized as depicted in the so-called Caucasus texts of Russian literature, and aims to show the flexibility and the shifting constellations of this relationship, ranging from rigid binary oppositions to complex forms of cultural interaction.

The Caucasus texts are an important contribution to Russian classical literature. Their historical context, the Russian conquest of the Caucasus, was a process that started at the end of the 18th century and reached a temporary high point with the inclusion of Georgia into the Empire in 1802. Military conflicts, always a danger to stability in the Caucasus region, escalated dramatically in 1829 when the Muslim tribes declared jihad, holy war, against Russia, but abated after Shamil, the last leader of the Chechens, surrendered to the Tsar in 1859.[1]

Against this historical background, a number of Russian writers were involved in a cultural creativity which construed an imaginary and Orientalized Caucasian world, not found on any map, a Russian Orient, even before the area had been scientifically researched and described.[2] Intense literary activity produced a whole set of well-known Western stereotypes and schemata which were projected onto the Caucasus highlands, transforming both its places and its people into images of otherness. As a result of these literary mythographies, the mountainous borderland was culturally restructured and came to represent the foreign, the primitive Asian and Oriental, the opposite of post-Petrine European Russia and the antithesis of civilization and Eurocentric development.[3] Consequently, as Bruce Grant (2005: 45) has asserted, one could suggest that "the literary Caucasus overrode the Caucasian Mountains (in the way,

---

[1] On the history of the Caucasus during the Russian Empire, see Baddeley (1969).

[2] On the development of the Caucasus texts and their enormous myth-making effect, see particularly Layton (1994) and Ram (2003).

[3] On the Caucasus as the Oriental other, see Helle (2009).

perhaps, that Edward Saïd (1978: 96) contended that "orientalism" overrode the Orient)".[4]

As has been pointed out by Jurij Lotman and others, the invention of an oriental alter as the primitive alien in Russian cultural consciousness may have been prompted by the desire in the post-Enlightenment and Westernized Empire to construct a picture of the other as an inversion of one's own self-image. In Lotman's words (1990: 142), this is "an image of the Oriental as a 'pre-logical savage', belonging to anti-spheres lying beyond the rational space of culture".

Lotman's observation here is hardly provocative. It is interesting, though, to observe how multi-faceted the literary approach to this invented pre-logical Oriental was: some Russian writers distanced themselves sharply from the alien, while others found in the alien a second and alternative self. Not surprisingly the first texts to take up the theme of colonial conquest, the nation-building odes from the 18th century, are characterized by a persistent opposition between "us" and "them", between the Russian conquerors and the Asian or Oriental tribes. Moreover, the odes generally establish an abyss between the Westernized Russian and the Oriental other, glorifying in the name of progress the Empire's military actions and reducing the indigenous population of the besieged territories to wild and barbarous villains. Because the distinction between Europe and the Orient is thus resolved as a matter of civilizational superiority and military invasion, these odes have been defined by some scholars as the beginning in Russia of a modern Orientalist ideology (cf. Ram 2003: 78). This ideology is clearly present in the following panegyric passage from the master of odic composition, Mikhail Lomonosov (1959: 562-63), in which he exalts the birth of the tsarevich Pavel Petrovich in 1754 and foresees his splendid colonial victories in the Ottoman peripheries of the Empire:

When we gaze at the East,
When we look at the South,
Oh what a vast expanse we see where news of you may thunder!

---

[4]    Saïd in his profoundly influential book *Orientalism* (1978) ignores Russia (and all Europeans east of the Rhine), referring mainly to Britain and France. His work has been criticized for frequently relapsing into the essentializing discourses it attacks, being as James Clifford (1988: 271) phrases it, "ambivalently enmeshed in the totalizing habits of Western humanism". This critique notwithstanding, Saïd's Orientalist thesis is without doubt of relevance to Russian colonialism, as a background for discussing and understanding the attitudes and worldview of Russian imperialism.

There the terrible Dragon has surrounded
The holy land, the splendid land
And raised its hundred heads to the clouds!
The whole world fears the monster,
The Russian Hercules is the only one
Who can boldly rush on.

The style of this and other 18th century odes has been termed "imperial sub-lime", because of its sublime rhetoric in the rendering of the imperial conquest (see especially Ram 2003). In Russia, more than elsewhere, a lofty aesthetics of the sublime seems to accompany political aggression, dialectically turning all brutal oppression into acts of eternal, sacred greatness. A sublime imperial triumphalism was used to justify and sacralize power and to transpose fear and pain into beauty, thereby illustrating Edmund Burke's classical definition of the sublime as "the concomitant of terror".[5]

Traces of this aesthetics (although usually in a less sophisticated form) can also be found in 19th century Russian literature, not least in works from the 1830s dealing with the escalating war against the Muslim mountaineers after their declaration of jihad (1829). A sublime and rapturous rhetoric that celebrates the state and the sovereign is here combined with crude depictions of military savagery against the tribes. The violent confrontations described more often than not demonstrate an unrestricted heroism in the accounts of the Russian side, while the Asian counterpart is portrayed as the embodiment of a backward and barbarous society.[6] Actively supporting the colonial policy towards the indigenous peoples, these texts make explicit the close connection in Russia between literature and Empire.[7]

---

[5]   Cf. Burke's famous formulation in *A Philosophical Enquiry into the Origin of our Ideas of the Sublime and the Beautiful* from 1757: "In short, wheresoever we find strength, and in what light soever we look upon power, we shall all along observe the sublime the concomitant of terror" (Burke 2008: 47). In this way the sublime becomes connected to hegemonistic and repressive historical processes, as e. g. Donald Peace (1984: 275) has argued: "The sublime has, in what we could call the politics of historical formation, always served conservative purposes". On sublime aesthetics and political terror in a Russian context, see particularly Etkind (2007: 624 ff.).

[6]   On the post-jihad Caucasus texts, see Layton (1994).

[7]   Ewa Thompson (2000) has studied this connection in her controversial work *Imperial Knowledge: Russian Literature and Colonialism*. Thompson argues that Russian literature is exclusively a literature of colonization, the story of a monolithic and univocal imperialistic power violating the colonized other. Lost in her highly binarized readings though, are the

The post-jihad literature on the Caucasus constructs a set of dichotomies that all present us with a uni-dimensional figure of the foe. A chief metaphor is the European lamp dispelling the Oriental darkness; and a much-exploited theme is the struggle between Holy Russia and heathendom. An axis of verticality, a well known topos of the sublime (*hypsos* – *ὕψος*), is created between the Russian invaders flying like victorious eagles in the heights of the Caucasian mountains and the Muslim tribes, crawling like wild hordes up from an underground and hellish realm, as the poet Aleksander Polezhaev has it in his highly chauvinistic poem "Erpeli" from 1832. This poem can be read as a "poetics of the fiend", portraying the highlanders as demonic shadows and dark spirits from a vicious subterranean world. Systematically depicted as the infernal offspring of Allah, raging animals and New Satans, they become a bulwark of evil against Russia's civilizing forces (see Polezhaev 1832: 45, 56, 62ff).

When such coarse emphasis is put on the bestial aspects of the Muslims, the contrast implied between Western enlightenment and Asian brutality becomes extremely conspicuous (and almost parodic, for a modern reader). Furthermore, when the native appears as a ferocious beast, the ruthless military conduct of the Empire could be elevated by a rhetoric of the sublime – and in line with Hegelian dialectics, as a necessary civilizing project. Besides, when tribes are reduced to pure barbarism, they administer *"une thérapeutique du Différent"* (Schwab 1950: 429), as it were. That is, by showing what the Russians were *not*, these writers sought to lend the colonial war of the Caucasus European legitimacy. Transformed into the negative Oriental other, the natives confirmed Russia's right to subjugate the colonized in the name of Enlightenment (or for their own good). Only the shelters of the European state could order and bring harmony to the wild and unruly mountaineers. Met with this mission, the Westernized Russians could in various degrees underwrite or accept the Empire's bloody conquest (not seldom in the form of genocide). As part of the "white man's burden" these inhumane acts were turned into noble sacrifices.[8]

Although Russia's quest for Empire was intended to establish her status as a European power, the country itself was frequently viewed as Asiatic by the

---

many literary texts where ambiguous bonds exist between colonizer and colonized, creating a boundary world of ambivalent loyalties and shifting cultural identities.

[8]    The imperial idea of "the white man's burden" was put in poetic form by Rudyard Kipling in his highly controversial lyrics from 1899, with the evocative (and provocative) first stanza: "Take up the White Man's burden, Send forth the best ye breed, Go bind your sons to exile, To serve your captives' need; To wait in heavy harness, On fluttered folk and wild, Your new-caught, sullen peoples, Half-devil and half-child".

West, which from the Enlightenment onwards construed Eastern Europe as a demi-Orientalized world.[9] Consistently criticized for being underdeveloped and dark, post-Petrine Russia might feel subordinate to the Western countries. Compared to the savage Caucasus, however, it could be seen as symbol of progress, an advanced European civilization. Consequently, descriptions of the Caucasus as a backward other serve to strengthen Russia's Europeanness and in due course to compensate for her feelings of cultural inferiority towards Western Europe. The nation's colonizing impulse was then fuelled to no small degree by a powerful compensatory urge. The Europeanized Russians strove to deflect the orientalizing image "to which they had themselves been subjected onto their conquered neighbors" (Ram 2005: 24). Paradoxically, in order to emerge as a Western power, Russia had to move east. Fedor Dostoyevsky (2004: 36-37) caught this ironic dilemma in his famous saying from 1881: "In Europe we were hangers-on and slaves, while in Asia we shall be the masters. In Europe we were Tatars, while in Asia we too are Europeans". Such shifting evaluations demonstrate, by the way, the flexibility of the concept of national identity and also the inherent contradictions of Russian Orientalism.[10]

When the Caucasus and the colonized peoples are presented as an absolute other and as the antithesis of the civilizing Empire, this is an antithesis which appears to be in line with the hegemonic West-East discourse of Saïd's typology, with its (tendentiously) uni-dimensional distinction between the Occident and the Orient. However, even if the Caucasus in some classical Russian literary texts becomes a mythologized anti-model to the Eurocentric Tsarist state, with seemingly untransgressible barriers between "us" and "them", in other texts these barriers turn into flexible borders, with literary treatments of acts of border crossing that undermine sharp polarizations. Actually, a rather

---

[9]     See particularly Wolff (1994). In this book Wolff shows how the West construed Russia and Eastern Europe from the 17th century onwards as a demi-Orientalized cultural zone, a place simultaneously included in and excluded from Western Europe.

[10]    Cf. Sahni (1997: 15), who points to the specific development of Russia's colonizing endeavor as a result of the nation itself being culturally and politically colonized by Western Europe in the post-Petrine period: "The Russian elite became mentally colonized without having ever been a colonial subject. This was the uniqueness of Russian history and created the inherent contradictions of Russian Orientalism, whereby the Oriental attitude directed at them was accepted by the Russians and subsequently employed to downgrade the conquered people". This is a valuable insight into the highly complex background and development of Russian Orientalism. Sahni herself, however, seems to forget this complexity, in her otherwise binarized and biased readings of Russia's relations with the colonized Orient.

large part of the classical literary works treating the Caucasus theme demonstrates a variety of mutual cultural mixing between the Russian invaders and the invaded Caucasians.[11] This fictional diversity of cultural bonds between imperial masters and colonial subjects tends to subvert received theories of hegemonic empire building and destabilize the programmatic pattern of the Saïdian binary system. In fact, as research has shown, cultural traffic between the imperial centre and the colonized periphery was a much more dynamic and reciprocal activity than previously presumed in post-colonial studies. Recently, historians have drawn attention to the mixed character of cultural exchange in the Caucasian mountains, and the instability of the borders.[12] It has been claimed that earlier versions of the post-colonial approach did not do justice to the enormous "grey" zones that lay between the imperial capital and the colonial frontiers. Cultural hybridization took place on both sides of the Christian-Muslim contact, which resulted in a porous mosaic rather then a straight borderline (cf. Etkind 2007: 621).[13]

When the borders are like porous mosaic or moving thresholds, this facilitates cultural interaction. Besides, even if Russia was an imperialist state politically, culturally it was coloured by a deep ambivalence: in addition to the usual Western stance of superiority towards the East, there was an extraordinary fascination and even in some cases an ambiguous identification with it. A kind of affinity rather than a difference can be observed. This blurring of clear demarcation lines undermines the Empire's Eurocentric aspirations, and the Oriental side of the Russian is foregrounded, activating the traditional idea of Russia as a two-faced Janus who looks "simultaneously toward Europe and Asia", as the Caucasus author Aleksander Bestuzhev-Marlinskii once put it (1958: 599).[14]

Accordingly, Rudyard Kipling's famous words, "East is East and West is

---

[11]   It might be mentioned that on closer reading, even some of the odes from the 18th century, written as programmatic and "sublime" celebrations of the post-Petrine Empire, could be interpreted as less polarized and more ambiguous with regard to the Oriental other than usually assumed. But this a discourse I cannot follow further here.

[12]   See e.g. Barrett (1999). In this study, colonization is presented as a fluid mix of cultures rather than a clear-cut imperialist conquest along Saïdian binary lines.

[13]   On cultural hybridization, see Bhabha (1994). Bhabha focuses on the paradoxically creative possibilities of colonialism which undermine the supposed segmented walls between colonizer and colonized.

[14]   In his writings about the Caucasus Bestuzhev-Marlinskii (1797-1837) often stresses the intermediary role of Russia as a link between the "settled activities of the West and the nomadic laziness of the East" (cf. 1958: 599).

West, and never the twain shall meet", are contradicted to no small degree by Russia's attitude to her Orient.[15] Even in the Empire's most chauvinistic periods, marked by constant attempts from the Tsarist side at creating a distinct divide between "us" and "them", we find examples, however inconsistent, showing that the indigenous peoples of the Caucasus never became quite foreign. The mountaineer, for all his backwardness, never sank to the level of the Guinea Negro, but belonged, in spite of his childlike immaturity to "our" superior race, as the ultra conservative journalist Rotislav Fadeev phrased it in 1860, in racist language typical for its time (cf. Layton 1994: 255).

Because of the positive dimension ascribed to the Caucasian Orient, it has been asserted that in the Russian Empire a cultural sympathy existed towards the colonized that was rarely found in other imperialist states (Figes 2002: 381). This is a rather complicated question, since examples of cultural crossings and ambivalent attractions between colonizer and colonized can easily be observed also in a West European context, like the British Empire and its cultural imaginations about exotic India.[16] But still it seems that the feelings of the Eurocentric Russian ruling classes towards their Orient were more complicated and contradictory than the feelings of other colonizing peoples (like the French and the English) towards their Orient.[17]

As has been argued, the aspect of geography is important to understand this specific situation (cf. Bassin 1991). Unlike the paradigmatic cases of countries like France and Britain, Russia in her quest for imperial hegemony conquered contiguous rather than overseas territories. Her colonies were not cut off from the imperial centre by oceans, but were rather a geographical extension of this centre. In Russia then, the separation of Europe and Orient as metropolis and periphery was not self-evident and the frontiers between East and West were

---

[15]  Cf. Kipling's controversial lyrics in "The Ballad of East and West" from 1889.

[16]  On the multiple reciprocal relations between the British and the Indians, see particularly Cannadine (2001), cf. also Inden (1992). The same ambivalent bonds can be observed no less in French Orientalism with its imaginings of colonized Africa; see for example Hosford & Wojtkowski (2010) and Dobie (2002).

[17]  Cf. Scimmelpenninck van der Oye (2010), in which this ambivalent reciprocity is a major theme. The book represents a significant departure from the Orientalism of Edward Saïd, demonstrating the specificity and profound ambiguity of Russia's relations with its Asian colonies. As Scimmelpenninck points out, Russian orientologists for example, "did not reduce the object of their inquiry to some uniform Saidian other. Their views varied widely, but on the whole, neither fear nor contempt dominated the academy" (2010: 238).

extremely elastic, being largely imaginative and constructed.[18] This situation undoubtedly resulted in the destabilization of fixed cultural and national traits, something that we find refracted also in the Caucasus texts.

The blurring and shifting of identities between the colonizer and the colonized are refracted not least in the works of two of the greatest Russian poets from the first part of the 19th century, Aleksander Pushkin and Mikhail Lermontov. In their romanticized and aestheticized contribution to the Caucasus mythology, the Caucasus is not only an other, but just as often a lost twin brother, or a secret, complementary self.[19] By the same token, the Asian is not the absolute alter, but rather a potent, but suppressed alter ego. This is an ego that has been suppressed in the Westernization (or cultural colonization) of post-Petrine Russia; but it lives on, hidden behind a mask of European civilization. The poetic and literary Caucasus then becomes a return to a more authentic being, untouched by the coercive norms of the European state. Even if the return to the nostalgic native condition is a common trend in European and Byronic romanticism, I would argue that this longing is articulated with special force by the post-Petrine Russians. The Russian Orient turns into a unique mythic space or a spiritual homeland, as expressed in the following declaration by Mikhail Lermontov in 1833 directed to the Caucasian landscape: "At heart I am yours, Forever and everywhere yours" (1955: 243).

Caucasus as a spiritual homeland is also a predominant motif in Pushkin's "southern poems", which abound with well-known Romantic *topoi*. The Russian Orient is created as the source of poetry and creativity, serving as a positive counter-point to the stagnated civilization of the Occident and to the decaying culture of *das Abendland*. Through cross-border confrontations, the fictional figures – Europeanized Russian officers and aristocrats – are drawn into scenery of breathtaking beauty, where they interact with the tribal highlanders, depicted not as subhuman villains and wild men, but as noble savages

---

[18] Cf. particularly Bassin (1991), who sees the geographical separation of European Russia from its Asian colonies as a matter of cultural imagination and ideology rather than a scientific fact. On the creation of an imaginative and literary Caucasian geography, see also Layton (1986). This fictitious border geography resembles Romantic exotic locations found in Western European literature of the time, see e. g. on border spaces in historical romances, Moretti (1998).

[19] As has often been pointed out, Russia's cultural and political relations to Asia make the Orient both self and other (cf. e. g. Emerson 1986: 148, 245).

and ideal Rousseauean children of nature.[20] This interaction is very evident in Pushkin's classic poem *Prisoner of the Caucasus (Kavkazskij plennik)* from 1822, a text that contributed more than any other to the invention of the literary and Orientalized Caucasus.[21] The poem does not primarily focus upon war and violence, but concentrates instead on the enigmatic prisoner, a nameless young Russian, held captive by Circassian tribesmen. His captivity, however, turns into a kind of liberation. Surrounded by fascinating wilderness and exotic settings, the hero finds in his imprisonment a refuge from the imperial state apparatus and gives himself over to a Byronic and Romantic rejection of the Europeanized *beau monde*. For some time, Pushkin's protagonist almost identifies with the bold mountaineers, undermining the distance between captive and captors, the captive clearly being captivated by the magnificence of his captors' world.[22]

To the disenchanted and over-cultivated Russian elite, the Caucasus symbolized regeneration and rejuvenation. To go there, in real life or in the imagined life of poems and novels, was equivalent to a sentimental journey away from inauthentic urbanity and the alienated existence of the modern metropolis. The ambiguous fascination with the Russian Orient is especially striking in the many literary depictions of the mountain warrior's virile masculinity (it is no coincidence that the word *dzhigit*, master rider, has become part of the Russian language and culture as an image of strength and fearlessness). Cer-

---

[20] The transformation of the native from the wild man into the noble savage is, by the way, a characteristic reversal in European cultural imagination that can be traced back to the late 17th century (cf. White 1972). The idea of the Savage, now turned Noble, could be used, as White (1972: 30-31) phrases it, "as an instrument of intracultural criticism" and serve as a contrasting image to Eurocentric perceptions of progress and civilization (cf. also Ram 1999: 6).

[21] On the importance of *Prisoner of the Caucasus* for the construction of the Russian literary Orient, see Zhirmunskij (1970: 145ff). See also Hokanson (1994).

[22] The ambiguous bonds between the captive and the captor have been depicted numerous times, manifesting the continuing vitality of Pushkin's theme in a Russian cultural context (for the "Captive" as a classical Russian literary topos, see particularly Austin 1984). For more recent manifestations of the theme, see Andrej Bitov's book *Kavkazskij plennik* (1996), Vladimir Makanin's story '*Kavkazskij plennyj*' (1997) and Sergej Bodrov's film *Kavkazskij plennik 1996*. Se also Ram (1999) and Grant (2005; 2009). In his interdisciplinary studies of sovereignty and captivity in the Caucasian region Grant suggests that the practices of kidnapping, hostage taking and hostage exchange contributed to controlling and diminishing rather than unleashing and increasing violence and conflicts between the Russians and the Caucasians.

tainly this warrior was a formidable foe, but nevertheless, as an unrestricted *Naturmensch*, he came to represent an alluring embodiment of the Russians' longing for freedom and independence.

In this respect, the attraction to the Caucasus seems to be more than a mere romantic reaction to a stagnated and over-urbanized civilization. The fictional (and real) Russians were disillusioned with the imperial power, so much so that they (however concealed and secret) identified with the tribes.[23] In a period when the Europeanized Russian community dreamed of liberalization and reforms within the autocratic Tsarist system (expressed for instance in the Decembrist insurgency of 1825), it is no wonder that an open or subconscious sympathy for the freedom-loving *dzhigit* could emerge. Thus, when Russian writers (sometimes even in the style of imperial sublime) describe how the highlanders perished in bloody combat with the military machine of the Empire, this can easily be seen as a symbolic suicide, since, however ambivalent, the fictional Russian protagonists tended to inject a second self into the other of the savage fighter.[24]

As I have argued so far, the Caucasus in classical Russian culture and literature is construed from one perspective as the alien, from whom the Westernized Empire had to be protected and segregated. But, on the other hand, the Caucasus is also constructed as a spiritual homeland where the Russian (male hero, I should add) regains and renews lost sides of himself, thereby dissolving the difference between himself and the Asian. Consequently, even if the fictional relationship between the colonizer and the colonized at one level reflects the constructions of barriers, the descriptions of them also disrupt these barriers and they turn into elastic border zones. In these border zones the cultural and ethnic oppositions between Western superiority and Oriental stagnation are undermined, even if rather subversively. Thus, however obliquely, the fictional Russian invaders and border crossers (and their readers) may gain new insights into mechanisms in their own culture as well as the culture of the other. In this manner they may even confirm a central concept of the border-thinker Mikhail Bakhtin, that creative, new understanding is born only when we are located outside our own cultural sphere in the border zone between ourselves

---

[23]  See also Etkind (2007: 620): "These Russian Europeans did not believe in the superiority of their culture and did not try to transform, successfully or not, the local Muslims … Russians were dissatisfied … so much so that they identified with their enemies who provided the only accessible alternative".

[24]  On the conflict between the Russians as exterminators of the Asian peoples in military action while at the same time subliminally identifying with them, see Layton (1994: 131).

and another, foreign culture: "In the realm of culture, outsideness is a most powerful factor in understanding. A meaning only reveals its depth once it has encountered and come into contact with another, foreign meaning: they engage in a kind of dialogue, which surmounts the closedness and onesidedness of these particular meanings, these cultures" (Bakhtin 1987: 7).[25]

One could easily maintain that not a few of the Caucasus texts demonstrate a considerable amount of reciprocal cultural dialogue and mingling, even hybridization, between the imperial masters and the Oriental tribes. But even if this (dialogic) mingling to a certain degree destabilizes the Saïdian picture of unidirectional manifestation of (Foucauldian) power/knowledge, it must be admitted that the hegemonic voice of Europe is still rather dominant. The relationship is still asymmetrical since in the Caucasus literature a mythologized Caucasian Orient plays a part of post-Petrine Russia's quest for a national identity, either in the role as foe or as friend, or as an other, or as a twin brother.

With the end of the tribal war, following the capture of Shamil, the literary myth of the Caucasus increasingly lost its formidable attraction both for readers and writers. In the Russian cultural consciousness the idea of the colonized Orient as an external alter was gradually dissolved and replaced by other constructions of orientalizing alterity.[26] One work that profoundly contributed to the dissolving of the Caucasus mythology is Lev Tolstoy's anti-imperialist novel *Haji-Murat*, written in 1904 and published in 1912, that is after the author's death, and even then only in a bowdlerized version. In his description of the Chechen highlanders, Tolstoy strives to invalidate all kinds of stereotypes, both the demonizing and the romanticizing ones, both the idea

---

[25]  Cf. also an early essay from 1924: "Every cultural act lives essentially on the boundaries, and it derives its seriousness and significance from this fact. Separated ... from these boundaries, it loses the ground of being and becomes vacuous, arrogant, it degenerates and dies" (Bakhtin 1990: 274).

[26]  As the myth of the Caucasus as Russia's external other faded, another myth, about the internal other, was evolving. In this myth, developed by the Eurocentric Russian gentry and intelligentsia, the Russian peasantry was imagined as a kind of internal noble savage and became an object of alien, exotic Orientalization. The Russian folk *(narod)* was regarded, by the Europeanized elite, as members of another race, and Russian ethnography became an imperialistic study of one's own people perceived as the other (cf. Etkind 2007: 626ff.). This internal colonization (which partly coincided with the Empire's external colonization) is a research field that opens up new and productive perspectives on the continuing cultural construction of otherness (see e. g. Etkind 2011).

of the Asian as an absolute alien or as a secret spiritual self.[27] Instead of turn-ing the main protagonist Haji-Murat into a figure of clichés and preconceived constructions (or a hero in the traditional sense), the author portrays him as a human being with rational motives and valid action patterns. By giving the mountaineer a voice of his own, a genuine, individual voice, we understand the reasons for his complex and contradictory conflict with the Russians in the 1850s, befriending them at one moment, fighting them at another. *Haji-Murat* is without doubt the most deep-reaching story ever told about the Tsarist conquest of the Caucasus, illustrating the extremely complicated bonds that developed between colonizers and colonized in the border zones of imperial war. Moreover, the story of the tribal warriors' struggle with the Russian Empire still has a regrettable relevance. Post-Soviet Russia's stereotyped images of the Caucasus and its present policy towards Chechnia remind us in a disturbing way of the imperialist regime of Nicholas I in the second quarter of the 19th century. Consequently, Tolstoy's critique and analysis are no less important today than they were 100 or 150 years ago, making explicit the challenges and problems of the borders of Europe and activating the questions of hegemony, aesthetics and border poetics.

## Bibliography

Austin, P. (1984). "The Exotic Prisoner in Russian Romanticism". *Russian Literature*, 16, 217-74.

Bakhtin, M. (1987). *Speech Genres and Other Late Essays*. Austin: Texas University of Texas Press.

Bakhtin, M. (1990). *Art and Answerability: Early Philosophical Essays*. Austin: Texas: University of Texas Press.

Baddeley, J. (1969). *The Russian Conquest of the Caucasus*. New York: Russel & Russel.

Barrett, T. (1999). *At The Edge of Empire: The Terek Cossacks and the North Caucasus Frontier, 1700-1860*. Boulder, Colorado: Westview Press.

---

[27]    On the one hand Tolstoy punctures established dichotomies, on the other, he consistently constructs new ones and most strikingly, he creates a new variant of the Rousseauean op-position between nature and civilization: In *Haji-Murat*, all good forces belong to nature, not only ordinary Chechen warriors, but also the Russian peasantry and the Russian con-scripted soldiers. The negative forces consist of the ruling classes, represented by the Russian Emperor, Nicholas I, the Chechen leader Shamil and generally everything connected to the civilized and official world.

Bassin, M. (1991). "Russia between Europe and Asia: The Ideological Construction of Geographical Space". *Slavic Review*, 50, 1-17.

Benjamin, R. (2003). *Orientalist Aesthetics: Art, Colonialism, and French North Africa, 1880-1939*. Berkeley and London: University of California Press.

Bestuzhev-Marlinskii A. (1958). *Sochinenija v dukh tomakh*. Vol. 2, Moscow: Chudozhestvennaja literatura.

Bhabha, H. K. (1994). *The Location of Culture*. London: Routledge.

Burke, E. (2008). *A Philosophical Enquiry into the Origin of our Ideas of the Sublime and the Beautiful*. New York and London: Routledge Classics.

Cannadine, D. (2001). *Ornamentalism: How the British Saw Their Empire*. Oxford and New York: Oxford University Press.

Clifford, J. (1988). *The Predicament of Culture: Twentieth-Century Ethnography, Literature, and Art*. Cambridge, Mass: Harvard University Press.

Dobie, M. (2002). *Foreign Bodies. Gender, Language, and Culture in French Orientalism*. Stanford: Stanford University Press.

Dostoyevsky, F. (2004). Dnevnik pisatelja za 1880-1881 gg. *Polnoe sobranie sochinenii v 18 tomakh*. Vol. 12. Moscow: Voskresen'e.

Emerson, C. (1986). *Boris Godunov. Transposition of a Russian Theme*. Bloomington Indiana: Indiana-Michigan Seriesin Russian and East European Studies.

Etkind, A. (2003). "Whirling with the Other. Russian Populism and Religious Sects". *The Russian Review*, 62 (4), 565-88.

Etkind, A. (2007). "Orientalism Reversed: Russian Literature in the Times of Empires". *Modern Intellectual History*, 4 (3), 617-628.

Etkind, A. (2011). *Internal Colonization. Russia's Imperial Experience*. Cambridge: Polity Press.

Figes, O. (2002). *Natasha's Dance. A Cultural History of Russia*. London: Alan Lane. The Penguin Press.

Grant, B. (2005). "The Good Russian Prisoner: Naturalizing Violence in the Caucasus Mountains". *Cultural Anthropology*, 20 (1), 39-67.

Grant, B. (2009). *The Captive and the Gift. Cultural Histories of Sovereignty in Russia and the Caucasus*. Ithaca, New York: Cornell University Press.

Helle, L. (2009). "The Multiple Meaning of Boundary Encounters: On the Caucasus as the Oriental Other in Russian Nineteenth Century Literature" in: Lindbladh, J., Paulsson, T., Sarsenov K. et al. (eds.). *The Arts in Dialogue. (=Slavica Lundensia 24)*, 65-79.

Hokanson, K. (1994). "Literary Imperialism, Narodnost' and Puskin's Invention of the Caucasus". *Russian Review*, 53, 336-352.

Hosford, D. & Wojtkowski, C.J. (2010). *French Orientalism: Culture, Politics, and the Imagined Other*. Newcastle: Cambridge Scholars Publishing.

Inden, R. (1990). *Imagining India*. Oxford: Blackwell.

Layton, S. (1994). *Russian Literature and Empire. Conquest of Caucasus from Pushkin to Tolstoy.* New York: Cambridge University Press.

Layton, S. (1986). "The Creation of an Imaginative Caucasian Geography". *Slavic Review*, 45, 470-85.

Lermontov, M. (1955). "Aul Bastundzhi". *Sochinenija v 6 tomakh.* Vol. 3, Moscow/Leningrad: Izd. Akademii Nauk SSSR.

Lomonosov, M. (1959). *Polnoe sobranie sochinenii v 11 tomakh.* Vol. 8, Leningrad/Moscow: Izd. Akademii Nauk SSSR.

Lotman, Ju. (1990). *The Universe of the Mind. A Semiotic Theory of Culture.* London/New York: I. B.Tauris & Co.

Moretti, M. (1998). *Atlas of the European Novel 1800-1900.* London and New York: Verso.

Peace, D. (1984). Sublime Politics. *Boundary,* 2 (12/13), 259-79.

Polezhaev, A. (1832). *Erpeli i Chir-Jurt. Dve poemy.* Moscow: V tipografii Lazarevych Instituta vostochnych jazykov.

Pushkin, A. (1994). *Polnoe sobranie sochinenii v 17 tomakh.* Vol 4, Moscow: Voskresen'e.

Ram, H. (1999). "Prisoners of the Caucasus: Literary Myths and Media Representations of the Chechen Conflict". *Berkeley Program in Soviet and Post-Soviet Studies,* 3-29.

Ram, H. (2003). *The Imperial Sublime: A Russian Poetics of Empire.* Madison, Wisc: The University of Wisconsin Press.

Sahni, K. (1997). *Crucifying the Orient. Russian Orientalism and the Colonization of Caucasus and Central Asia.* Bangkok and Oslo: White Orchid Press.

Saïd, E. (1978). *Orientalism.* New York: Vintage Books.

Schimmelpenninck van der Oye, D. (2010). *Russian Orientalism. Asia in the Russian Mind from Peter the Great to the Emigration.* New Haven & London: Yale University Press.

Schwab, R. (1950). *La Renaissance Orientale.* Paris: Payot.

Thompson, E. (2000). *Imperial Knowledge: Russian Literature and Colonialism.* Westport, Conn. and London: Greenwood Press.

White, H. (1972). "The forms of Wildness: Archaeology of an Idea" in: Dudley, E. & Novak, M. (eds.). *The Wild Man Within. An Image in Western Thought from the Renaissance to Romanticism.* Pittsburgh: University of Pittsburgh Press.

Wolff, W. (1994). *Inventing Eastern Europe. The Map of Civilization on the Mind of the Enlightenment.* Stanford, California: Stanford University Press.

Zhirmunskii, B. (1970). *Bajron i Pushkin. Iz istorii romanticheskoj poemy.* The Hague: Mouton.

# Time and Causality in Flaubert's Novels *Salammbô* and *Bouvard et Pécuchet*

*Helge Vidar Holm*

In this chapter, I shall be referring to three quite different theorists, in the hope that each of them may contribute to a better understanding of two novels written by Gustave Flaubert: *Salammbô* (1862) and *Bouvard et Pécuchet* (1881, posthumous edition). I am especially concerned with the conceptual mechanisms that form the temporal dimensions of the novels, as well as with the role played in these novels by the novelist's attitude to dominating ideological patterns in his time, such as the new paradigm in the 19th century in the philosophy of history.

Let us turn first to the German theorist of history and historiography Reinart Koselleck (1923-2006). Through his various works on the history of concepts, he develops a new understanding of how concepts from our social and political reality change through history while helping to enhance our apprehension of this reality. In *Vergangene Zukunft* (1979), he analyses this development by comparing various concepts with each other in constellations he calls *countering concepts*, in which one of the concepts describes "us", e.g. the situation or the characteristic that "we" (the actual speakers) think of as "ours"; while the other concept characterizes "the Others". Examples from history could be Greek/Barbarian or Christian/Heathen – the point being that the concept which defines the Other implies a disregard or a negative evaluation compared to the concept which defines Us. In Koselleck's terminology, this leads to an *asymmetrical* pair of countering concepts.[1]

One of the questions that I want to discuss is whether Koselleck's constellation of conceptual asymmetry may help us deepen our understanding of the narrative and conceptual mechanisms which structure the "creative chronotopes" in the two major flaubertian novels mentioned above. *Chronotope* is a term developed in one of Mikhail Bakhtin's major essays on the history and the theory of the novel genre,[2] "Forms of time and chronotope in the

---

[1]  *Asymmetrische Gegenbegriffe.*
[2]  From *chronos* (Gr. "time") + *topos* (Gr. "place").

novel".[3] The creative chronotope differs from the other forms of chronotope discussed in his essay. According to Bakhtin, the chronotope is decisive for the unity of a literary work in its relation to reality,[4] but whereas the internal chronotopes in a literary work (like those of the road and of the threshold, also in the metaphorical sense of these words) belong to the fictional universe, the creative chronotope is part of the universe that the fictional work reflects.[5]

The third theoretical reference in this chapter will be Edward W. Saïd (1935-2003), especially the essay that made him a central catalyst in postcolonial literary theory, *Orientalism. Western Conceptions of the Orient* (1978), by giving the term "Orientalism" a completely new meaning. Despite – and perhaps also as a consequence of – a number of publications containing well documented, partly negative criticism of this seminal essay over more than thirty years,[6] Saïd's definition of the term "Orientalism" is not only the dominating one today, but it has practically made it impossible to use the term in the traditional meaning, prior to the publication of his essay.[7]

The relatively neutral meaning that used to prevail before 1978 concerning the term "Orientalism" and thus to define an academic discipline, dominated by Western "Orientalists" (e.g. specialists of Oriental languages, literature and cultures), no longer applies. The term has even extended its semantic field to areas which have little or nothing to do with the Orient, but which, on the other hand, relate to the implications of Koselleck's constellation of conceptual asymmetry. Orientalism may today be detected, for instance, in a description of the Inuits and their culture given by a Norwegian, or similarly, one given of the Lapps by a non-Lappish European. It is not only a question of our tendency to define the Other by our own standards. It is rather a matter of the fundamentally fictional narrative we produce in presenting the

---

3    The major part of this essay was written in 1937-1938, but the concluding chapter, "Final observations", was added in 1973, two years before the death of the great Russian thinker. Concerning the creative chronotope, see Bakhtin 1978: 394.

4    Bakhine 1978: 384: «Le chronotope détermine l'unité artistique d'une oeuvre littéraire dans ses rapports avec la réalité».

5    See Bakhtine 1978: 394.

6    Varisco 2007 gives an excellent overview of this criticism and makes some good points concerning Saïd's selection of texts and his biased interpretation of them. However, Saïd's reading of *Bouvard et Pécuchet*, shows us that although Saïd may be biased, he is perfectly capable of performing analyses which may place an "Orientalist" like Flaubert in the opposite camp as well.

7    See Saïd 1996 and 2000 for discussions of other aspects of his commitment to Oriental values than his negatively based definition of the term "Orientalism".

Others as we see them through our falsifying conceptual lenses, which, according to Saïd, have created an Orient which only exists in the works of the Occidental Orientalists – be they great scientists or artists – and absolutely not in the minds nor the world of the Oriental population. Studies of the modern concept of Orientalism have thus become an important aspect of a new academic discipline, *borderology*, which has primarily concentrated until now on philosophical themes and cultural/political issues related to the Northern spheres of Europe.[8] Semantic implications of the notion of Europe through modern history, especially through the last two centuries,[9] are largely based on an opposition between a constructed European progressive universality and an imagined backward-looking Oriental civilization, a constellation which corresponds closely to Kosseleck's description of how asymmetrical pairs of countering concepts work in our minds.

The existence of such asymmetrical pairs of concepts as those presented by Koselleck implies logically that their opposite, symmetrical conceptual pairs, also exist. However, such symmetrical pairs rarely come into practical use when one of the two countering concepts applies to "us". At any rate, the understanding of symmetry in a conceptual pair will necessarily depend on the given context. Plato and Aristotle discussed the concept of democracy as one of several possible forms of political governance, whereas this concept has gained an ideological and ethical meaning during the last centuries which depends on the speaker's idea of the opposite concept in the pair, dictatorship. For instance, the speaker may think of the Marxist concept of dictatorship of the proletariat.

Not only the ideological orientation of the speaker, but also the time and the place of the utterance, may be of decisive importance. This fact leads us back to Bakhtin and the chronotope, as well as to his theory of the utterance (Bakhtin 1998: 53). According to this theory, no utterance can be repeated as such, because its *utterance situation*, its time-and-place situation, can never be exactly the same, in the first place due to the continuous passing of time. The logical consequence of this understanding of the utterance's status relates both to the Bakhtinian chronotope and to the understanding of concepts that we find in Koselleck, especially in his *Vergangene Zukunft*.

---

[8]   The first philosophical conference on borderology, "Thinking about Limits and Borders", was held in June 2006 at the Barents Institute in Kirkenes, arranged by the Norwegian Kant Society.

[9]   See our introductory chapter, in the first section of this book.

Any understanding of conceptual pairs like democracy/dictatorship will consequently depend on their discursive context, and in a wider perspective on their time/place setting. Koselleck calls the discursive context a "unity of action", decisive for the understanding of the concept in question (See Jordheim 2001: 173). We have here interesting parallels to the Bakhtinian idea of the "aesthetic event" represented by the reader's perception of a fictional text (Bakthine 1984: 43). In both cases, the phenomena are understood as unique, impossible to repeat as such, regardless of whether they pretend to be based on factual texts (Koselleck: historiography) or fictional ones (Bakhtin: novels).

Koselleck's description of the concept of *progress* (*Fortschritt*) explains the asymmetrical dimension of conceptual thinking. This concept creates a "horizon of expectation" that relates asymmetrically to the "space of experience" (*Erfahrungsraum* and *Erwartungshorizont*), to the knowledge and the experiences accumulated by mankind. In earlier days, at least until the last part of the 17th century, this knowledge and these experiences were regarded as a stable, practically unchanging basis for the expectations any person could have for his or her future. During and after the age of Enlightenment and the following Romantic period, this basis lost its primordial importance. The idea of History as a lineal phenomenon, not a cyclic or circular one, created new expectations for a different future. Koselleck, referring to Immanuel Kant, puts it this way: "*Progress* is the first genuinely historical concept that formulates the temporal difference between experience and expectation".[10] During the historical period following the creation by Kant of this use of the term "progress", the relation between the space of experience and the horizon of expectations becomes increasingly asymmetrical: our parents' life experience, added to our own, no longer provides a sufficient basis for us to form well founded expectations for our own and our children's future lives. We are no longer convinced that there will be a close, clear continuity between what has been and what is to come.

This line of argument leads us to a central point in the new paradigm created by Koselleck's works on the history of conceptual development: that the history of the fundamental concepts in the socio-political life of different cultures in specific periods and places enables us to discover the experiences and expectations of people constituting specific socio-cultural groups. Koselleck's paradigmatic point in historical research has close affinities to the Bakhtinian position on a chronotopic understanding of the history of the novelistic genre.

---

[10]    Quoted (in my translation) from Jordheim 2001: 168.

By analysing the chronotopes of the greatest novels from different cultures and periods, we may reach a better understanding of the axiological basis of these peoples and their visions of reality as well as of their religious, philosophical and metaphysical orientations.

However, the historical period treated in a novel is not necessarily what really makes up the novel's subject matter. According to Bakhtin, the chronotope of creation will always primarily convey the novelist's understanding of human existence and thereby reflect his/her own historical and ideological background. It will also be strongly influenced by the background of the reader. This second part (which might be called the chronotope of reception) will of course always vary according to the reader's orientations, ideological or any others. The first part will not vary as such, but its role in the "aesthetic fulfilment of the literary work" constituted by the perception of the novelistic text will always depend on the reader's interpretation of the work.[11]

In Flaubert's novel from 1862, *Salammbô*, the creation chronotope will thus be related to France in the first years of the Second Empire (1852-1870) even though its plot takes place in and around Carthage at the time of the 3rd Punic War, about 140 BCE. The novel narrates the complicated love story between the Libyan warrior Matho and Salammbô, the daughter of Hamilcar, leader of the Carthaginian army. Matho's desperate love for Salammbô makes him commit "blasphemic" actions which lead to his death. Lots of details in the presentation of the subject matter are strongly marked by Flaubert's fascination for exotic as well as grotesque, often rather superficial elements,[12] a fascination which was probably a result both of his thorough and detailed study of the different aspects of history of Carthage and of his lifelong interest in the Oriental world.[13]

One of the most prominent literary critics in France at the time of Flaubert, Sainte-Beuve, accused the author of *Salammbô* of having created too much of a mental distance between his readers and the novel's subject matter through an exaggerated exposition of historical details, be they as correct as

---

11  *L'oeuvre dans sa plénitude événementielle* (Bakhtine 1978: 395).

12  Flaubert had forced himself to suppress as much as possible of this fascination during the five years he was stubbornly working on his preceding novel, *Madame Bovary* (1856), whose setting and plot are all but Oriental.

13  Flaubert went twice to the Orient. The first trip, when he travelled mostly in Egypt, lasted from 1849 to 1851; the second one brought him for two months in 1859 to Tunisia (Carthage).

they might be.[14] To Sainte-Beuve, a historical novel should make readers relate to the characters and the events, not only teach them something about a culture and a historical period which was long gone and practically forgotten. Sainte-Beuve's critique is interesting because it exposes a certain idea of the historical novel. But as we shall see, the most important historical dimension in Flaubert's novel might well be the one which provides *Salammbô* with its basic chronotope of creation (the Second Empire in France), and in a wider context with the philosophy of history prevailing in this country during most of the 19th century.

In his preceding novel, *Madame Bovary* (*Moeurs de province*), Flaubert succeeded in developing a main technical innovation for the narrative genre: a new, subtle and sometimes quite ambiguous form of focalisation or "point-of-view" narration, where we as readers feel that we see the world and human existence mainly through the perception of the characters, not through that of the author or even that of the narrator.[15] This "perspectivism" has its parallels in Koselleck's understanding of conceptual history, in that the German historian insists upon a discursive and thus not an "essentialiste" definition of historical concepts. What is special about them is their ambiguity, or rather: their wide range of meanings, according to their specific historical and discursive situation. One has to interpret them as part of a specific utterance, in a "perspectivistic" mode.[16]

In fact, we find a good understanding of such a perspectivistic mode in the comments made by Edward Saïd (1978) on the unfinished, last novel written by Flaubert, *Bouvard et Pécuchet*. The novel presents a satirical view on the prevailing positivistic belief in science as one of the pillars of human progress. There can be little doubt today that Flaubert had quite another understanding of the dominating historically situated concept of progress than had most of his fellow intellectuals at the time, the prevailing understanding being one based on Hegelian historicism. In his notes on the final chapter of *Bouvard et Pécuchet*, the novelist lets the two main characters discuss the future of mankind. Whereas Monsieur Pécuchet is a notorious pessimist who sees everything in black, Monsieur Bouvard is an unbeatable optimist

---

14    In Sainte-Beuve 2010 (1862), critique refuted by Flaubert in a personal letter to Sainte-Beuve in December 1862. See Flaubert: 1991.

15    Flaubert's innovative use of *style indirect libre* is decisive here. See Holm 2011: 59-96.

16    See Koselleck: "Vorwort" in *Geschichtliche Grundbegriffe*, vol. 7, p. VII; commented upon in Jordheim 2001: 172.

claiming that modern man moves forward continuously through progress, and he thinks that Europe will be reborn thanks to Asiatic influence. According to Bouvard, the idea that the process of civilisation passes from the Orient to the Occident can be regarded as a historical law, leading eventually to the integration and complete assimilation of the two cultures some time in the future.

Like the other "great" ideas discussed by the two main characters in this novel, the vision of the future of mankind conveyed by Bouvard's discourse is based on a comprehensive, holistic perspective on mankind and its history. In Flaubert's view, such a perspective is typical for the scientists and artists of his time, and there is little doubt that this satirical novel sets out to make a discourse of this kind seem ridiculous. However, satire is rarely unambiguous, and the novel *Bouvard et Pécuchet* is definitely not a unilateral attack on the belief in progress for humanity. It is rather a satirical novel which applies a narrative technique of discursive perspective to apparently progressive ideas of practical value (for instance in agriculture) and of theoretical importance (like the one just mentioned with regard to the philosophy of history), by relating them to specific speakers (like Mr Bouvard and Mr Pécuchet) or writers (like various authors of encyclopaedic works, handbooks on agriculture and academic articles, quoted to a great extent throughout the novel).

If we return to *Salammbô*, we may note that Flaubert avoids all serious attempts to describe an Orient which would relate closely to the Orient of his own time. The Orient of this novel is basically pure imagination, although it is based on long and meticulous research combined with the author's own experiences from his two visits to Oriental countries. An interesting fact is that Flaubert chose a historical event about which our sources of knowledge are few, with his most important source, the Greek historian Polybius (about 200-118 BC), being one of the first historians to present history as causal, as sequences of causes and effects. It is difficult to find such presentations of the historical events that frame the action in *Salammbô*, where the lack of such a causal narration has been commented upon by several critics.[17] For instance, Gisèle Séginger (2000b) maintains that although the temporal dimension in *Salammbô* does not allow for historical rationalization, one may find another form of temporal, historical philosophy in this novel: a

---

[17]   Among others: Séginger 2000a and 2000b, Lörinszky 2002 and Bender 2007.

naturalistic conception of history, opposed to the dialectic model prevailing in Flaubert's century.[18]

Actually, Flaubert made a choice of a historical event which in fact led to "nothing" (the main historical event in *Salammbô*, the insurrection of the mercenaries, having turned into a hopeless defeat) and of a historical setting, Carthage, which not only was destroyed by the Romans, but which, at the time of Flaubert, was nothing more than a few rather insignificant ruins situated 16 km from the modern town of Tunis. One might conclude, a little daringly, that the novelist's choice provided him with a freedom of creative perspectivism and historical "circularism" that enabled him to make *Salammbô* into a new kind of historical novel,[19] where the reader not only is transposed to another time and a different place, but where the time-and-space dimension differs totally from our own, because of the lack of traditional causal narration. The satirical presentation of Hegelian historicism given by Flaubert through Monsieur Bouvard's belief in historical progress in the notes to the final chapter of the posthumous novel *Bouvard et Pécuchet* is to be found in germ in *Salammbô*, in the total lack of a "progressive" historical dimension in this historical novel's representation of time.

Based on elements from the two novels discussed above, I propose two pairs of countering concepts, of which one describes the basic time dimensions of the story told, whereas the other relates to the way in which discourse is presented in the narrative:

1) Linear progress vs. Cyclic repetition:
   *Bouvard et Pécuchet*: the basic conclusion of the novel is quite unambiguous: Most "great" ideas are quite short-lived and they are all doomed to fail sooner or later, thus continually "pulling all players back to start". (Cyclic repetition)
   *Salammbô*: The narrative presents no clear causality between the various events, and the major time references are practically non-existent. (Cyclic repetition)

---

[18] "Le temps représenté dans *Salammbô* ne se laisse pas transformer en Histoire. Flaubert montre que les événements résistent aux tentatives de rationalisation, alors que son siècle s'efforce de maîtriser le temps par le discours en pensant l'Histoire. … Dans *Salammbô* le rythme binaire oppose à la pensée dialectique ce qu'il faut bien considérer comme une autre pensée, une conception naturaliste de l'histoire.» (Séginger 2000b: 172).

[19] Or "naturalism": see the quotation from Séginger 2000b in the preceding note.

2) Omniscience vs. Perspectivism

Perspectivism (or internal focalisation through the Flaubertian form of *style indirect libre*) is a basic narrative structure both in *Salammbô* and in *Bouvard et Pécuchet*. In *Salammbô* it is primarily used as a means of strengthening the subject status of the main characters, whereas the use in the latter novel is part of an ironic narration that makes any idea of pretended omniscience, narrative or factual, seem both ludicrous and vain.

The two Flaubertian novels defend, through their treatment of time and discursive perspective, a conceptual understanding which undermines the first part of the two pairs of concepts above. In doing so, the novels criticize, indirectly but strongly, two of the main pillars of Orientalism: 1) the dominating European 19th century philosophy of history; 2) the hegemonic, Occidental way of seeing the Other as an object, not as a subject in his/her own right. I shall further elaborate these two statements in the rest of this chapter.

Saïd (1978) points to the fact that the idea that Europe was supposed to be heading towards a new renaissance inspired by Asia, e.g. the "historical law" advocated by Bouvard in the notes to the final chapter of *Bouvard et Pécuchet*, was an idea widely accepted at the time of Flaubert and especially in his younger days. In those days the influence from the Romantic period was still quite strong, and the idea was defended by several important European philosophers and poets. Novalis and Schlegel, as well as Wordsworth, Chateaubriand and Comte recommended studies of Indian and other Oriental cultures and religions to their fellow Europeans, as a remedy against growing materialism in European culture.

Saïd does not really believe in the seriousness of this romantic interest in Asian countries. To him, the inheritors of the Romantic ideas were more interested in making use of Asian richness and culture in a reborn, modern Europe than in studying Oriental philosophy and literature. According to Saïd, Flaubert not only understood this, he quite clearly saw the dangerous hegemonic attitude prevailing in this kind of "great" and comprehensive ideas. Saïd gives Flaubert credit for his perspicacity regarding the *hubris* hidden in the cultural attitude and the philosophy of history expressed by many of the French novelist's fellow Europeans:

> In regularly allowing Bouvard and Pécuchet to go through revisionist notions from start
> to comically debased finish, Flaubert drew attention to the human flaw common to all
> projects. He saw perfectly well that underneath the *idée reçue* "Europe-regenerated-by-Asia"
> lurked a very insidious hubris. Neither "Europe" nor "Asia" was anything without the vi-

sionaries' technique for turning vast geographical domains into treatable, and manageable, entities. At bottom, therefore, Europe and Asia were *our* Europe and *our* Asia – our *will* and *representation*, as Schopenhauer has said. Historical laws were in reality *historians'* laws (Saïd 1978: 115, his emphasis).

As we can see, the chronotope of creation does not only apply to fictional texts. Applied to the conceptual thinking that we have seen in Koselleck, this Bakhtinian concept gives us a larger understanding not only of the genre of the novel, but also of historiography. Like most of the "great" projects and ideas presented by the novelistic character Bouvard, his conviction regarding the place of the Orient within a historical progress framework comes from epistemological paradigms dominating most of the 19th century. At the time, the Orient was viewed by several important European historians both as an actual, contemporary neighbour and as an imagined place somewhere far away in the past. In Flaubert's homeland, the most famous of them all, Jules Michelet, represents this paradigm. To him the Orient is the cradle of the Occident; it is the place where our religion and our culture were born thousands of years ago, to later expand, by Occidental means, throughout most of the world. The conceptual asymmetry is evident: our values are hegemonic because they have become superior through a historical process where "progress" is the key word.

We may see this from the philosophy of history expressed in two of Michelet's historical works, which were well known to Flaubert, "Introduction à l'histoire universelle" (1831) and *Histoire romaine* (1839). From the first title, we understand that Michelet wants to present us with a universal history, e.g. not only a World History, but something more, with deeper philosophical pretensions: a universal understanding of the History of our world in historical times. And this is what he sets out to do. Inspired by a Hegelian, dialectic model of the great movements in History, Michelet presents a narrative where the Occidental man moves forward on a line based on time and space, from antiquity to modern times, from Asia to Europe. The ideology of progress is the fundamental paradigm, related to ideas which were to change the dominating understanding of History not only during the Romantic period and its sequels, but through most of the 20th century as well.

Reinhart Koselleck describes in an essay from 1967, "Historia Magistra Vitae", how this new vision of History structures the Occidental understanding of human existence from the beginning of the 19th century onwards. This new vision implies a comprehension of the limitation and the relativity of human knowledge. After more than two thousand years of regarding human life according to a circular paradigm, as cyclic movements of infinite repetition (the

*Historia Magistra Vitae*),[20] the time has now come for a new conception – and concept – of History.

To Flaubert, this "great" idea is as ridiculous as many other "great" ideas from his contemporary scientists and artists, at least in the presentation we find in his satirical novel *Bouvard et Pécuchet*. This presentation is *discursive*, in the sense that it is formulated by one of the characters in the novel, and we might think that it is just another example of Flaubert's *perspectivism*. This is in fact the case, but if we look to his much admired contemporary historian Jules Michelet, we can see that Flaubert is mocking, through Bouvard's discourse, an important element in his time's historiography. A brief quotation from Michelet's "Introduction à l'histoire universelle" may illustrate my point. The context is Michelet's metaphorical presentation of the development of the human mind and society in historical times as a long march towards freedom, from East to West, facing all kinds of obstacles imposed by uncivilized nature. At last the march culminates in the middle of Europe, in France, Michelet's own home country: "By every step we make during this long march from Asia to Europe, from India to France, we can see how the fatal powers of nature diminishes".[21]

When it comes to *Bouvard et Pécuchet*, Saïd is quite unambiguous in qualifying Flaubert as an anti-Orientalist, whereas the discussion of *Salammbô* in Saïd's essay is meant to support the author's qualification of Flaubert as one of the most important Orientalists among the 19th century's fictional writers. Although Saïd in parts of his famous essay convincingly presents Flaubert, especially in his letters from the Orient, as rather a typical Orientalist, there are, in my opinion, not many convincing arguments in Saïd's essay to prove that *the novelist* Flaubert fits this description. More to the contrary, I would say. I shall revert to my arguments against Saïd's characterisation of *Salammbô* as an Oriental novel after presenting the following concluding quotation from his presentation of *Bouvard et Pécuchet*, which in my opinion shows the importance of Flaubert's perspectivism, his discursive, indirect argumentation against ideas presented by the novel's protagonists. This quotation leaves no doubt as to Saïd's understanding of the French novelist's comprehension of the futility of the ideas that have framed the Occident's Orientalism:

---

20   This title is taken from a central concept in the historiography of Polybius, a classical Greek historian who is Flaubert's main historical source in *Salammbô*. To Koselleck, this expression represents a paradigm of the pre-modern philosophy of history.

21   Quoted (in my translation) from Bender 2007: 885.

Bouvard and Pécuchet have learned that it is better not to traffic in ideas and in reality together. The novel's conclusion is a picture of the two of them now perfectly content to copy their favourite ideas faithfully from book onto paper. Knowledge no longer requires application to reality; knowledge is what gets passed on silently, without comment, from one text to another. … In a highly compressed form this brief episode, taken out of Flaubert's notes for *Bouvard et Pécuchet*, frames the specifically modern structures of Orientalism, which after all is one discipline among the secular (and quasi-religious) faith of nineteenth-century European thought (Saïd 1978: 116).

As for *Salammbô*, the "secular (and quasi-religious) faith" concerning the Orient, criticized here by Saïd, is in my opinion definitely not a structuring principle of this novel.

The Orientalism in *Salammbô* is more of a superficial décor than an important aspect of the novel's subject matter. In spite of their "exotic" behaviour, the central characters of *Salammbô* are strongly marked by individual psychological reactions to the events that they encounter, and the discursively based presentation of their innermost thoughts belongs far more to the 19th century than to antiquity, for instance in the perspectivism which dominates the scene of the death of Matho:

Salammbô was leaning on the balustrade; these horrifying pupils were contemplating her, and inside her rose the conscience of all that he had suffered for her. Even though he was in agony, she saw him once again in her tent, on his bended knees with his arms around her waist, mumbling sweet nothings: she thirsted to feel them again, to hear them; she didn't want him to die! (Flaubert 1862/1970: 467, my translation).[22]

At the time of Flaubert, Carthage was, as it still is, a reminiscence of antiquity, a collection of ruins with practically no significant remains of the original town structures. As already mentioned, it must have been an excellent setting for Flaubert's fictional use of historical knowledge and of his own impressions from his visits to the Orient, the sites of Carthage included. Saïd realizes this, and

---

22    "Salammbô était penchée sur la balustrade; ces effroyables prunelles la contemplaient, et la conscience lui surgit de tout ce qu'il avait souffert pour elle. Bien qu'il agonisât, elle le revoyait dans sa tente, à genoux, lui entourant la taille de ses bras, balbutiant des paroles douces; elle avait soif de les sentir encore, de les entendre; elle ne voulait pas qu'il mourût!» (Flaubert 1862/1970: 467, my translation).

when he comments on Flaubert's narrative technique in novels like *Salammbô*, he actually hits the nail on the head:

> Flaubert puts his voyages to ingenious use. Most of his experiences are conveyed in theatri-
> cal form. He is interested not only in the content of what he sees but – like Renan – in
> *how* he sees (185-186).

Saïd's emphasis of the word "how" in this quotation shows that he has grasped a fundamental aspect of Flaubert's thinking about the Orient, an aspect that the French novelist set out to practice in what I call his *perspectivism*, a discursive way of presenting the character's individual ideas and their ways of reacting to actions and surroundings. To me the fact that Saïd insists on calling the Flaubert of *Salammbô* an Orientalist is quite paradoxical. However, admittedly he grants Flaubert (together with Gérard de Nerval) a status apart in this context.[23]

Let us now return to Koselleck and his constellation of countering concepts. In the constellation "linear progress versus cyclic repetition", there is no doubt that the latter concept is what characterises the time dimension in *Salammbô*. By insisting on presenting recurrent battles with little or no logical development between them, by refusing to give any specific dates for the various events or to indicate the periods of time they last, Flaubert places himself indirectly in opposition to any "great" historico-philosophical interpretation inspired by his Carthage novel. In *Bouvard et Pécuchet*, he openly attacks the ruling historical paradigm of his time, such as we have seen it exemplified in Michelet's historiography. The discursive, satirical presentation of Bouvard's "great" idea about a new Europe reborn through Asian influence is a novelistic proof.

In *Salammbô*, Flaubert gives the action a setting which is a sort of nowhere, beyond time and place. The "referential" historical event is the third Punic War, but the war seems more like a fictional setting than a historical reference. This setting is a place where people live, love, fight and die, and the chronology of the events as well as their importance in a broader temporal perspective are completely neglected. There is no trace of a philosophy of history such as the one we find in Michelet and other historians of the 19th century. More than anything, the universe of the novel *Salammbô* is that of a myth (See Lörin-

---

23   "Flaubert's work is so complex and so vast as to make any simple account of his Oriental
writing very sketchy and hopelessly incomplete" (Saïd 1978:185).

szky 2002), but not the kind of myth that has created Orientalism as "one discipline among the secular (and quasi-religious) faith of nineteenth-century European thought", as we have seen Saïd put it. The kind of myth Saïd refers to is based on the concept of progress as it was developed in the philosophy of history that dominated the 19th century, a "great" idea clearly turned down by Flaubert in the two novels discussed in this chapter.

Moreover, it is important to note that the perspectivism of Flaubert refutes Orientalism as such. An Oriental novel will be dominated by the hegemonic ideas of its author, either by a narrative omniscience or by manipulating the novelistic characters' thoughts so they fit such ideas.[24] In my reading of the two Flaubertian novels in question, such a manipulation of characters does not take place. One reason is the fact that these novels do not pretend to present a true story or factual events; even *Salammbô*, a "historical novel", has no such pretensions as to the story of the protagonists. The other reason is a consequence of Flaubert's perspectivism, as I see it: the main characters of these novels, and again I am thinking particularly of *Salammbô*, seem to be subjects in their own right, and not objects corresponding to the author's hegemonic view of the Other, as will be the case for Oriental characters in Oriental novels.

As we have seen, Flaubert's attitude to the concept of *progress* as presented by a prominent French historian like Jules Michelet is clearly expressed in *Bouvard et Pécuchet* by means of a discursive perspectivism. In *Salammbô*, Flaubert's sceptical attitude to a dominant ideological structure of his time has other consequences. Not only does it influence the temporal dimensions which structure the novel strongly – it also gives the setting of the novel a mythical dimension which liberates it from being a mere historical reference.

Both Koselleck's conceptual pairs and Bakthin's creative chronotope have proved important for the discussion leading to my conclusions. These conclusions imply that the dominant European paradigm concerning the philosophy of history and the concept of progress at the time of Flaubert have played important roles in structuring his "Oriental" novel *Salammbô* and in convey-

---

[24]  This may also be the case in journalistic works. A fairly recent example from the Norwegian scene could be a much debated "journalistic novel", *The Bookseller of Kabul*, by Åsne Seierstad (*Bokhandleren i Kabul*, Cappelen, Oslo 2003). The book is presented by its author, a famous journalist, as a factual reportage, but she admits to having employed a literary, discursive technique that manipulates the factual persons' pretended thoughts.

ing a narrative irony to *Bouvard et Pécuchet*. Flaubert's use of irony provides the unfinished parts of this novel with a serious contemporary critique of civilization, especially concerning important European intellectuals' ideas of the Orient with regard to both its historical past and its imagined future.

We have also seen Flaubert's perspectivism give the main characters of the novel a subject status which makes them appear quite differently from most objectified characters in most Oriental novels. There is no doubt that the narrative technique developed in Flaubert's novel from 1856, *Madame Bovary (Moeurs de province),* has contributed largely to giving the characters in the two later novels their own *voice,* as Bakhtin would have put it, and to their becoming *characters in their own right* (See Bakhtine 1970: 32-33). My conclusion concerning Flaubert's alleged Orientalism is that his fiction, exemplified by the two novels discussed in this chapter, proves to be more anti-Oriental than Oriental, thus adding some important nuances to Edward W. Saïd's descriptions of the works of the great French novelist. However, what Saïd and others might say about the Orientalism of Flaubert's *Correspondances* is quite another story.

## Bibliography

Bakhtin, M. (1998). *Spørsmålet om talegenrane.* Bergen: Ariadne forlag.

Bakhtine, M. (1970). *La Poétique de Dostoïevski.* Paris: Seuil.[25]

Bakhtine, M. (1978). Formes du temps et du chronotope dans le roman. *Esthétique et théorie du roman.* Paris: Gallimard.

Bender, N. (2007). Pour un autre Orientalisme: Flaubert et Michelet face à l'Histoire. *Modern Language Notes 122.* Baltimore, Maryland: The Johns Hopkins University Press.

Flaubert, G. (1970/1862). *Salammbô.* Paris: Folio classique, Gallimard.

Flaubert, G. (1991). *Correspondances IV.* Paris: Bibliothèque de la Pléiade, Gallimard.

Flaubert, G. (1997/1881). *Bouvard et Pécuchet.* Paris: Pocket.

Flaubert, G. (2001/1856). *Madame Bovary (Moeurs de province).* Paris: Folio classique, Gallimard.

Holm, H.V. (2011). *Mœurs de province. Essai d'analyse bakhtinienne de Madame Bovary.* Berne: Peter Lang SA Editions scientifiques européennes.

Jordheim, H. (2001). *Lesningens vitenskap. Utkast til en ny filologi.* Oslo: Universitetsforlaget.

---

[25] In French, the family name of the Russian philosopher is spelt with an "e" at the end: Bakhtine.

Koselleck, R. (1967). Historia Magistra Vita. *Preussen zwischen Reform und Revolution*. Stuttgart: Klett und Cotta.

Koselleck, R. (1972). Vorwort. *Geschichtliche Grundbegriffe, VII*. Stuttgart: Klett und Cotta.

Koselleck, R. (1979). *Vergangene Zukunft*. Frankfurt a.M.: Suhrkamp.

Lörinszky, I. (2002). *L'Orient de Flaubert. Des écrits de jeunesse à Salammbô: la construction d'un imaginaire mythique*. Paris: L'Harmattan.

Michelet, J. (1980/1831). "Introduction à l'histoire universelle". *Oeuvres complètes*. Paris: Flammarion.

Michelet, J. (2003/1839). *Histoire romaine*. Paris: Les Belles Lettres.

Saïd, E.W. (1978). *Orientalism. Western Conceptions of the Orient*. New York: Pantheon Books.

Saïd, E.W. (1996). *Representations of the Intellectual (The 1991 Reith Lectures)*. New York: Vintage Books: Random House.

Saïd, E.W. (2000). *Reflections on Exile*. London: Granta Books.

Sainte-Beuve, C.A. (2010/1862). *Nouveaux lundis, IV*. Charleston, S.C.: Nabu Press.

Séginger, G. (2000a). *Flaubert. Une poétique de l'histoire*. Strasbourg: PUS.

Séginger, G. (2000b). *Flaubert. Une éthique de l'art pur*. Paris: Sedes/HER.

Seierstad, Å. (2003). *Bokhandleren i Kabul*. Oslo: Cappelen.

Varisco, D.M. (2007). *Reading Orientalism. The Said and the Unsaid*. Seattle: University of Washington Press.

# Mozart's Opera *The Abduction from the Seraglio* and Bakhtin's Border Poetics

*Torgeir Skorgen*

Mozart's opera *The Abduction from the Seraglio* represents a particularly interesting example of how the emergence of 18th century nationalism is interconnected with the launching of the concept of Europe and the European on the threshold of 19th century romanticism. This article aims at investigating some ways in which the harem motif in Mozart's opera marks the aesthetic, cultural, moral, political and historical border between Europe and its Oriental 'other'. *The Abduction* was an elaboration of Christoph Bretzner's Singspiel *Bellmont und Constanze*, ordered by the progressive Austrian emperor Joseph II as the first German 'Nationalsingspiel', celebrating the 100th anniversary of the Turkish siege of Vienna. At the same time the emperor wanted to honour the Russian Grand Duke Paul, hoping that the Russians would help him drive the Turks out of the Bosporus. The Turks in Mozart's opera are therefore depicted in a rather offensive way, in particular the gloomy harem supervisor Osmin. Appealing not only to emerging Austrian patriotism, but also to contemporary demand for Oriental, in particular Turkish, motifs, the opera experienced tremendous success on all stages all over Europe.

*The Abduction* is also considered the final breakthrough of the German 'Singspiel'. According to Adorno's aesthetics, the truth of a work of art has a historical core which in turn is dependent on its inherent form. At the end of this article, I will therefore discuss some formal elements of the opera with special regard to its intermediality. I will also examine the extent to which Mozart's opera crosses the borders between 'high' and 'low' culture in a rather carnivalesque manner, thereby challenging some romantic clichés about the asserted purity of Mozart's music. After Herder's critics against the pomp and circumstance of the Italian opera seria, a demand for a popular 'Singspiel' grounded on the German mother tongue had been raised several times. Eventually this demand benefited from the powerful support of the Austrian Emperor Joseph II. The 'Singspiel' is regarded as a compromise between the baroque opera seria and the later opera buffa, which was an adaption of French comic opera. Hence a 'Singspiel' could encompass both serious and comic parts and grotesque motifs, as long as they served a moral educating purpose (Mehnert 2005: 72).

Confirming both European and Austrian self-esteem, the opera also linked Enlightenment ideas of freedom and equality to notions of religious and moral superiority. In the story of the freedom-loving and bold Spanish nobleman Belmonte, infiltrating the court and seraglio of the brutal pasha Selim and his ridiculous supervisor Osmin in order to free the honourable and virtuous Spanish lady Konstanze, Mozart seems to excel in Orientalist clichés. The abduction motif was already well established as a popular motif in contemporary 'Turk operas' (Johann Adolf Hasse's *Die Pilger aus Mekka* and Christoph Willbald Gluck's *La Recontre imprévue*) (Mehnert 2005: 69). Osmin could be interpreted as an example of the comic version of Orientalism with carnivalesque features. In his famous study *Orientalism: Western Images of the Orient*, Edward Saïd showed how Europeans depicted non-Europeans as a kind of negative reflection of themselves, with the image of the sensual but silent Oriental woman and the barbaric and irrational Oriental man confirming the self-image of the Europeans as being rational and progressive. Saïd points at the works of Mark Twain and Gustave Flaubert, depicting the Arabs and the Orient as a living tableau of peculiarities, frequently linked to bazaars and marketplaces. In these tableaus, the distinction between private and public is dissolved in a carnivalesque manner.

Mozart's opera sets off in the seraglio of Pasha Selim, where Konstanze is held prisoner. Together with her maid Blonde and servant Pedrillo, she has been ambushed and kidnapped by pirates and shipped to a slave market. Even so, Edward Saïd did not consider it an unambiguously Orientalist opera. As a matter of fact, Pasha Selim offers the ladies rather humane conditions after having bought them at the slave market. One should also consider the fact that the opera plot takes place in the middle of the 16th century, at the time when the Ottoman Empire reached its zenith under Süleyman, including Anatolia, the Middle East, parts of Northern Africa and parts of Southern Europe. Even though the Ottomans were no longer considered insuperable since the defeat at Lepanto in 1571, they still represented an imperial superpower. And the contemporary relation between Austria and Turkey would hence fit very badly into Säid's Orientalism scheme. In Saïd the relation between Europe and the Orient is conceived of as a relation between a manipulative defining power and its passive, colonized other. Although the concept of Europe had been launched in 1549 as a church political slogan by Pope Pius II in order to mobilize the Catholic principals to 'dislodge the Turks from Europe by God's hand', most Europeans in Mozart's time did not yet consider themselves Europeans. From the 16th century onwards to the end of the 18th century the notions "Europe" and "Christianity" were frequently used as synonymous terms. As a political slogan the notion "Europe" emerged in two historical crises: In the 15th century, when it was launched by Pope Pius II as a mobilizing slogan against the Muslim Turks. In the 17th century it was used by Protestant and Catholic states, which felt that their entire existence was threatened by the dominant super power of France. In medieval times the distinction between Christians and pagans was the most powerful criterium for making identities on macro level. In the case of the Church fathers, the notion "nations" mainly referred to pagan tribes as opposed to Christians. These kind of axes are referred to by Reinhard Koselleck as 'inside-outside-relations' (Koselleck 1989). On the other hand the concept "nation" mostly referred to nobility or families, which were privileged by birth and property and defined by way of contrast to the unprivileged layers of the population. According to Koselleck, these groups were defined by a vertical above-below-relation.

As a notion "Europe" was only used on rare occasions, such as the convention of Mantua in 1459, where Pope Pius II called upon the most powerful princes of Christianity in order to mobilize them to engage in a common crusade against the new infidel enemy, the Ottoman Turks. Consequently the convention decided, 'by the help of God to dislodge the Turk from Europe' (Christensen 1988: 67). By using this slogan the convention confirmed the idea of the European continent as the home of the Christians, even though there were at the time older Church communities in Africa and the Middle East. Furthermore the formula European = Christian marked the beginning of a transition from an educated cosmographical description level to the current political level of the Church. As a consequence of this formula the concept of Europe was launched as a realm which belonged to Christians, and where the Turkish Muslims were excluded.

In a letter to the German humanist, Cardinal Nicolas of Kues, Pope Pius points out that the conquest of Jerusalem by the Turkish Ottomans in 1453 was the greatest tragedy in the history of Christianity. In particular he expressed his concerns about the loss which European culture had experienced after the Ottoman conquest of Greece, which he described as the source of European art and science. This resulted in the Ottoman Turks being launched as Europe's 'Other' along an east-western axis. Pope Pius also stressed that the Catholic Christianity should be the leading confession, despite the fact that he knew there were forces on the continent aiming to create independent national churches and to break with the Catholic Church as a guardian in the field of Church rituals and organization. Hence the identification between Europe and Catholic Christianity also implied a hierarchical above-below-relation with the true Catholic Christians on top, and the so called heretics at the bottom.

The notion "Europe" was commonly restricted to a context where the enemies of Christianity as well as their actions were mentioned (Christensen 1988). Afterwards "Europe" vanished from spoken language until it was re-launched at the turn from Enlightenment to Romanticism in the 18th century. From then on, in accordance with the concept "nation", "Europe" as a notion was loaded with political and ideological meaning and also received a historical time dimension through the utopian narratives of a great past (i.e. medieval times) and a glorious future, which could include all Europeans and mobilize them against the infidel and backward peoples and nations.

In this narrative the siege of Vienna in 1683 played a crucial part, confirming both European unity and European virtues, such as liberty and braveness on the one hand, and Ottoman backwardness, barbarism and cowardice on the other. In reality the remaining Austrian defenders and five thousand civilians were quite close to giving in to the more than 100.000 Ottoman attackers with their fifteen thousand tenants, accompanied by their cooks, wives and concubines. The King of Austria, Leopold 1., was also titled Emperor of the German-Roman Empire, which was not a national state, but rather a conglomerate of countries and principalities in Western and Central Europe. The German-Roman Empire was partly concurrent with the Western Roman Empire, which had collapsed already in 476 AD together with its capital Rome.

The Emperor was crowned by the Pope in Rome and considered himself the legitimate successor of the former Roman Emperors. On the other hand the Eastern Roman Empire with its capital Constantinople had lasted until 1453, when it was conquered by the Ottoman Sultan Mehmet 2., who considered himself the legitimate successor of the former Emperors of the Eastern Roman Empire. Consequently there were a Sultan in the East and an Emperor in the West, who were both claiming the same throne. Unfortunately King Leopold was at the same time at war with France. But to Pope Innocens II and the profoundly religious King Leopold the war against the Ottomans was far more important, because it was conceived as a war between Christianity and Islam. The Pope therefore proclaimed Holy War and succeeded in mobilizing the King of Poland, Jan 3. Sobieski, who signed an agreement, according to which the Poles should assist King Leopold in case of an attack against Vienna, and Leopold should assist the Poles if they were attacked (Stoye 1965: 200 ff.). During the battle of Vienna, atrocities were carried out on both sides, confirming Austrian stereotypes of Ottoman barbarism. In a song called "The Bloody Siege of VIENNA", the anonymous poet, who claims he has participated in the battle, describes the ravaging Turkish army in the following poem:

Three Hundred Thousand Turks in Rage,
Who never spared Sex nor Age;
In Seven Hundred Leagues they Marcht,
Till they VIENNA did Invest:
They raised Batteries round the Town,
Which did Command the highest Towers;
Candy, nor Rhoads, nor Christian Crown,
Was never assaulted by such Powers (Anonymous 1688: 1).

Eventually the ten thousand Austrian defenders were only rescued by the brave intervention of Polish troops under Jan Sobieski's command. According to an Ottoman eyewitness it looked as if "a river of black pitch came streaming down the hill, burning and destroying everything which stood in its way" (Stoye 1965: 256 ff). In Vienna Sobieski was celebrated as the liberator of the town, passing on the following statement to the Pope: "We came, we saw and God conquered". In the abandoned Ottoman tenant camp the luting Polish and Austrian troops found supplies, which would alter the European kitchen and fashion for centuries: Coffee beans, turbans, music instruments led to a new taste for cappuccino, croissants and janissary music, which was later imitated by both Haydn and Mozart.

To the Austrians, who had resisted the Ottoman sieges in both 1529 and 1683, Mozart's opera had a special meaning: it did not only confirm European self-esteem and Austrian nationalism in a particular mixture, with Enlightenment ideals of freedom and equality being associated with notions of religious and moral superiority. Representing a closed and mysterious world to European men, the Ottoman harem also represented a political and philosophical threshold between the Orient and the Occident. That is: between oppression and freedom, between stagnation and progress, between despotism and individualism and between unreason and reason, which in this case could also be synonymous with Christianity. But as in Montesquieu's novel *Lettres Persannes* and Voltaire's tragedy *Zaïre*, the Oriental motifs could also be interpreted as a disguised attack on the feudal conditions applying in contemporary Europe, allowing the princes and nobility to implement legislation and treat their subjects in a high-handed and abusive way. According to this reading, the gates of the harem represent an inner moral border between oppression and freedom, in the Orient as well as in the Occident, and between the arbitrary abuse of power and human dignity. This partly static dichotomy, resembling the Orientalist schema in Saïd, is however disrupted by the border-crossing motifs in the play. These motifs are Selim's conversion from Christianity to

Islam, Belmonte and Pedrillo's infiltration of the harem, and finally the abduction itself, which is only allowed thanks to Selim's rehumanization.

Mozart's operas *The Magic Flute* and *The Abduction* both depict Orientals with human features. But why does Pasha Selim turn 'nice' at the end of the opera as he forgives Belmonte and liberates him together with the three other European characters? The answer turns out to be that Selim was originally a Christian nobleman who later turned to Islam. Both in Bretzner's 'Singspiel' and Mozart's opera, Pasha Selim appears as a Christian renegade who turned to an inner exile in Turkey after personal disappointments. At the end of the novel, Selim recognizes Belmonte as his long-lost son, whom he had to give up as a four-year-old to the monastery of St. Sebastian, more or less in accordance with the pattern of the Greek-Hellenist adventure novel, as we shall see. However, this scene was altered by Mozart, allowing Selim to recognize Belmonte as the son of his arch enemy, who once caused his disaster. Hence Selim's transgression of the border between the Occident and the Orient coincides with the transgression of an inner religious threshold, even though in Mozart's rationalist-optimistic conclusion this transgression appears to be reversible.

According to Mikhail Bakhtin's famous chronotope essay, the chronotope marks a process in which time is visualized in a literary work of art and the categories of time run together with spatial categories. This also means that in the chronotope, the space appears in an intensified manner in the sequences of time. Only when visualized as space does floating time gain outlines, direction and intelligibility. In this sense, the chronotope also marks the 'border of the borders':

> In the literary artistic chronotope, spatial and temporal indicators are fused into one carefully thought-out, concrete whole. Time, as it were, thickens, takes on flesh, becomes artistically visible; likewise, space becomes charged and responsive to the movements of time, plot and history. This intersection of axes and fusion of indicators characterizes the artistic chronotope (Bakhtin 2008: 84).

In his essay on the chronotope, Bakhtin outlines the way in which different historical genres are defined by specific chronotope schemas which are remarkably stable throughout history. The first example mentioned by Bakhtin is the adventure time of the Greek romance. The adventure chronotope schema can also be recognized in the libretto of Mozart's opera *The Abduction:* the coincidental meeting between a young man and woman, Belmont and Constanze, who are overwhelmed by a sudden passion for one another. Then certain obstacles and obstructions occur: an urgent journey into exotic countries, and Constanze's slavery after being attacked by pirates on open sea, followed by her imprisonment in Pasha Selim's harem, her resistance to Selim's advances, and the adventurous escape after the intervention of Pedrillo and Belmont. And finally her happy reunion with her beloved.

One of the characteristics of the adventure time is the number of coincidences and the uncertain duration of the action: at the end of the story the characters seem to have met only yesterday. Hence Mozart's and Bretzner's libretto seems to follow more or less the composite schema of the 'adventure novel of ordeal' outlined by Bakhtin:

> There is a boy and a girl of marriageable age. Their lineage is unknown, mysterious (but not always: there is, for example, no such instance in Tacitus). They are remarkable for their exceptional beauty. They are also exceptionally chaste. They meet each other unexpectedly, usually during some festive holiday. A sudden and instantaneous passion flares up between them that is as irresistible as fate, like an incurable disease. However, the marriage cannot take place straightaway. They are confronted with obstacles that retard and delay their union. The lovers are parted, they seek one another, find one another; again they lose each other, again they find each other. There are the usual obstacles and adventures of lovers: the abduction of the bride on the eve of the wedding, … their journey, a storm at sea, a shipwreck, a miraculous rescue, an attack by pirates, captivity and prison, an attempt on the innocence of the hero and heroine, the offering-up of the heroine as a purifying sacrifice, wars, battles, being sold into slavery, presumed deaths, disguising one's identity, recognition and failures of recognition, presumed betrayals, attempts on chastity and fidelity, false accusations of crimes, court trials, court inquiries into the chastity and fidelity of the lovers. … The novel ends happily with the lovers united in marriage. Such is the schema for the basic components of the plot (Bakhtin 2008: 87f.).

On a philosophical level, the harem seems to concentrate and spatialize a certain European philosophy of history. A major precondition for the emergence of this new philosophical discipline, and along with it the rise of modern nationalism, was a fundamental shift of the European time conception, which Walter Benjamin has described as a turn from the Messianic time conception of the Middle Ages to the modern conception of time as 'empty' and 'homogenous' (Benjamin 1997: 700-703). According to the Messianic time conception, time was inseparably linked to place and to the expectation that the Messiah would return at any point of time. It was therefore unnecessary to conceive of time in more extensive historical lines. To the medieval mind, there was a 'now' that was inseparably linked to a 'here'. Time only existed if it 'took place' and was conceived of as an expandable moment which was inseparably tied to the locality in which it was experienced. Places far away were accordingly projected far back in time. In the wake of new 18th century discoveries and technical inventions, such as the invention of the chronometer and the synchronization of the homogenous global time by the division of time meridians, time could be gradually separated from space, and a new conception of time as empty and homogenous emerged (Anderson 1996: 22-36).

To the medieval mind, time had been filled with mythological and religious meaning and stories, serving as moral examples. In the new homogenous time conception, these stories were replaced by history, which in turn was filled with new meanings and narratives, such as the concept of progress. European experiences of non-European civilizations had confirmed a certain feeling of accelerating progress among Europeans, allowing them to think of history in a linear or helical scheme of technical, scientific and political progress, for instance in terms of the Enlightenment, freedom and human rights. Within this new historical scheme of self-interpretation, some cultures could be thought of as modern and progressive, while others were conceived of as backward. The German historian Reinhart Koselleck has also referred to this period as 'Sattelzeit' (saddle time) or 'Schwellenzeit" (threshold time); that is a time in which the Europeans experienced a growing gap between the current realm of experience and their horizon of future expectation, allowing new political ideologies and utopian narratives to emerge, such as those of the national community and its future prosperity (Koselleck 1989a: 349-375). Accordingly, Voltaire and Kant launched competing utopian drafts of a future European League of Nations, ruled by democratically elected governments, thereby securing the welfare of their citizens and striving towards the regulative ideal of the perpetual peace and happiness of mankind by mutual agreements and obligations (Kant 1987).

Kant's liberal Utopia of a democratic League of Nations would later on be disputed by the German poet Novalis, or Fredrich von Hardenberg, who in his essay "Christianity or Europe" idolized Christian medieval culture as a state of religious-aesthetic harmony, hoping that the alienating process of modernization eventually would dissolve itself and make room for a new religious spirituality in a future Europe (Novalis 1989: 327-346). In our time, the definition of Europe as being synonymous with medieval Catholic Christianity has been relaunched along with the Siege of Vienna and radicalized in a rather dangerous and martial manner inside the anti-jihad movement, which brought fuel to the fire that exploded so tragically in Norway on 22 July 2011.

In Mozart's opera however, the historical time inside the Turkish harem appears to be static, allowing despotism, immaturity and unreason to overwinter. The harem also appears as a historical space in which enlightenment and humanity could be reversed, as in the case of Selim. In contrast, the Europeans Belmonte and Constanze and their allies Blonde and Pedrillo epitomise the future optimism of European Enlightenment and its conception of time as a progressive and linear medium of enlightenment and liberation, at least to the Europeans themselves. In the seraglio, static and cyclic Oriental time confronts the progressive and linear time represented by the Europeans. At the same time the meetings and separations of the characters seem to represent an intercultural exchange, triggering off the action of the opera. Hence the presence of Constanze and Blonde in the seraglio gains a different meaning than the presence of Selim and the other harem concubines. The harem motif itself represents the negation of European humanist and emancipatory ideas, allowing for a new reflexive legitimation and renegotiation of Europeanness.

In a gender perspective it is also interesting to notice Constanze's virtuous resistance to the partly threatening and seductive Selim's advancements, and the English character Blonde's anticipating ideas of gender equality. Similar ideas of a more just social hierarchy between men and women and women's educational rights had already been advocated at the turn from the 17th to the 18th century by early feminist writers like Mary Astell (O'Brien 2009). In the opera, they have a metonymical and allegorical function as images of the Austrian nation's patriotic virtues and resistance to the political and military threat of the Ottoman Empire. At the same time, Constanze and Belmonte represent the law of free romantic love, from which Selim is excluded and alienated because he has become internally oppressed through the disappointments and insults he has suffered in his own past. His inner exile in a Turkish seraglio may be interpreted as an image of the inner forces of mankind, keeping it from seizing its own freedom and from recognizing the freedom and dignity of others. Two years later, Kant would make his famous statement in his Enlightenment essay "What is Enlightenment?": "Aufklärung ist der Ausgang des Menschen aus seiner selbstverschuldteten Unmündigkeit". (Enlightenment is the exodus of Man from his self-inflicted immaturity.) (Kant 1994: 9).

In Mozart's opera the seraglio appears as a chronotope battlefield, where both immaturity and man's exodus from his inner and outer subjugation is visualized. Reading Mozart's libretto as a romantic love comedy, cleansed of any political or bodily impurity, would be nothing less than a banal underestimation of the opera.

The romantic expectation of "pure" love and music contrasts with the carnivalesque dimension of Mozart's elaboration of Bretzner's libretto *Belmonte und Constanze*. Threats about rape and savage torture ("Martern aller Arten") go hand in hand with drinking and fighting scenes. Both the musical janissary motif of the overture and the libretto establish an ideological and philosophical contradiction between the Orient and the Occident, between despotism and individualism, between oppression and free love. Nevertheless, the text had to obey the musical demands for beautiful sound, as Mozart points out in one of his letters to his father Leopold. At the same time, Mozart benefits from the musical drama to perform some breathtaking shifts and turns of the harmony keys that would not have been possible in a purely instrumental work. This can be illustrated by Mozart's transformation of the harem supervisor Osmin from a stereotype into a character, bearing individual features, as prescribed by Lessing in his *Hamburgische Dramaturgie*. "Osmin's rage", Mozarts writes in a letter to his father, "is made ridiculous by using Turkish music" (Geck 2006: 264). Furthermore, he writes that 'the janissary orchestra offers everything one could demand – short and funny, written all according to the Vienna taste" (Kvist 2009: 176).

In the same manner as the janissary music stresses and makes fun of Oriental warrior culture, Osmin's solemn aria stresses Oriental unreason and brutality through a number of logical self-contradictions:

Erst geköpft, dann gehangen,
Dann gespiesst auf heissen Stangen,
Dann verbrannt, dann gebunden
Und getaucht; zuletzt geschunden (Mozart 2005: 12)

(First beheaded, then hanged
Then impaled on hot poles
Then burned, then tied up
And ducked under, finally skinned).

This was not sensational in contemporary theatre and opera, which was far more carnivalesque than is commonly recognized today. The popular Vienna Burgtheater, directed by Mozart's friend Emanuel Schikaneder, was no exception to this rule. The example also shows how the music medium itself can work ideologically and does not depend entirely on the text medium and dramatic performance for its ideological content. In the letters concerning *The Abduction*, Mozart develops an entire form of opera aesthetics, leaving behind the representation of a dominating passion, such as rage, as prescribed by the baroque opera seria. Instead, Mozart managed to depict the characters in dialogic cooperation. As in Osmin's part, the music does not only illustrate but also gesticulates and allows a harmonic boldness which could only be possible within the musical drama. Hence the text and action release an astonishing vitality in the music. Another example is the romance "In Mohrenland gefangen", where Belmont's servant Pedrillo expresses his homesickness in seven times and with seven different keys, without being at home in any of them.

In romanticist culture, the gesture of carnivalesque culture, transforming high and low and dwelling with all kinds of bodily inputs, outputs and openings, was gradually repressed by a sublime official culture. The idolization of Mozart as a melancholic-immaculate genius, as depicted in Eduard Mörike's short story "Mozart auf der Reise nach Prag", and even in some current music criticism (Wikshåland 2007), illustrates this repression. Any reader with some knowledge of Mozart's life, correspondence and historical environment is familiar with this misrepresentation. For instance, some of Mozart's letters are so bizarre that they were censored for a long time or interpreted as expressions of madness or anal fixation. As in the case of the letters he wrote to his cousin Maria Anna Tekla Mozart, called Bäsle, which is Austrian for cousin. In 1778 Mozart writes to Bäsle:

> ... victoria! – unsre arsch sollen die friedens-zeichen seyn! – ich dachte wohl, dass sie mir nicht länger widerstehen könnten. ja ja, ich bin meiner sache gewis, und sollt ich heut noch machen einen schiss, obwohl ich in 14 Tagen geh nach Paris. Wenn sie mir also wolln antworten, aus der stadt Augsburg dorten, so schreiben sie mir baldt, damit ich den brief erhalt, sonst wenn ich etwa schon bin weck, bekomme ich statt einen brief einen dreck. Dreck! – dreck! – o dreck! – o süsses wort! – dreck! – schmeck! – auch schön! – dreck, schmeck! – dreck!leck – o charmante! – dreck, leck! – das freüet mich! – dreck, schmeck und leck! – schmeck dreck, und leck dreck! – Nun um auf etwas anderes zu kommen; ... (Mozart 1978: 117).

> (victoria! – our arses shall be signs of peace! – as I expected you would no longer be able to resist me. yes, yes, I am sure of it, and if today I were to take a shit, though in a fortnight I leave for Paris. If you will answer me, from the town of Augsburg yonder, then do it quickly, so that I receive the letter, otherwise if I am gone already, instead of a letter I will get a piece of shit. Shit! – shit! – oh shit – oh sweet word! – shit! – taste! – also sweet! – shit, taste! – shit!lick – oh charming – shit, lick! – it pleases me! – shit, taste and lick! – taste shit and lick shit! – Now to speak of something else; ...)

But Mozart's mother also sometimes spiced up her letters with carnivalesque effects (Kvist 2009: 165):

> Adio ben mio good health to you! Put your arse to your mouth. I wish you good night! Shit in your bed until it creaks. It's already up to your ears, and now you can rhyme yourself.

Actually these letters expressed quite common social codes at the courts and among the upper citizenry of Mozart's contemporary Vienna. Mozart and his family were living in a time when crime was punished with inhuman torture and public executions.

Both Mozart and his father were to be considered villeins as long as they were employed at the Salzburg court. And Mozart would risk penalty if he left the court without permission. The Oriental harem eunuchs shared their fate with the castrati, performing in Mozart's early operas. Accordingly, the masquerades and bodily humour at the Vienna courts and among the citizenry can be interpreted as carnivalesque, although they were invented by the upper class.

One last problem should be mentioned, namely Mozart's claim that the libretto texts were excessively determined by the music in his operas. In other words, that there was a hegemony of music over literature. In a letter to his father in 1781 Mozart writes:

> To music verses are probably pretty indispensable – but rhyme for rhyme's own sake is most harmful. Those who view things so pedantically will go to the dogs along with their music (Kvist 2009: 165).

And he adds: "The opera text is always the obedient daughter of the music" (Kvist 2009: 176). In his staging of Mozart's opera at the Nordic Impulses Festival in Bergen in 2007, the director Calixto Bieito turned the Orientalist edge of the 'Singspiel' into a critical mirror reflecting the current Occident, moving the plot into the brutal world of modern Western trafficking. Accordingly, Bieito showed how violence and brutalization could haunt both offenders and victims, letting Belmone and Pedrillo, blinded by hatred, kill the remaining harem concubines, while Konstanze shoots Pasha Selim during her escape. By showing violence, including sexual violence, as a universal inner threat both to 'Oriental' and 'Occidental' societies, Bieito challenged some of the cultural borders and dichotomies of Mozart's opera. Hence the Catalonian director transgressed not only the Western image of the Oriental and its physical and cultural borders, but also our stereotypical concepts of violence, love monogamy and individual and political freedom as cultural border markers between Orient and Occident. But Bieito's twist could also be viewed as a dialogisation of Saïd's concept of Orientalism and of Franz Fanon's disclosure of colonized identity as excessively determined by the colonizer's gaze, and of post-colonialist culture as a sub-conscious reflection of hegemonic colonialist culture and dichotomies (Fanon 1988).

Depicting the violence not only as a legitimate strategy for liberation, but also as a sub-conscious continuation of colonialist logics, Bieito reveals the sad dialectics of such liberation, which is implemented as a pure negation of hegemonic power. To overcome this antagonism, another exodus must take place: the transgression of the dichotomy between subjugators and subjugated, colonizers and colonized, leading to a mutual recognition of human freedom and dignity:

Nichts ist so hässlich als die Rache;
Hingegen menschlich, gütig sein
Und ohne Eigennutz verzeihn,
Ist nur der grossen Seelen Sache (Mozart 2005: 57).

(Nothing is so hideous as revenge;
Yet to be human, kind
And to forgive without self-interest
Only great souls are capable of)

## Bibliography

Anonymous (1688). *The Bloody Siege of VIENNA. A Song Wherein the Turks have lost One Hundred and Sixty Thousand Men; being the greatest Victory that ever was obtained over the Turks, since the Foundation of the Ottoman Empire. Written by an English Gentleman Volunteer, that was at the Garrison during the Siege.*

Bakhtin, M. (2008). "Forms of time and of the chronotope in the novel" in: *The Dialogical Imagination. Four Essays by M.M. Bakhtin*, transl. Emerson, Caryl & Holquist, Michael. Austin: University of Texas Press.

Bakhtin, M. (1986). "Toward a Methodology for the Human Sciences" in: *Speech Genres and Other Late Essays.* Emerson, Caryl & Holquist, Michael (ed.). transl. McGee, Vern W. Austin: University of Texas Press.

Benjamin, W. (1997). *Über den Begriff der Geschichte* in: Benjamin, W. *Gesammelte Schriften,* vol. 1.2. Frankfurt a.M.: Suhrkampf.

Bretzner, C.F. (1785). *Arien und Gesänge aus der Oper: Die Entführung aus dem Serail.* Hamburg.

Christensen, S. (1988). "Europa som slagord". *Europas opdagelse. Historien om en idé.* Boll-Johansen, Hans & Harbsmeier, Michael (ed.). København: Christian Ejlers'forlag.

Fanon, F. (2008). *Black Skin, White Masks,* transl. by Charles Lam Markman. London: Pluto Press.

Geck, M. (2006). *Mozart. Eine Biographie.* Hamburg: Rowohlt.

Kant, I. (1994). "Beantwortung der Frage: Was ist Aufklärung?". *Was ist Aufklärung? Thesen und Definitionen.* Ehrhard Bahr (ed.). Stuttgart: Reclam.

Kant, I. (1987). *Zum ewigen Frieden. Ein philosophischer Entwurf.* Malter, R. (ed.). Stuttgart: Phillip Reclam jun.

Koselleck, R. (1989a). "'Erfahrungsraum' und 'Erwartungshorizont' – zwei historische Kategorien" in: Koselleck, R. *Vergangene Zukunft. Zur Semantik geschichtlicher Zeiten.* Frankfurt a.M.: Suhrkampf, 349-375.

Koselleck, R. (1989b). "Zur historisch-politischen Semantik asymmetrischer Gegenbegriffe" in: Koselleck, R. *Vergangene Zukunft. Zur Semantik geschichtlicher Zeiten.* Frankfurt a.M.: Suhrkampf Verlag.

Kvist, B. (2009). *Mozart. Mennesket bak musikken.* Oslo: Opera Forlag.

Mehnert, H. (2005). "Nachwort", Mozart, Wolfgang Amadeus: *Die Entführung aus dem Serail.* Stuttgart: Reclam.

Mozart, W.A. (2005). *Die Entführung aus dem Serail.* Stuttgart: Reclam.

Mozart, W.A. (1978). *Mozarts Bäsle-Briefe,* published and commented upon by Joseph Heinz Eibl and Walter Senn. Stuttgart: Reclam.

Novalis. (1989). "Die Christenheit oder Europa" in: *Novalis. Werke in einem Band.* Berlin and Weimar: Aufbau-Verlag, 327-346.

O'Brien, K. (2009). *Women and Enlightenment in Eighteenth-Century Britain.* Cambridge: Cambridge University Press.

Røssaak, E. (1998). "Orientalisme". *Vinduet,* vol. 52, No. 3.

Skorgen, T. (2007). "Mozart som orientalist". *Bergens Tidende,* 17.07.2006.

Wikshåland, S. (2007). "Når kjærlighet blir et fremmedord". *Dagbladet,* 04.06.

# The Female Body, Landscape and National Identity

*Sigrun Åsebø*

The concept of landscape, and consequently landscape art, plays an important part in the construction of Norwegian identity both historically and today. Norway is sold to tourists as a place of untouched nature, and Norwegians in general identify strongly with the idea of landscape in its national romantic tradition. Going hiking or spending time alone in the mountains is highly rated as a recreational activity, and symbolically it seems to unite Norwegians. Learning to appreciate landscape aesthetically and to take pride in peasant culture was essential in the construction of the nation in the 19th century, and the tradition of landscape and the concept of nature runs through Norwegian canonical art history up until the 1960's and beyond.

The goal of this chapter is to show how the construction of gendered bodies and identities are dependent upon and inherent in the boundaries that put in place "Norwegian landscape" as a tradition at the root of our national art historical canon. A central element in dealing with landscape is our perception of space, and how space is formed in and by social, psychic, and cultural subjectivities and in turn shapes those very same categories. The borders of the nation are both imaginary and "real". Political and physical border spaces are easily identified, and as a space the nation seems at first sight to be a given entity. Any topographical area within the politically set borders of Norway could be a Norwegian landscape. Still, if we take a closer look at our visual culture, we may all agree that the boundaries separating "Norwegian" landscapes from the mere "ordinary" landscapes are far from identical with the actual political borders: not all landscapes are elevated and given status as expressions of "Norwegianness". Landscapes are as much a way of seeing as they are a matter of mere physical topography, if such a thing even exists.

This article deals with the imaginary borders and boundaries that take part in the construction of a national art historical canon and its landscapes. Borders may in many ways be cultural constructs, but they have "real" consequences for the people who are affected by them. Traditionally women and men are accorded different access to the imaginary, psychic, social or geographical spaces that form the basis of landscape art, and are hence placed differently in relation to national identity. How does this affect women artists working with the concept and tradition of landscape? Here I will deal with A K Dolven and Mari Slaattelid, who are known for art projects that quote or in other ways reference canonical art history and art practices. How do they deal with gender and the body in relation to landscapes? To what extent may we read their re-workings of the tradition of landscape painting as more than mere postmodern play with history and visual culture? And in what sense do their practices have feminist effects, making them specifically important to those of us living partly under the sign of "femininity"?

## Femininity, women artists and contemporary historical landscapes

In her article "Where the visual gets the last word", written in connection with Slaattelid's exhibition *Loud and Close. Kisses and Dust* in 2006, Bente Larsen points to the dialogic aspects of Slaattelid's work. She claims that Slaattelid "engages in an on-going dialogue with art history so as to claim it, in a sense, as her own" (Larsen 2006).[1] In my view, that little "her" in this quotation must be understood as more than a grammatical necessity. I am not arguing that Slaattelid *is* a "woman artist" in a traditional sense of the word, and that her art expresses a stable gendered identity. Neither Slaattelid nor Dolven place themselves *outside* of the art historical canon or insist on inherent femininity. Instead, I see their work as entering canonical art history and painting, from a position that destabilizes ideas of fixed identity and deconstructs sexual difference.[2] I read Dolven and Slaattelid's art as an example of what Teresa de

---

[1]   Larsen does not deal with gender or sexuality explicitly.

[2]   I do believe it is important to question categories like "woman artist", so as not to pass on ideologies of canonical art history into contemporary feminism. The term "woman artist" doesn't refer simply to artists who happen to be women. Historically it is a particular type of artist; the female type, who invests art with all her feminine creativity. See e.g. Pollock & Parker 1981. In a contemporary context, however, it also refers to the women's movement in the 1970's, who "appropriated" the term with all its connotations, in an attempt not only to valorize historical and contemporary women's artistic practices, but also to form discourses resisting an artistic norm that favoured white masculinity. Few contemporary artists identify with this feminism. Most Norwegian women who are artists do not want to be known as "women artists", but simply as artists. They are opposed both to canonical and feminist uses of the term. Still, removing the "woman" from artists who are women does not necessarily install utopia. Often it just conceals the contradictions of women acting as artists, upholding the illusion that artist as a term is gender neutral.

Lauretis calls a "view from elsewhere", defining this as "the elsewhere of discourse here and now, the blind spots, or the space-offs, of its representations" (de Lauretis as cited in Pollock 1999: 7). This involves moving our attention away from the spaces that are represented in or by a certain representation, to spaces that are implied, perhaps unseen, but still vital to the representation in question and its meanings. Feminism comes about in art not through the individual artist's beliefs and intentions, but as an effect of the artistic practice and its modes of meaning.

Throughout this chapter I refer to both gender and sexual difference, with gender being understood as a social category. The category "woman" and the concept of femininity refer to a specific group or political constituency. Femininity is an identity and an imaginary space that women are expected to inhabit. But as a space, femininity may also be understood as a structure of meaning. Femininity refers to the spaces "beyond the visible forms of gender, [it serves] to signal a radical alterity in relation to culture that dominates in the name of Man" (Pollock 1996: 70). In my view, Slaattelid and Dolven engage in the displacement of gender and insist on heterogeneity, the unsaid, the unnameable, as a potential that might open up for "critical confrontations with all forms of xenophobia: fears of difference, of the stranger, of the other" (Pollock 1996: 70).

Referencing is vital to the production of images and of meaning in general. Images always remind us of something we have seen before, and signs must be readable to qualify as signs and escape the status of non-sense. Art historical canons are built up as a system of reference. Art historians are not the only ones to insist on organizing historical material according to artist, themes and nationality. Artists choose their own predecessors and set up versions of the past, too. Often art history treats predecessors as *prior* to contemporary art, and we forget how history is always constructed to serve the needs of the present. In my view, quotations not only re-actualize the "original", but by doing so, they obliterate older images and create new versions of them (Bal 1999: 1). Any engagement with the past and its images must therefore be read as an active intervention. As such it has important implications for history. Accepting this means abandoning the idea that art history is a quest for intentions and inherent meaning. Iconographic readings of images, seeking meaning within the framed field or behind it in the artist/context, must give way to a study of the process of images, the effects of pictures and picturing. What are images doing for their users? (Pollock 1988: 147). What are the effects of Slaattelid and Dolven's practices for Norwegian art history and our conceptualization of the border separating "Norwegian landscapes" from mere nature?

## A K Dolven: *between two mornings*

When it comes to quoting, paraphrasing and referencing in general, Dolven is perhaps best known for her projects on Edvard Munch, an artist whose imagery we also find in Slaattelid's work. In this chapter, however, I turn towards work referencing romanticism and neo-romanticism, the sublime and the position of the body in relation to those spaces. Sublime landscapes and the tradition of the female nude are amongst the main topics referred to in the video *between two mornings*, which was first shown at Dolven's 2004 Music Festival Exhibition *Moving Mountain* at Bergen Kunsthall. *between two mornings* is a four-minute film showing four female nudes on a calm but rocky beach. A distant sun low on the horizon causes the scene to be bathed in yellow, orange and light purple. The bodies are motionless, and the only changes in the scenery are the relentless waves. Silence and tranquillity dominate despite the very loud film projector intentionally chosen to show the film. Books, mirrors, a necklace, lipsticks and sunglasses are scattered in the sand. Those objects break the illusion of otherworldliness brought about by the amputated torsos and the atmosphere, tying the bodies to the everyday life of women and our handbags. The camera is static; the film is unedited and uncut and relies on natural light. Art historians watching Dolven's videos almost all immediately see the reference to German romanticism and C.D. Friedrich. Norwegians, at least, will also recognize this as the sublime landscapes of national romanticism and especially J.C. Dahl (1788-1857). It is also likely that many will make the connection to Peder Balke (1804-87) and others known for representing Northern Norway or what the 17th and 18th centuries imagined as a Northern arcadia.[3]

---

[3]    We could read the imagery as comments upon the geography of "Norwegianness", with different areas being privileged at different periods in art history, and Northern Norway generally being constructed as a place of both nostalgia and raw and "real" nature. At the beginning of the 19th century we get the impression that "Norway" takes place in the fiords in the West and in the mountains, or that it could perhaps be seen in its pure and arcadian form in the northern part of the country. From the 1880s however, the untainted Norwegian soil and its people are to be found mainly in the woods or the inner parts of Eastern Norway, perhaps also along the southern coast of West Norway, such as Jæren and Ryfylke in the art of Kitty Kielland and Lars Hertervig. The North doesn't make the transition from a space for the experience of the sublime to a place for the everyday life of realism and plein-air painting. This can only take place amongst the farmers on the big farms in the east, whereas nostalgia and neo-romanticism demand moorland and woods and not the midnight sun. It is a paradox that coastal culture has been largely left out of

*Fig. 1. A K Dolven, "between two mornings", 2004, film still courtesy Galleri MGM Oslo, Wilkinson Gallery London og carlier | gebauer Berlin.*

A sensation that time has halted, that something is being held back, and a strong sense of beauty but also deep loss, dominates the effect. Dolven makes use of well known iconography from national romanticism and apparently stages contemplation, but disrupts our possibility to take pleasure in landscape or to transcend our fears and get access to the sublime in subtle ways.[4] The women appear amputated or as body fragments, and their baldness is deeply disturbing. It makes us think of cancer and death. For those of us familiar with the tradition of the female nude, the lack of hair stands in stark contrast to the

---

the canon, given that most people live along the long coastal line. For a discussion of the geography of Norwegian painting and the place of Northern Norway within this narrative, see Høydalsnes 2003.

4     This video should be seen in connection with another film by Dolven; *moving mountain,* which in the exhibition in question seemed to function almost as a mirror to *between two mornings* dealing with the same issues in reverse form. *between two mornings* is also closely connected to the film/installation called *between the morning and the handbag,* staging a similar female body and a beige handbag as if they were two items of the same type. For a more thorough discussion of the relation between the sublime and the feminine body, see Battersby 2007. Seip (2007: 203-237) reads the relation between landscape and the bodies in Dolven's video from a phenomenological point of view.

traditionally flowing hair symbolizing feminine sexuality. The sensuousness of the skin and the lack of hair make them highly ambivalent as representations of feminine beauty or femininity. By removing the hair Dolven explores the meaning of bodily boundaries and their relation to concepts such as nature and landscape.

## Mari Slaattelid and Lars Hertervig

Slaattelid is amongst Norway's best known artists, and works mainly with acrylic or oil paint on hard material such as plexi-glass or aluminium. She sometimes also uses photography. Her projects often manage to integrate a conceptual textuality or density with painterly problems. According to art historian Sverre Wyller, her art is filled with a latent melancholia. This is obvious in her recurrent choice of the artist Lars Hertervig (1830-1902) as her precursor and field of intervention (Wyller 2007).[5] Like Munch and the Swedish artist Carl Fredrich Hill, both of whom have been paraphrased by Slaattelid, he is known for being mentally ill. Hertervig was diagnosed with melancholia and for long periods of time he was cut off from his contemporaries.

Hertervig seems an obvious case for the study of the relation between the artist and painting, and between the artist and landscape. Many see Hertervig as carrying on the tradition from C.D. Friedrich, J.C. Dahl and the German painter and scientist Carl Gustav Carus's romanticist view of landscape and the artist. Carus saw art as science, and through the meticulous study of nature, the sensitive artistic subject could provide us with a deeper understanding of the processes and phenomena of nature itself. To art history, the connection between the artistic *soul* and landscape becomes very important. Not only does the neo-romanticism of his landscapes suggest that the trees should be read as expressions of his soul, his mental illness also strengthens art historical ideas of the artistic subject and creativity. Hertervig, Hill and Munch are all obvious examples of a certain artist's mythology, with talent being seen as inherent and bound to come through. Creativity borders

---

5    Wyller's article is available on the Mari Slaattelid's website, http://www.marislaattelid. com/a_good_painting_is_a_sensation.html. The title, "A Good Painting is a Sensation", refers both to sensation in the bodily sense of the word, and to the rarity of good paintings. Wyller claims that Slaattelid's quest for the perfect painting is part of her melancholia.

on madness. Lack of recognition serves as proof of the artists' being either ahead of their time, or too creative (contemporary culture only recognized the madness and not the genius).[6] Art history constantly grapples with the question: should his art be interpreted as an expression of his mental illness, or can the dying trees and the gloomy woods and moorlands simply be re-inscribed into the traditional narratives of art history as expressions of artistic problems?

Slaattelid negotiates the boundaries between the artist's body, mind and the spaces that are supposed to mirror them in both her exhibitions on Hertervig. The first of these was at Rogaland Art Museum in Stavanger in 2002, and the second was at the National Museum of Art, Architecture and Design in Oslo in 2004. In both she included Hertervig's paintings, texts on or by him, and her own re-workings in the form of photography and paintings. The installations seemed driven by a wish to move in closer on both the artist and his work, and to investigate the mythology of the artist's soul as present in the landscape.

The half-dead trees of Hertervig's paintings are often read as self-portraits, indicating his solitude, his isolation from other artists and lack of recognition, not to forget his melancholia. Slaattelid deals with trees as the embodied self in several smaller paintings, for example *Actual Mental and Bodily Incidents in Düsseldorf*, which was shown in the 2002 exhibition in Stavanger. The text written underneath the trees (which is also the title) could be read as an attempt to strengthen the symbolism of the trees, by repeating the message art history generally reads in them. The effect, however, is parallel to Barbara Krüger's textual manipulations by revealing the underlying structure of meaning, the illusion of the image is broken. Instead of getting closer to the artistic soul and to nature itself, Slaattelid leaves us with a feeling of loss and distance. How could these trees ever *incarnate* Hertervig's mind?

Slaattelid goes on to study his paintings by way of photography. It is an analytical approach. She photographs sections of his paintings. In some she leaves the flash visible on the surface, and in others she treats the film with acid or light, making the surface appear damaged. The series *Haunted Landscape* from 2002 is one example. The same interest and intervention on the surface of the painting is also present in the series *Romantic Backdrop* from 2004 and the largest photograph of the 2004 exhibition: *Solitaire*. They all show the same

---

[6]   For a discussion of the reception of Hertervig within Norwegian art history, see also Renberg (2002) which sums up the main tendencies in the reception of Hertervig.

*Fig. 2. Mari Slaattelid. "Actual Mental and Bodily Incidents in Düsseldorf", 2002, Acrylic on paper, (100 x 115 cm), copyright M. Slaattelid/BONO.*

part of Hertervig's painting *Skogtjern* (1865), photographed by Slaattelid, who has left the reflection of the flash visible on the surface. *Solitaire* is a converted version, a negative, and the flash appears as a big black sun weighing down the brownish sky behind white, dying trees.[7] To sum up, both Slaattelid and Dolven deal with a specific moment in Norwegian art history, romanticism, and with the place of the body and the artistic subject in relation to a romanticist view of landscape. What part does this play in Norwegian art history, how might it be related to gender and sexual difference?

## The birth of the nation and of art

Norwegian intellectuals imported their definition of nation directly from Germany. The cultural theorists and philosophers J.G. Fichte and J.G. Herders's ideas of the nation as a unified geographical, cultural and spiritual entity became very important. Nordic nations constructed themselves upon a founda-

---

[7]     This has been interpreted as a reference to Julia Kristeva's book, *Soleil Noir, Depression et mélancolie*, from 1985. Bente Larsen, op. cit., and Paasche 2004.

tion of kinship and custom. This might be seen as opposed to a French model as articulated by historian Ernest Renan in 1882, defining the state as a mutual consent to a form of citizenship defined by social contract (Facos 1998: 28).[8]

The strong hold of landscape on Norwegian identity can partly be seen as an effect of this ideology with all its metaphors of roots and connections between geography and mentality. This is historically related to the work done to establish Norway as an independent nation at the beginning of the 19th century. Norway had been colonized by Denmark since the Middle Ages, but broke loose partially in 1814. However, Norway was forced into a union with Sweden in 1815 by the Treaty of Kiel, to compensate Sweden for the loss of Finland to Russia after the Napoleonic Wars. The union with Sweden lasted until 1905. Norway enjoyed a degree of self-determination, and a Norwegian constitution was signed in 1814.

Both the nation and Norwegian painting were apparently born from nature itself. Most books claiming to present an overview of Norwegian art through the ages trace art back to the Viking era or the Middle Ages, with specific focus on the medieval stave churches and wooden crafts. However, it seems hard to dispute the fact that Norwegian art originated in romanticism, and was fathered by the painter J.C. Dahl. According to Gunnar Danbolt in his book on Norwegian art history, J.C. Dahl was the first to realize that Norway did not only consist of nature, but also of *landscapes* (Danbolt 1996: 154). The moment of revelation, when J.C. Dahl finally *saw* that the land was sublime, puts Norway in contact with international art. This merging of C.D. Friedrich, German romanticism and Norwegian topography in the art and mind of J.C. Dahl liberated the visual field from its status as a supporting discipline in travel literature or as a handicraft: a typical example of the narrative of purification of the visual field so important to traditional art history. The act of seeing, or more precisely access to a specific way of looking, is vital to the establishment of the boundary between ordinary nature in Norway and "Norwegian landscape". Nature must be elevated, it must be seen by or filtered through a creative mind in order for it to be landscape and for Norwegian art history to begin.

If we read on in Danbolt's text we find that J.C. Dahl not only discovered the wilderness, he also saw that this *virginal* nature was sublime. The description is gendered in traditional ways: the artist is a masculine character

---

8    Facos's book (1998) also deals with Norwegian art and nationality after Norway joined the union with Sweden and until 1905.

approaching a feminized nature. Nature may be tamed by the act of painting; metaphorically painting is a sexual act. Furthermore, in Danbolt's description landscape is transformed from a space surrounding the artist into a body. It is experienced through vision and is met as an object to a masculine look. The story has all the characteristic traits of canonical art history and its mythologies of art and artistic genius. The metaphor of fatherhood is common in art history, where artists follow one another in a line of father and son, with the occasional daughter as an exception to the rule. But is it in any way important that our painterly father cast his eyes upon landscape?

## The female body and the Nordic feeling for nature

In his book *Landscape* from 2007, John Wylie opens by stating that landscapes are a matter of tension. With reference to Cézanne's many representations of Mont Saint-Victoire, he problematizes the frictions between proximity and distance, abstraction and realism, the appeal both to sensuousness and to detached observation that haunt Cézanne and our ideas of landscape in general. Is landscape to be understood as our lived environment, Wylie asks, is it a world we inhabit or live *in*? Or should we perceive it as a scene that presents itself to our eyes, something we look *at* from afar, a cultural genre of picturing that involves visual strategies and devices for distancing and observing? Is landscape a question of objectification, mastering and the gaze, or is it rather a matter of space, embodiment, and relations between self and land? (Wylie 2001: 1).

Within traditional art history, landscape has been defined as a genre concerned with looking at landscape "for its own sake", so to speak. The human figure and mythological or other narratives are intended to play supporting parts. Landscape expresses man's natural ability to take pleasure in an aesthetic look at nature. Despite the attempts at problematization, this idea is at the heart of Danbolt's narrative as well as the recent exhibition *A Mirror of Nature. Nordic Landscape Painting 1840-1910*, which toured the major Nordic national art museums and the Minneapolis Institute of Arts in 2006/7.[9] The Nordic

---

9    In terms of art history it seems that landscapes are often understood along two lines. One is the modernist narrative with landscape taking part in the development and purification of painting, which reached its peak in 20th century abstraction. The role of the beholder is contemplative, and paintings are seen first and foremost as "Painting". Narrative, verbal or historical elements are secondary. Paintings and images are separated and hierarchized: once a view has become a painting, it is presented as having inherent value. The other

feeling for nature is taken as a starting point. The climate is harsh and we live far apart; nature simply imposes itself upon us, begging us to paint it. Paintings are a matter of perception and the expression of inherent identity.[10]

The catalogue for *A Mirror of Nature* as a whole is highly conventional. The tension described by Wylie underpins the text. One example of this is the section "in the open air", which deals with the so-called Nordic light. The section includes a bathing scene with four female nudes by Swedish artist Anders Zorn. The catalogue insists that the female bodies and the stones are equally interesting. Zorn lets bodies and landscape melt, as if they were of the same matter, both surrendering to Zorn's overriding wish to capture the light, colour and crisp air of Nordic summer nights. It is the painterly effect as an expression of nature that is important.

The body however, does return to this narrative, but it is devoid of sexual-

---

approach focuses on interpretation. Landscapes and the visual in general can be read as a series of visual signs. Forms and structures take part in narrative typologies such as the sublime and picturesque. Trees, mountains and nature in general may serve as symbols in religious, psychological or other allegories. What both these perspectives have in common is a tendency to see meaning as something to be found on the surface of the painting or within the frame of the picture. We look for what is already there, and do not take the underlying structures that produced it into consideration. See Mitchell (1994) 2002. Both Danbolt and the catalogue for *A Mirror of Nature* recognize interpretation, and also see landscapes as spaces of meaning.

[10]  In his article in the catalogue, Philip Conisbee claims that seen from the outside, Nordic painting appears as one tradition. The nuances in time and place will be more apparent to those who feel more familiar with the art works in the exhibition. According to Conisbee, Nordic painters were closer to nature, and did not let pictorial conventions dominate their images. See Moorhouse et al. 2006: 199. See also Messel & Yvenes 2008. Messel writes about how both painters and scientists "discovered" the mountains at the beginning of the 19th century, and asks himself whether Norwegian painters wanted to make use of the mountain as a symbol of something more. After all, landscape and the mountains were recurring symbols in German romanticist paintings dealing with nostalgia, religious longing and pantheism. Or should the mountains be seen as part of a political rhetoric of nationality? Messel insists that Norwegian painters were pragmatic and didn't deal with ideas of the mountain. They were interested in the concrete mountains as they appeared before their eyes seen "from the north", or with the topography of particular places. Romanticism in this view is seen as an art historical style, but not as a set of ideas, and Messel never questions the difference between what is actually pictured and what might be the latent content of the pictures. Dolven's video and photographs with the titles *1 am North, 1.30 am North, 4 min. at 2 am 22 July of 2003* and others seem to play with the gap between an insistence on the "Real", on time and place as the only content of landscapes and the ideologies images take part in.

ity, gender or any social meaning. The catalogue insists that the experience of *plein air* painting is more complex than a mere *visual* registration of hills and light. When looking at a painting the body reaches for its past experience, with vision, touch, smell, hearing and taste all being mobilized. The lack of previous physical experience of the specific meteorological conditions of this particular landscape leaves the beholder having to trust vision, thought and emotions alone, the article claims. Those who have grown up along the coast of Sweden or Finland watching Zorn's paintings will re-experience the sensation on their very skins of the light chill of past clear and bright summer days (Moorhouse et al. 2006: 25 and 104).

The story is parallel to J.C. Dahl. The female body and landscape are interchangeable, and are only the material basis of art making (Nead 1992; Nochlin 1999). Any social questions, structures of desire and sexuality are rendered irrelevant. It is hard to contest the fact that summer nights are chillier in Norway than in Southern Europe, and cities are far apart. But the privileging of topography, meteorology and vision serves to naturalize a specific story that leaves Nordic people devoid of culture, social interaction and real bodies.[11] To return to Wylie's opposition, it seems that landscape within art history is a matter of men's looking, whereas for women it poses itself as a matter of embodiment and relations between the self and nature. The boundary separat-

---

[11]    One example of the importance of nature or landscape to discourses of gender within a Norwegian contemporary context might be the appointment of a Men's Panel to discuss masculinity and equality issues by the former Minister for Children and Equality Karita Bekkemellom in 2007. The Men's Panel was highly criticized in the media for being elitist and urban, and it was characterized as a "gay panel" or feminized. The panel's members were politicians, researchers and all types of men, including working-class men and gay men, but according to former Minister for Agriculture Lars Sponheim, no "real men" such as hunters, fishermen and the like had been appointed. Much debate followed this statement, and many pointed towards Norwegian explorer Lars Monsen as an example of (Norwegian) masculinity. Monsen is known from the media for his television in programmes showing him alone in the wilderness, walking, fishing and generally preoccupied with surviving with as little equipment as possible and enjoying the roughness of the wilderness. He stood out as an exemplary Norwegian man, living close to nature and knowing how to survive alone and enjoying wild nature as "landscape". Real Norwegian men apparently don't discuss their masculinities or gender roles, but live out their inner authentic masculine selves in nature. For a more thorough discussion of Norwegian masculinity, the male body and sexuality, see Langeland 2009. For information about the Men's Panel, see the official pages of the Norwegian government: http://www.regjeringen.no/en/dep/bld/Topics/equality/men-and-gender-equality/conclusive-memorandum-of-the-mens-panel.html?id=521783.

ing artist/look/masculinity and landscape/body/femininity seems watertight. If painting is defined as a question of looking, as it often is, then landscapes along with most other genres and motives are reserved for masculinity. The body of aesthetics is masculine and only skin deep.

## The female body and landscapes

In her article "Painting, feminism, history", feminist art historian Griselda Pollock states that the:

> complex relations between painting (art), feminism and history can be rhetorically tracked in the contradictory placements and significations of two bodies: the 'body of the painter' and the 'feminine body' (Pollock 2001: 75).

Often however, when studying the bodies of art history, we tend to take the female body for granted. Either we study it as it is represented or alluded to in visual representation, or we focus on the bodies of women artists and the social constraints under which they have lived historically.

On the one hand landscapes are packed with bodily metaphors. Art history is full of Venuses being born from the sea and women bathing. Hills, fields and landscapes from Cézanne's Mt Saint Victoire to Monet's haystacks, or for that matter Norwegian artist Harald Solberg's *Winter at Rondane*, are all metaphorically feminized (Paul Smith in Adams & Gruetzner Robins 2000). Writers fantasize about their homeland with its hills and rugged contours as a caring mother figure or an attractive, inspiring, beautiful woman whose arms and body they desire. Nations are also generally premised upon gender divisions. Men are privileged as historical and political agents, and women are seen as naturally associated with the household, family and tradition. The nation, as an abstract entity with its own civil virtues, however, is often allegorised as a stereotypic female body.[12]

But this distinction between public and private that is at the heart of

---

12   This was common in a Swedish context, where bourgeois intellectuals saw the hills of their maternal Sweden as a cure for alienation offering a psychological rootedness which was greatly longed for. See Facos 1998: 27. See also Cusack & Síghle Bhreathnach-Lynch 2003. To my knowledge there is no dominant feminized symbol of Norway that would correspond to the likes of the Finnish maiden, the French Marianne or Mother Russia.

our understanding of nations, and so important in our treatment of women artists, often leaves landscapes on the outskirts of discourse, if not outside it altogether. Much landscape painting does not depict the human body, so the discussion of "images of women", fetishism and popular culture seems irrelevant. Seen as part of a larger economy of vision, it could also be argued that landscapes offer themselves as spaces of freedom for women artists. Women might not have had access to art education on equal terms with men, but the controversial point here was sexuality. The most prestigious of genres within the academic theory, history painting, required to drawing classes and the nude. Women were rarely granted such training and both history painting and later in the century, modernity's prostitutes and public entertainment culture, were therefore themes and spaces that were closed to respectable bourgeois women in the 19th century. The strong hold of landscape within the Nordic tradition, however, could also be read as one of the reasons why women artists had a strong position here (Smith 2002).[13] As long as you are able to carry the equipment and walk the distance, you may enjoy the view. Still, it might be argued, the hills of a farm mean different things to those who are allowed to inherit them, and the mountains look different if you walk them as a scientist taking part in the mapping of the nation. Landscape must not only be read as a discourse complicit with ideology, but also as a space for counterstrategies.[14]

## Slaattelid, Dolven and the desire for more

Landscapes take part in psychological, social, imaginary and geographical processes and are complex spaces that can never be reduced to a simple mirror of nature, of the artist or the essence of the nation as a whole. Landscapes

---

[13]   It is important in this context to make a distinction between romanticism and neo-romanticism as opposed to realism, plein-air painting and impressionism. Plein-air painting, and the moderate form of naturalism practiced by Nordic artists at the end of the 19th century, could be seen as offering a space of temporary freedom for many women artists. However, few women artists actually chose to paint landscape. Romanticism does not offer the same spaces of ideological freedom.

[14]   For a problematization of masculinity and gendered identities in a Nordic context, see e.g. Lorentzen & Ekenstam 2006. Women had a stronger position in farming societies in the 19th century as opposed to the bourgeois ideal of the passive woman of the home. Daughters were allowed to inherit land. This became a topic of dispute in the parliament. For a survey of the rights and gendered roles of women in the 19th century, see Vogt et al. 1985-88.

are structures of meaning, and are hence put in place through the establishment of boundaries. As American anthropologist Mary Douglas insists in her famous study *Purity and Danger* from 1966, there is no reason to treat bodily boundaries as more natural or primary than other boundaries. "The body", she claims, "is a model which can stand for any bounded system. Its boundaries can represent any boundaries which are threatened and precarious" (Douglas 1966/2003: 273). Bodily boundaries, sexuality and gender are deeply implicated in the establishment of the boundary between landscapes and mere nature and landscape and artist, as well as in the establishment of a nation and national identity.

A mere glance at canonical art history reveals that landscapes take part in the traditional ideologies of looking, where man is the bearer of a look and the female body is metaphorically both his object and the material art is made from (Rose 1993; Nash 1996). As long as "woman" is seen as an extension of nature, her subjectivity can be erased from discourses of painting, simply by insisting that painting practices are a matter of truth, purity and flatness (Garb 1985: 3). The national art historical canon and the visual culture we now recognize as "Norwegian landscape" is put in place by re-presenting the boundary between mind and body, subject of looking and beautiful/sublime object, masculine and feminine. Not only is landscape painting part of the general masculine narcissism of the art historical canon. Landscape, as it marks the border of culture and the social, is perhaps particularly susceptible to being treated as a space of truth, authenticity and the essence of man. Landscape is a spectacle and a "stand in" for the body. Landscape *is* body, and thereby guarantees that the artistic identity is preserved as spiritual and creative, elevated and detached from its body.

Dolven and Slaattelid intervene in this narrative through a constant engagement with boundaries, and especially the boundaries of bodies and their spaces. Dolven's videos make us uneasy as a result of her manipulation of space. *between two mornings* juxtaposes two genres of painting, the female nude and sublime landscape. The traditions of the sublime are primary sites for the investigation of the borders between the self and its other, the material and the transcendent. Human bodies facing the mysticism of nature are well known from C.D. Friedrich and J.C. Dahl.[15] However, within the tradition of sublime landscape, the represented body is reinserted as the centre of pictorial

---

[15]    The midnight sun is also important in this investigation of the sublime, since it is a natural phenomenon that is not easily understood within the laws of time and space, or within the structure we generally regard as nature.

space and meaning. Man faces the sublime, the possibility of terror, but is able to transcend it. He re-establishes a stable autonomous (and masculine) self by insisting on nature as female.

Dolven repeats this iconography, but by juxtaposing it with the scheme of the female nude the effect is deeply disturbing. The female bodies follow the prerogative of containment and clear boundaries that governs the female nude: the bodies mimic Velasquez, Ingres, Man Ray and numerous other backs with which we are familiar. But it has gone too far, the cleansing and beautification of the surface has deprived them of their sign of sexuality, the hair, leaving us with only the bare skin. The make up, normally meant for the surface of the body, is scattered in the sand and appears abjected, making us aware of how "natural" femininity is a construction. The traditional shallow space of the female nude reassuring us that the body is there for us to enjoy visually has been replaced. Dolven's juxtaposition of spaces undermines the notion of a strong autonomous subject looking at the world, and draws attention to embodiment. She lets the female bodies take part in the looking, placing them before landscape as our point of identification within the picture. Dolven does not provide a proper object to their look, a masculine body that might reassure us or hint at any essential femininity or stable gender identity. We are left at the border of life and death, beauty and terror, unable to transcend the body.

Slaattelid's approach is slightly more analytical and distanced. She enters the spaces of painting by investigating the mythology of the artist and the artist's body. The combination of text and isolated sections of images, as we have seen, seems to drive a wedge between the artist and his imagery. This releases Hertervig from the "Hertervig" of art history, but also leaves the artist as an open space that might eventually be structured differently. The idea of the artist, in this case Hertervig, observing so intensely that he eventually *is* in the painting; living, breathing and dying with it, is deconstructed (Wylie 2007: 5). Instead of trying to replace Hertervig's body as the body of the painter, by insisting on the stroke as the index of the painter's body, and as the index of her "female" body, she breaks the illusion that the picture plane is transparent. This does not give us access to real landscapes, nor to the artistic personality or the truth of painting. The trace left by the flash becomes almost ironic as a representation of the aesthetics associated with Nordic light.[16]

---

16    The text also destabilises the meaning of "Düsseldorf" in Norwegian art history. The Düsseldorf school is one of two main schools in Norwegian painting in the middle of the 19th century, the other one being the Dresden school and J.C. Dahl. Hertervig studied in

The feeling of melancholia and loss that dominate both are not a result of the general nostalgia of romanticist ideas of landscape or a repetition of the psychological state of Hertervig. It comes from the ambivalence of trying to make sense of the female body in a culture and a structure that insists on treating femininity as its other. The desire that underpins both these artists' practices is not a specifically female desire, but the desire for more, or for something else, and not a desire to take the place of the artist's body and have access to Norwegian landscape and painting as they are. Both artists accentuate the space that separates the one from its other, which at the same time is the space that connects us and opens the possibility of real dialogue. In my view the constant referencing of traditions such as Romanticism, Modernist abstraction and landscape could be read as an investigation of what being or performing as a "woman" might mean within the spaces of a Norwegian and Nordic canonical tradition.

## Bibliography

Adams, S. and Gruetzner Robins, A. (eds.). (2000). *Gendering Landscape Art*. Manchester: Manchester University Press.

Bal, M. (1999). *Quoting Caravaggio. Contemporary Art, Preposterous History*. Chicago and London: University of Chicago Press.

Battersby, C. (2007). *The Sublime, Terror and Human Difference*. London and New York: Routledge.

Betterton, R. (1996). *An Intimate Distance: Women, Artists and the Body*. London: Routledge.

Cusack, T. and Bhreathnach-Lynch, S. (eds.). (2003). *Art, Nation and Gender. Ethnic Landscapes, Myths and Mother Figures*. Hampshire UK and Burlington USA: Ashgate Publishing.

Danbolt, G. (1996). *Norsk kunsthistorie. Bilde og skulptur frå vikingtida til i dag*. Oslo: Det norske samlaget.

---

Düsseldorf, and the debate over whether his painting should be read as a continuation of this school is recurrent. Slaattelid removes "Düsseldorf" from a sign of a particular style, not only by using brighter colours instead of the brownish tone that is characteristic of the Düsseldorf school, but also by insisting that it was a place of *actual incidents* that had both psychological and bodily consequences, and not only a place of "art" in the sense of strokes of paint etc. This reinscribes the body into the narrative, a body that is no longer a surface that responds to the Nordic light, but is a living, breathing and vulnerable body instead.

Douglas, M. (1966). "External Boundaries" in: Jones, A. (ed.). (2003). *The Feminism and Visual Culture Reader*. New York: Routledge, 373-75.

Facos, M. (1998). *Nationalism and the Nordic Imagination. Swedish Art of the 1890s*. Berkeley, LA. London: University of California Press.

Garb, T. (1985). "Renoir and the Natural Woman". *Oxford Art Journal*, 8:2, 3-15.

Høydalsnes, E. (2003). *Møte mellom tid og sted: bilder av Nord-Norge*. Oslo: Forlaget Bonytt.

Jaukkuri, M. et al. (eds.). (2001). *Skulpturlandskap Nordland/ Artscape Nordland*. Bodø and Oslo: Press Nordland fylkeskommune.

Langeland, F. "Den norske kroppen" in: Mühleisen, W. & Røthing, Å. (eds.). (2009). *Norske sexualiteter*. Oslo: Cappelen Akademisk Forlag, 37-58.

Larsen, B. (2006). *Where the visual gets the last word*, http://www.marislaattelid.com/where_the_visual_gets_the_last_word.html [31.05.2009]

Lorentzen, J. & Ekenstam, C. (eds.). (2006). *Män i Norden. Manlighet och modernitet 1840-1940*. Stockholm: Gidlunds Forlag.

Malmanger, M. (1993). "Fra klassisisme til tidlig realisme 1814-1870" in: Wichstrøm, A., Christie, S., Anker, P., Malmanger, M. & Berg, K. (eds.). *Norges malerkunst. Bind I, Fra middelalderen til i dag*. Oslo: Gyldendal Norsk Forlag, 187-350.

Messel, N. and Yvenes, M. (2008). *Oppdagelsen av fjellet*. Oslo: Nasjonalmuseet for kunst, arkitektur og design.

Mitchell, W.J.T. (ed.). (2002). *Landscape and Power*. University of Chicago Press, Chicago.

Moorhouse, L. Ahtola, Gunnarson, T. & Haverkamp, F. (eds.). (2006). *A Mirror of Nature: Nordic Landscape Painting 1840-1910*. Copenhagen: Statens Museum for Kunst.

Nash, C. (1996). "Reclaiming Vision: Looking at Landscape and the Body" in: *Gender, Place and Culture*, #3, 149-69.

Nead, L. (1992). *The Female Nude: Art, Obscenity and Sexuality*. London: Routledge.

Nochlin, L. (1999). "Courbet's Real Allegory: Rereading the Painter's Studio" in: Nochlin, L. *Representing Women*. London: Thames and Hudson, 106-153.

Pollock, G. & Parker, R. (1981). *Old Mistresses. Women, Art and Ideology*. London: Routledge & Kegan Paul.

Pollock, G. (1988). *Vision and Difference. Femininity, Feminism and the Histories of Art*. London and New York: Routledge.

Pollock, G. (1996). "Inscriptions in the feminine" in: Catherine de Zegher (ed.). *Inside the Visible. An Elliptical Traverse of 20th Century Art in, of, from the Feminine*. Cambridge, Massachusetts, and London: MIT Press, 67-87.

Pollock, G. (1999). *Differencing the Canon: Feminist Desire and the Writing of Art's Histories*. London: Routledge.

Pollock, G. (2001). *Looking Back to the Future: Essays on Art, Life and Death*. Amsterdam: G+B Arts International.

Paasche, M. (2004). "Den kritiske distansen". *kunstkritikk.no*, available at http://www.kunstkritikk.no/article/7023_[20.05.2009].

Renberg, I.M. (2002). *Stanse tiden: temporale aspekter i Lars Hertervigs landskapsmalerier 'Gamle furutrær' og 'Borgøya' belyst ved Walter Benjamins allegoribegrep*. M.A. Thesis in Art History, University of Oslo.

Rose, G. (1993). *Feminism and Geography: The Limits of Geographical Knowledge*. Cambridge: Polity Press.

Schlieker, A. (2004). *A K Dolven: Moving Mountain*. Bergen: Bergen Kunsthall.

Seip, I. (2007). "Å se med kroppen. Fiksjon og fenomenologisk realisme hos Espolin Johnson og A K Dolven" in: Vaa, Aa. (ed.). *Å låne øyne å se med. Kåre Espolin Johnsons kunstnerskap*. Tapir Akademisk Forlag/Galleri Espolin, 203-237.

Smith, S.B. (2002). "Outdoor Spaces" in: *As Women Tell it. Nordic Women Painters 1880-1900*. Copenhagen: Kunstforeningen, 111-122.

Vogt, K. et al. (1985-88). *Kvinnenes kulturhistorie, Bind II, Fra år 1800 til vår tid*. Oslo: Universitetsforlaget.

Wylie, J. (2007). *Landscape*. London and New York: Routledge.


**Internet resources:**

The official website of the Ministry of Children and Equality and the Norwegian Government:

http://www.regjeringen.no/en/dep/bld/Topics/equality/men-and-gender-equality/conclusive-memorandum-of-the-mens-panel.html?id=521783

Artscape Nordland:

http://www.skulpturlandskap.no/Skulpturlandskap/artscape/about.html

Mari Slaattelid's homepage:

http://www.marislaattelid.com/

A K Dolven's homepage:

http://www.akdolven.com/

Third section:
Poetics and Aeshetics of
Borders and Border Crossing in
Contemporary Literature and Art

# On the Borders of Poetry and Art

*Jørgen Bruhn*

## PART I

### Introduction

Since the beginning of reflections on art in Western thinking, and long before Baumgarten created the discipline of aesthetics in the 18th century, theories on art have been forced to deal with the question of the degree to which media are mixed or pure. A question that may be reformulated as the question of the existence and importance of aesthetic borders. We might think that "intermedia" (the artist and philosopher Dick Higgins coined the term in the 1960s) is a modern phenomenon (be it a possibility or a problem). Or we may tend to believe that aesthetic thinkers before our own vexed time had fewer problems with understanding questions of pure media or un-pure media.

In this article I wish to begin with a brief outline of the history lying behind this contemporary discussion of aesthetic borders. The historical outline will lead me to reconsider the very core of these discussions, namely: What is a medium, and what constitutes the border of a medium? My attempt to define a medium, and its borders, will lead me to a terminological suggestion that may prompt new ways of thinking about media and media borders.[1]

---

[1] Isolated parts of this article resemble two of my earlier articles on the history and theory of intermediality, and thus media borders; "Intermedialitet. Framtidens kulturvetenskapliga grunddisciplin" (*Tidsskrift för litteraturvetenskap*, 4, 2008) and "Heteromediality" in Lars Elleström (ed.), *Media Borders, Multimodality and Intermediality*, Palgrave Macmillan 2010.

A terminological specification might be useful to begin with. Following numerous contemporary critics, I use the term medium as a substitute for the somewhat problematic term art and art form, and the internal division of art. For instance, literature, sculpture and music are defined as media in my discussion below (see also Clüver 2007, for an argument supporting this terminology). Likewise I follow Clüver's suggestion to use the term text for any semiotic artefact, not only verbal products.

## *Ut pictura poesis*

An early theoretician of the borders of art and media, and a starting point for many investigations of the history of comparative arts or intermediality, is the Roman author Horace (whose poetics, as is well known, was a creative recycling of Aristotle's *Poetics*). Horace famously coined the term ut pictura poesis, 'as is painting so is poetry' – which was interpreted in terms of 'as is poetry so is painting'.[2]

Taken from a more complicated context, the words "ut picture poesis" has, in the long history of theoretical and artistic reception, been read as one of the first instances of the tradition of "sister arts", and the fragment is often quoted along with the Greek poet Simonides, who is believed to have claimed that painting is mute poetry, whereas poetry is painting with the aid of words. Both are instances of "the story about the long Western tradition of comparing the visual and the textual under the auspices of mimesis", a "doctrine that asserted the direct comparability of visual and textual imitation of the world" (Melville & Readings 1991: 8). In other words; the differences between the arts are merely surface phenomena: the conventionally differentiated arts aim at expressing the same content and achieving the same functions. Many examples from western cultural history could be quoted here, but one example referred to by Umberto Eco may suffice: Honorius from Autun, a medieval commentator, defines the triple purposes of (religious) art as follows: (a) "the house of God should be thus beautified"; (b) to remind [the spectators] of the life of the Saints; and (c) to be "the literature of the Laity" (Eco 2002 [1959]: 18). In other words: the purpose and the effect of religious art are identical across the boundaries of media.

A famous instance of this concept of sister arts is, paradoxically, the notorious paragone debate in the Renaissance. The paragone debate, with one vehement partaker by the name of Leonardo da Vinci, deals with the hierarchy of the arts (Leonardo championed the superiority of painting). This debate turned the harmonious concept of sister arts into a competitive battle, but the underlying theoretical foundation was nevertheless unaltered. The battle of dominance rests on the firm assumption that the arts may compete in describing identical content – the paragone debate concerns *which art* should lead the way.

---

2     The most comprehensive *Wirkungsgeschichte* of the ut pictura poesis term, going from Aristotle and of course in particular Horace, to Renaissance culture, is to my knowledge still Lee 1967. The quote is from page 3.

The ut pictura poesis conception, albeit in new and modernised versions, is far from being forgotten, and important trends in 20th century cultural theory continue the idea. For structuralists, for instance Claude Bremond, in the sixties and seventies, narrative content could be transported across media borders because the effects created by different media were relatively similar. And a little later, in 1980, Seymour Chatman claimed that:

> One of the most important observations to come out of narratology is that narrative itself is a deep structure quite independent of its medium. In other words, narrative is basically a kind of text organization, and that organization, that schema, needs to be actualized: in written words, as in stories and novels; in spoken words combined with the movements of actors imitating characters against sets which imitate places, as in plays and films; in drawings; in comics strips; in dance movements, as in narrative ballet and in mime; and even in music, at least in program music of the order of *Till Eulenspiegel* and *Peter and the Wolf* (Chatman 1980: 121).[3]

To sum up, in the tradition referred to above as the sister arts tradition, the borders between the media and the arts are neglectable, something that the arts, so to speak, are designed to overcome, even if warnings against mixing in unwarranted ways were issued already in the very first verses of Horace's *Ars poetica* when he strongly warned against "idle phantasies", which should be avoided because they constituted unnatural, "monstrous" phenomena.

## Lessing's Laokoon – establishing aesthetic borders

There was a decisive and for cultural history unusually clear break with the ut pictura poesis line of thinking in the middle of the 18th century. In 1766 the German author and philosopher G.E. Lessing strongly opposed the sister arts tradition in his extremely influential *Laokoon: oder über die Grenzen der Malerey und Poesie,* 1766. A few of the (oft-cited) claims of Lessing deserve to be quoted here. First one of the paragraphs where Lessing defines the signs of the media in opposition to each other:

> I argue thus. If it be true that painting employs wholly different signs or means of imitation from poetry – the one using forms and colors in space, the other articulate sounds in time

---

[3]    For a more recent and directly comparable position, see Rozik 2008.

– and if signs must unquestionably stand in convenient relation with the thing signified, then signs arranged side by side can represent only objects existing side by side, or whose parts so exist, while consecutive signs can express only objects which succeed each other, or whose parts succeed each other in time.[4]

And it is these sign essences (which we would now call semiotic differences) that according to Lessing should define the eponymous borders (Grenzen) of his essay dividing the arts. Borders that create a healthy and friendly atmosphere:

> Painting and poetry should be like two just and friendly neighbours, neither of whom indeed is allowed to take unseemly liberties in the heart of the other's domain, but who exercise mutual forbearance on the borders, and effect a peaceful settlement for all the petty encroachments which circumstance may compel either to make in haste on the rights of the other.

The history of reception of Lessing's Laokoon reading is long and complicated, and his work has been discussed in a wide variety of ways in recent years as well: as a political treatise in disguise (Mitchell), as a misunderstood masterpiece of aesthetic common sense (Scholz), or as a proto-semiotic theoretical work (Sonnesson).[5] In the postwar period Lessing's ideas were more or less synonymous with the ideas on medium specificity propounded by Clement Greenberg (see below).

Lessing's text is a rich, labyrinthine and partly internally contradictory essay, but in this particular context I wish to focus on the learning of the phenomenon of border that we can retrieve here. The essay's distinctions can be shown in a simple dichotomy, and it is relatively simple to move from the explicit distinctions to the more hidden dichotomies underlying the argument. On the left side we find painting and sculpture, on the right side literature, with painting being identified from the outset with space, whereas literature is identified with time.

| **Space** | **Time** |
|---|---|
| – Natural signs | Arbitrary signs |
| – Narrow sphere | Infinite range |
| – Imitation | Expression |
| – Body | Mind |

---

4     Lessing quoted in Mitchell 1984: 98-115, quote on p. 98. In a lecture in Växjo 2008.
5     (Scholz 2007; Sonneson, no year; Sternberg, 1999).

| | |
|---|---|
| – External | Internal |
| – Silent | Eloquent |
| – Beauty | Sublimity |
| – Eye | Ear |
| – Feminine | Masculine |

The point in the influential reading of Lessing conducted by W.J.T. Mitchell is that these distinctions lie on the surface of the text, whereas Mitchell wishes to go one step further and get to the core of Lessing's distinctions. The dichotomies which seem at first hand to be intuitively sensible, devoid of any ideological or political sub-texts, thus carry with them a much more wide-ranging message. What appear to be descriptive elements (convenience, "das bequäme") of the different kinds of signs thus have normative undercurrents. Mitchell suggests that the distinctions should be "translated" into differences between the sexes (psychology, anthropology), borders between religion and art (ontology), and even geographical borders between England/Germany vs. France (politics).

However, what is perhaps more interesting in this context is that the very distinctive process – the borders – carry with them significant meaning. And thus, according to Mitchell, our understanding of Lessing might be taken one step further to be a treatise not only on the aspects of the content lying between the borders, but on the phenomenon of borders itself. Consequently, at a deep level the essay distinguishes between blurred genres or art forms and distinct art forms:

| Blurred genres | Distinct genres |
|---|---|
| Moderns | Ancients |
| Adultery | Honesty |
| Monsters | Beautiful bodies |
| Mothers | Fathers |
| French "refinement" | English/German manliness |

Mitchell's reading does not stand un-criticized (see Scholz's very tough critique in *Changing Borders*), and I am not sure whether I can support the entire argumentation. But what interests me is the way that Mitchell manages to add an ideological meaning to the apparently objective distinctions and borderlines. Mitchell tries to ideologize the idea of borders as a phenomenon. In other words, borders of aesthetics become ideological borders.

Before the second part of my essay I will mention a few post-Lessing formulations of an aesthetics based on the idea of legitimate aesthetic borders. This tradition is normally called the tradition of medium specificity.

Medium specificity is a strong aesthetic trend in comparative thinking in modern art, in addition to the structuralist claims for medium-unspecificity mentioned above, and it is directly modelled on Lessing's example. Art critic Clement Greenberg (1909-1994) is the classic proponent of twentieth century modernist, medium specificity, and a classical Greenberg formulation may suffice here to state the position. As Clement Greenberg writes:

> ... the unique and proper area of competence of each art coincided with all that was unique in the nature of its medium. The task of self-criticism became to eliminate from the specific effects of each art any and every effect that might conceivably be borrowed from or by the medium of any other art. Thus would each art be rendered 'pure', and in its 'purity' find the guarantee of its standards of quality as of its independence ("Modernist Painting", 1960).

After Irving Babbitt's "A Newer Laocoon" (1919) and Greenberg's elaborate medium specificity theory, it is in particular Michael Fried who has continued this tradition, for instance in his classic essay "Art and Objecthood".[6]

So, to sum up once again. The media have been compared and discussed from the moment that they were first theorized in Western thinking. Two traditions can be distinguished: one tradition sees the differences between the arts as surface phenomena, whereas the second trend strongly divides art forms into different groups according to their essential properties. I call the first tradition the sister arts tradition, whereas I call the second trend the medium specificity tradition. But these are merely distinctions and historical surveys, of course, and they do not answer any of the questions I want to raise. Nor do they give us any hints as to how to consider the phenomenon of borders in aesthetic thinking. For what is a medium, and what is a border?

---

6     In "The Politics of Intermediality" (*Film and Media Studies, 2 (Acta Univ. Sapientia, 2010)*), Jens Schröter gives a valuable contribution to the ideological reading of intermedial questions, showing for instance that proponents of the mixing of media (Dick Higgins and others) share many political agendas with the most vehement critics of media mixing (for instance Greenberg).

# PART II

In this part of the article I do not seek to answer historical questions regarding the origin of the ways in which we discuss relations between the media. Instead I want to suggest ways of describing what a medium is – and how the borders between the media can be described. And this will lead me to the third part of this article, where I will try and suggest ways of thinking about borders between media in a fruitful way.

## From interart studies to intermediality studies

Since the beginning of the twentieth century the relations between the arts have been investigated, partly independently of and partly inspired by the two trends in comparative arts outlined above. A comparative tradition, often called *interart studies*, with subcategories such as 'word and image studies' and 'music and image studies', has been a subfield of comparative literature and art history. The three art forms referred to most often are literature, the visual arts and music, and these art forms are more or less automatically, but not without problems, connected to words, images and music. Interart studies basically dealt with the relations *between* the arts, and the object of research in this field has been conceptualized along various lines, but often the focus was placed on, for instance, studies of ekphrasis, of so-called artistic *Doppelbegabungen*, or adaptations from music to poetry. But under the general impression of both the basic tenets of cultural studies from the sixties and onwards (the critique of the traditional hierarchy of the arts), and new trends in artistic and technological products (hybrids in the arts such as performance and happenings, the development of new digital media), interart studies have been supplanted since about 1990 by "intermediality studies", studying the phenomenon of intermediality (cf. Clüver 2007).

The shortest definition of intermediality that I have encountered claims that intermediality is "intertextuality transgressing media boundaries" (Lehtonen 2000: 71). Intermediality studies constitute a rather young field of investigation, and consequently the object as well as the theory and methods of the field are still relatively loosely defined. At conferences as well as in publications, discussions are still at a fundamental (but often sophisticated) level concerning the basic elements of the field: What is a medium? What is the difference between interartiality and intermediality and multimodality? These questions show that this is a discipline that has not yet defined its own object and limits.

Several schematizations of the field of intermediality have been suggested, for instance by Werner Wolf in the very influential *The Musicalisation of Fiction. A Study in the Theory and History of Intermediality*, and by Hans Lund in *Intermedialitet. Ord, bild och ton i samspel* [Intermediality. Word, Image, Sound in Collaboration] (2002). Lund suggests a useful division in which the field of intermediality is divided into *combination* (divided into the subcategories 'interreference' and 'co-existence'), *integration* and *transformation*.[7]

| COMBINATION (including inter-reference and co-existence) | | INTEGRATION | TRANSFORMATION |
|---|---|---|---|
| Interreference | Co-existence | Concrete poetry | Verbal ekphrasis |
| Illustration | Advertisement | Sound poetry | Musical ekphrasis |
| Emblems | Stamps | Typography | Program music |
| Picture & title | Songs | Print picture | Novel into film |
| Music & title | Video | Sprechgesang | Iconic projection |
| Photo journalism | Comics | Conceptual art | Word into music |
| Picture books | Opera | Picture alphabet | Cinematic novel |
| | Liturgy | Iconicity | Theatricalization of text |
| | Posters | Image containing verbal signs | |

Intermedial research has proven its worth in many different subcategories, and researchers like Siglind Bruhn, Claus Clüver, Hans Lund, Irina Rajewsky, Werner Wolf and numerous others have shown the necessity of interdisciplinary work as a revolt against inexpedient academic borders. But nevertheless I would claim that contemporary intermediality studies suffers from problems which I think may be solved by a change of direction. First of all, I think it is crucial that intermedial studies tries to establish a manageable working definition of the core concept of medium.

## Defining medium

As mentioned above, the important strategic move from interart studies to intermediality studies involved broadening the field of investigation from the traditional arts to (in principle) all existing media. As a result, intermediality studies can analyze the entire traditional field of aesthetic objects as well as

---

7    Lund 2002: 21, as translated in *Changing Borders,* p. 15.

musical videos, corporate logos, book covers, the medieval Christian mass and the opening of the Olympic Games.[8]

But defining media has proved difficult. In Marie-Laure Ryan's introduction to the important anthology *Narrative Across Media* she enumerates a large number of different definitions of media circulating in academic research (pp. 15-16) ranging from radio to spiritual medium in touch with other worlds, and she seems to decide for a relatively pragmatic definition of medium. But "[c]uriously", Werner Wolf has noted, "problems of definition and typology have not hindered intermediality research. The most obvious among these is the problem of defining 'medium' itself".[9] Consequently, Wolf suggests

> a broad concept of medium: not in the restricted sense of a technical or institutional channel of communication but as a conventionally distinct means of communication or expression characterized not only by particular channels (or one channel) for the sending and receiving of messages but also by the use of one or more semiotic systems (Quoted in Rajewsky 2002: 7).

This is an attractive definition because of the pragmatic idea that medium should be defined by 'conventions', but the definition ends up by saying, basically, that the term 'media' is more or less identical with what was previously known as the arts, which does not solve the original problem.

The multimodal model proposed by Lars Elleström and Mitchell in recent publications may prove to be a good starting point for future discussions of intermediality. Mitchell's suggestions (in "There are No Visual Media", for instance) have been of a rather metaphorical kind, whereas Lars Elleström has developed a much more elaborate model combining intermedial studies and multimodality. Elleström tries to avoid a problematic media essentialism by operating with four necessary conditions for every medium: a *Material modality*, a *sensorial modality*, a *spatiotemporal modality* and a *semiotic modality* concerning types of signification using Peirce's distinction between iconic, symbolic and indexical signification. The four necessary conditions (modalities) constitute what Elleström calls "basic media", such as still images, written words, oral words and organised sound. However, these basic media will enter

---

[8]  The last two examples are Claus Clüver's. Clüver believes that these are highly significant (but as yet almost un-analyzed) examples of intermediality in contrast to interart phenomena. See the final remarks in 'Intermediality and Interart Studies', *Changing Borders*, p. 34.

[9]  See Werner Wolf's entry on 'Intermediality' in Herman, Jahn & Ryan 2005.

or be transformed into, more elaborate culturally and aesthetically conventional forms, which Elleström chooses to call "qualified media".

The idea that every medium consists of a number of elements called basic modalities common to all media (in specific constellations), means that these modalities (in particular combinations) also form the basis of other media. Consequently, multimodality is a fact of any conceivable text in any conceivable medium. The idea that texts are mixed is of course banal when dealing with openly mixed media such as the mixture of sound, image, words, music in cinema or performance art, or the pictures and words in commercial advertising or in comics. The new, and less obvious, insight is that the mixed character of texts is also a fact of the traditionally pure media. The main point is that even the apparently monomedial text always consists of several modalities. The mixed medium is the default position; and even though it may be possible to imagine pure media, pure media are very rare. In my understanding of Elleström's model, this leads to the following step, namely that the pure, distinct medium and its equivalent on the level of specific texts, is a historical as well as an ontological illusion.

This is probably what W.J.T. Mitchell has in mind when he claims that "the attempt to grasp the unitary, homogeneous essences of painting, photography, sculpture, poetry, etc., is the real aberration" and that the conception of purity and unity of media "is both impossible and utopian" and therefore media ought not to be investigated as an existing fact but as the result of ideological construction and evaluation (Mitchell 1994: 96).

Pure, unmixed media may be, and have been, a desired object in specific historical periods and in particular ideological surroundings, but they only very rarely exist in the form of a real, existing phenomenon. Consequently, research – and teaching – should take as its starting point the fact that "all arts are 'composite' arts (both text and image); all media are mixed media, combining different codes, discursive conventions, channels, sensory and cognitive modes" (Mitchell 1994: 94).

Thus the implications of a new, multimodal concept of medium is that interartial/intermedial models are transgressed and the meetings of media are no longer privileged exceptions but become a condition of every text.

## *Media borders and intermediality*

The position outlined here is gaining acceptance in contemporary intermedial thinking. It would probably be hard to find a scholar doing intermedial studies that would disagree with the claim that media are constructed entities and that defining media is difficult if also necessary. As I have suggested elsewhere, I believe that even if media do not exist as essential entities in themselves, they are nevertheless crucial participants in cultural history and in contemporary discussions. Consequently, they should be investigated in the same way that modern literary studies have studied literary genre, after it has been agreed upon that genre does not exist as a Platonic idea but is, instead, instigated by historical forces with various intellectual, economic and ideological interests steering it.

In taking this position, I align myself with a recent reflection on the question of media borders, namely Irina O. Rajewsky's "Border Talks: The Problematic Status of Media Borders in the Current Debate about Intermediality". Her point of departure is the constructed, discursive character of media and art forms, and she questions the nature of the borders between media. In other words: Rajewsky would subscribe to the common definition of intermediality that I referred to above, "Intertextuality crossing media boundaries" (Lehtonen) – but she strongly questions the nature of the boundaries, or borders, referred to in the definition. What is the role of media borders if it is a foregone conclusion that media are mixed, that "all media are mixed media" as Mitchell claims, a claim that Rajewsky suggests may be slightly changed into "all media are multimodal (media)" (Rajewsky 2010: 66).

We might reformulate the question somewhat in relation to the historical outline with which I began this essay. How can we consider the question of media borders in the light of two (interrelated) aspects: first the historical debates where ut pictura poesis (no significant aesthetic borders) stand against Lessing's *Laokoon* (aesthetic borders are crucial), and second, the insights of contemporary media theory and intermedial studies strongly stating the constructed character of media and art forms, and in particular a modality-based definition of media?

Before answering these questions, it is crucial to mention a few basic elements concerning a definition of medium. I agree completely with Rajewsky, who stresses that even though most researchers in the field agree that medium is a constructed phenomenon, this does *not* mean that the question of the function, form and history of media, in contemporary thinking or in historical studies, becomes obsolete: in any epoch media – and here media resemble genres – play a crucial role in debates about the correct production, reception and dissemination of media. (see Bruhn 2010) And another equally crucial fact is that no matter what particular definition of medium is used, it is impossible to gain access to any medium as such. Rajewsky: "in dealing with medial configurations, we never encounter 'the medium' as such, for instance, film *as* medium or writing *as* medium, but only specific individual films, individual texts and so on" (Rajewsky 2010: 53).[10]

But despite my basic agreement with Irina Rajewsky concerning the basic questions of the nature of media (being at one and the same time absent as concrete phenomena and present as discursive and ideological conditions), I still want to conclude on a different note than she does.

I think that part of the problem may reside in terminology. Rajewsky has a point when she argues from a common-sense position that the term intermediality, because of its prefix "inter-", necessarily must apply to border crossing. She states:

> Hence, 'intermediality' can be said to serve first and foremost as a flexible generic term 'that can be applied, in a broad sense, to *any* phenomenon involving more than one medium' [quoting Werner Wolf] and thus to any phenomenon that – as indicated by the prefix *inter* – in some ways takes place *between* media. Accordingly, the crossing of media borders has been defined as a founding category of intermediality (Rajewsky 2010: 51-52).

But perhaps the very term intermediality needs to be reconsidered, perhaps even changed, to fit contemporary theoretical thinking? What if intermediality as a term is founded on anachronistic ideas of media? What if intermediality as a term is part of the problem instead of offering a solution of seeing media as either mixed or pure, either in the sister arts tradition or in the Lessing line?

I believe that the term intermediality is too limited to satisfy the demands of the new multimodal theory of medium. Therefore I will suggest a new umbrella term to describe any conceivable text, whereas I reserve the term intermediality to cover parts of my new term. I suggest that we consider using the term "heteromodality" in order to frame what we are talking about in a better way, and that this term should be used to reflect the fact that all texts share a limited set of modalities, though in a number of very different ways.

With heteromodality the focus shifts from comparisons *between* media and art forms, roughly consisting of the numerous possibilities suggested in Lund's diagram, where music represents poetry, novel becomes movie, words and picture combine on the poster, etc. to a method investigating the expanded

---

10   Rajewsky suggests that this problem is solved by using Niklas Luhmann's distinction between "Medium" and "Form". In a number of publications, Joachim Paech has outlined the value of a "Medium-Form" approach to intermediality studies.

field of media relations *inside* the text. With heteromodal studies we shift the focus from relations between media (always concretized in forms, in 'texts'), to medial relations within texts, in other words. Therefore the prefix 'hetero' (Greek meaning 'different' or 'other') is more suitable than 'inter' for these investigations.

My proposal, in other words, aims at creating a new, universal concept of text, the heteromodal text. However it will be useful to operate with pragmatic subcategories of the heteromodal text so that we do not create a monolithic concept that risks not explaining anything at all. So I shall continue to use the terms intermedial text (examples of which are listed in Lund's diagram, where media is defined as Wolf's "conventionally distinct" forms in contradistinction to the multimodal definition) and intertextuality (the theoretical concept designating the fact that all texts are dialogically connected but without taking media specificities into consideration).

Intertextuality defines the overall phenomenon of texts being mosaics of other texts (according to now classic definitions by Barthes and Kristeva). Heteromodality defines the existence of several modalities in all conceivable texts. And intermediality is my term for one particular subgenre of heteromediality, characterized by the traces of more than one medium. Consequently, *all* texts are heteromodal, and they will *always* cite and will be cited by other texts (intertextuality); but only part of the immense category of heteromediality is intermedial in the restricted sense of the word, where we meet conventionally distinct media, crossing one or more media borders.

So media borders do exist, but they are impossible to identify "outside" media. Media borders, I suggest, should be understood as parts of internal struggles inside texts. Any text consists of different modalities, thus including parts of other media, and the real meaning of borders is, and will remain, discursive constructions outside media: borders whose main purpose in the discursive and ideological economy is to create distinctions. And these distinctions can and will later on be processed, managed, interpreted and digested by human beings – "outside" that particular media, but "inside" the borders of other media.

# Bibliography

Bruhn, J. (2008). "Intermedialitet. Framtidens kulturvetenskapliga grunddisciplin". *Tidsskrift för litteraturvetenskap*, 4.

Bruhn, J. (2010). "Heteromediality" in: Elleström, L. (ed.). *Media Borders, Multimodality and Intermediality.* London: Palgrave MacMillan.

Chatman, S. (1980). "What Novels Can Do That Films Can't (And Vice Versa)". *Critical Inquiry* Vol. 7 no. 1.

Clüver, C. (2007). "Intermediality and Interart Studies" in: Arvidson, Askander, Bruhn & Führer (eds.). *Changing Borders. Contemporary Positions in Intermediality.* Lund: Intermedia Press.

Eco, U. (2002). *Art and Beauty in the Middle Ages.* New Haven and London: Yale UP.

Lee, R.W. (1967). *Ut Pictura Poesis, The Humanistic Theory of Painting.* New York: Norton.

Lehtonen, M. (2000). "On No Man's Land. Theses on Intermediality". *Nordicom Review*, 4.

Mitchell, W.J.T. (1994). "Beyond Comparison". *Picture Theory.* Chicago: Chicago UP.

Mitchell, W.J.T. (1984). "The Politics of Genre: Space and Time in Lessing's Laocoon". *Representations*, no. 6.

Paech, J. (1997). *Litteratur und Film.* Weimar: Metzler Verlag.

Rajewsky, I. (2002). *Intermedialität.* Tübingen & Basel: A. Francke Verlag.

Rozik, E. (2007). "Medium Translations between Fictional Worlds" in: Arvidson, Askander, Bruhn & Führer (eds.). *Changing Borders. Contemporary Positions in Intermediality.* Lund: Intermedia Press.

Scholz, B. (2007). "'A Whale that Can't be Cotched?': On Conceptualizing Ekprhasis" in: Arvidson, Askander, Bruhn & Führer (eds.). *Changing Borders. Contemporary Positions in Intermediality.* Lund: Intermedia Press.

Schröter, J. (2010). "The Politics of Intermediality". *Film and Media Studies, 2 (Acta Univ. Sapientia).*

Sonneson, Göran. "Den allra nyaste Laokoon. I ljuset av modern semiotik", at http://www.lu.se/o.o.i.s?id=12588&postid=540189, accesed 2 April 2011, 14.00.

Sternberg, M. (1999). "The 'Laokoon' Today: Interart Relations, Modern Projects and Projections". *Poetics Today,* vol. 20.

Wolf, W. (2005). "Intermediality" in: Herman, D., Jahn, M. & Ryan, M.-L. (eds.). *Routledge Encyclopedia of Narrative Theory.* London & New York: Routledge.

# Writing Exile, Writing Home: Translocation and Self-Narration in Eva Hoffman's *Lost in Translation*

*Øyunn Hestetun*

Seeing the world through this other tongue I see it differently. It is a different world
(David Malouf, *An Imaginary Life*).

The practice of autobiographical writing bears witness to the writer's urge to revisit and reconstruct places and experiences that belong to the past, but which have left lasting traces in memory. As Jerome Bruner observes in "The Autobiographical Process", "autobiography is life construction through 'text' construction" (Bruner 1995: 176). The compulsion to tell one's own story becomes perhaps particularly pronounced for the category of writers who have lost their home of origin, and who in their memoirs write *as* exiles, and *of* exile from the lost home.[1] Retrospection tends, however, to be accompanied by the projection of future possibilities, and the mourning of the lost home by the effort of constructing a new home elsewhere. In "Reflections on Exile" Edward Saïd writes: "The exile knows that in a secular and contingent world, homes are always provisional", and he ventures to suggest the productive and creative potential of the exilic experience when he adds: "Exiles cross borders, break barriers of thought and experience" (Saïd 2000: 185). The creative potential of border crossing is also brought into focus by Theodor Adorno, when he states in an oft-cited passage from *Minima Moralia* that, "In his text, the writer sets up house. ... For a man who no longer has a homeland, writing becomes a place to live" (Adorno 2005: 87).[2]

Saïd and Adorno are among the many exiles and border crossers who could be said to have made writing their "place to live", and so has Polish-American

---

[1] For a discussion of different usages and implications of terms such as exile, migrant, Diaspora, traveler, and tourist, see e.g. Kaplan 2005: esp. ch. 3, entitled "Travelling Theorists: Cosmopolitan Diasporas".

[2] See e.g. Saïd 1999: 114 and 1994: 54-59. As will be noted below, Hoffman herself includes a reference to Adorno, but to a different passage.

Eva Hoffman, if on a less grand scale.[3] Her memoir *Lost in Translation: A Life in a New Language*, published in 1989, provides an account of her early formative years, during which she experienced translocation twice, first from Poland to Canada at the age of thirteen, and next to the United States as a young adult. As her title indicates, her memoir foregrounds how the crossing of geographical borders is paralleled by *cultural* transplantation and *linguistic* transposition. Her account articulates her sense of loss at leaving her home of origin and her efforts to make herself a new home – and as her subtitle reads "A Life in a New Language" – in North America. It is obvious that the retrospective reconstruction of the migrant experience is made by someone who has an intimate sense of – and love of – language. Commenting on the textual constructionist stance that permeates Hoffman's memoir, Danuta Zadworna Fjellestad writes: "For Hoffman, the space between the *memory of her selfhood* and her *intellectual understanding of herself as a script* becomes the space of exile" (Fjellestad 1995: 143). Not surprisingly, as becomes clear in the final part of her memoir, Hoffman has made language and the written word her profession as an academic, editor, and writer.[4]

Hoffman's story of migration during the post-WWII era, in which Europe figures as the home of origin, finds parallels in numerous stories of the present time, except that in more recent years, Europe has tended to represent a place

---

[3]   Much critical space has been devoted to the question of how to categorize Hoffman's ethnic and cultural belonging. While many comment on Hoffman's own usage of "American" as a denominator for both Canada and the United States, Mary Besemeres, for instance, describes Hoffman as Polish-Canadian and emphasizes her ethnic identity as Jewish (Besemeres 1998: 327). Hoffman was born as Ewa Wydra in Cracow, Poland, July 1, 1945, and immigrated at the age of 13 with her parents to Vancouver, Canada, in 1959. At 19 she left for university studies in the United States on a scholarship from Rice University, Texas, went on to Harvard for her PhD, and chose New York for her professional life for many years. She is currently based in London, but divides her time between London and the United States. In a 2005 interview she explains that she holds two passports; while the Canadian one grants her access to Britain, she is not ready to give up her American citizenship (Hoffman 2005).

[4]   In addition to her memoir, Hoffman has to date written three works in which she looks back on her European heritage: *After Such Knowledge: Memory, History and the Legacy of the Holocaust* (2004), *Shtetl: The Life and Death of a Small Town in the World of Polish Jewry* (1997), and *Exit into History: A Journey Through the New Eastern Europe* (1993). She has also published *Time: Big Ideas, Small Books* (2009), and two novels: *Appassionata* (first published as *Illuminations* 2008), and *The Secret* (2001). She worked for *The New York Times* 1979-90, and has also contributed to publications such as *The Atlantic Monthly* and *The Yale Review*.

of arrival rather than departure. In an increasingly globalized world where migration is the order of the day, for numerous people arriving from different parts of the world – in similar ways as the United States of earlier times – Europe epitomizes the land of opportunity, adventure, freedom and fulfillment. While Hoffman's memoir constitutes a testimony of the seminal consequences of migration for her own personal life, her story may also contribute to a more general understanding of the experience of the crossing of borders. Her tale of uprooting, translocation, and acculturation transcends the specific historical moment and geographical place, and articulates an experience that also has more general relevance. In the following I will take a closer look at how Hoffman's memoir is structured and evokes tropes often found in immigrant writing within various genres; how it epitomizes the liminal position of the border crosser, and how – in "writing exile, writing home" – it constitutes an effort of self-definition and finding at-homeness in narrative construction.

## Three Parts: Nostalgia, Alienation, Reconciliation

The titles of the three parts of Hoffman's memoir repeat tropes that resonate with religious significance: Paradise, Exile, and The New World. Evoking Hoffman's Jewish background, these titles also bring to mind their scriptural foundation and the history of the Diaspora. In addition, the title of the last part connects her memoir to the archetypal American immigrant experience of leaving the Old World of Europe behind for a life in the New World of promise and freedom. The three parts loosely correspond to Hoffman's migration across national borders from one geographical location to the next, and to the different stages of life, from childhood, through adolescence, to young adult life. Concurrently, the narrative mood shifts from nostalgia, through alienation, to conciliation. While the retrospective voice of the narrating self informs the text throughout, it manages to convey a vivid sense of the gradual shifts in the voice of the experiencing or narrated self, which slowly but surely develops into the assured voice of someone who has found a sense of at-homeness in the adopted place.

The first part of Hoffman's memoir takes us back to her childhood years in Cracow, Poland, in the 1950s. If the dominant mood in this first part is nostalgia, it is fuelled by what André Aciman calls "compulsive retrospection" which, he argues, is what "even a 'reformed' exile will continue to practice … almost as a matter of instinct" (Aciman 1999: 13). Hence, in Hoffman's retrospective meditation on her home of origin, Cracow is construed as "Paradise." The opening lines indicate her state of mind on leaving her own private paradise at the age of thirteen: "It is April, 1959, I'm standing at the railing of the *Batory*'s upper deck, and I feel that my life is ending" (3). Going back in time from this moment of departure, she reconstructs her lost home, offering a description of place as a palimpsest of recollections, presenting glimpses of cherished places, episodes she remembers, and people she loved, interspersed with comments on objects, smells, sights, and emotions that she recalls. Her account thus exemplifies Lawrence Buell's notion of "place-sense" as "a kind of palimpsest of serial place-experiences" (73). Reflecting on the way in which she construes her lost home, Hoffman remarks:

> But the wonder is what you can make a paradise out of. … I grew up in a lumpen apart-ment in Cracow, squeezed into three rudimentary rooms with four other people, surrounded by squabbles, dark political rumblings, memories of wartime suffering, and daily struggle for existence. And yet, when it came time to leave, I … felt I was being pushed out of the happy, safe enclosures of Eden (5).

In this and other passages the narrating voice evinces awareness of the con-structed nature of her life story; she aims to capture the emotions of the experiencing self, the child she once was, while at the same time adding the self-reflective thoughts of her mature self.

The Hoffman family left Poland at a time of growing anti-Semitic senti-ment. In her memoir Hoffman mentions that the Polish authorities lifted the ban on emigration for Jews in 1957, after which "the exodus beg[an]", cul-minating with "an 'anti-Zionist' purge" in 1968 (83). In a later piece entitled "The New Nomads", she writes:

> My emigration took place during the Cold War, though not in the worst Stalinist years. My parents chose to leave, though that choice was so overdetermined that it could hardly have been called "free". But I happened to be a young and unwilling emigrant, yanked from my childhood, which I had believed to be happy (Hoffman 1999: 45).

These comments may be read as a response to the critique directed at her memoir for the way in which it constructs the Polish home as Paradise, not only with reference to the general treatment of Jews in Poland at the time, but also because almost all members of her own family were Holocaust victims.[5]

---

5     Such critique has been voiced by, among others, Marianne Hirsch and Sarah Phillips Casteel. For responses to criticism along these lines, see e.g. Besemeres (1998: 329-30 note 8), and

While it is true that her memoir does not dwell on the anti-Semitic sentiments that ruled, Hoffman does not repress all memory of this dark side of her land of origin. She notes, for instance, that her family's emigration was motivated by the realization that "Poland is home, in a way, but it is also hostile territory" (84), while she also acknowledges her tendency to shy away from the stories that her mother tells her: "I can't go as near this pain as I should. But I can't draw away from it either" (25). As Heidi Slettedahl Macpherson observes, "Hoffman problematizes her own construction of Poland as 'paradise'" (Macpherson 2006: 63). Looking back on her own experience of dislocation in "The New Nomads", Hoffman proposes that exile may trigger mechanisms of "self-defense and self-preservation", and explains:

> My own tendency was certainly to nostalgia and idealization – perhaps because I was ejected before my loss of innocence, before I could develop more considered opinions and preferences or revise my feelings about the place I came from. And once you leave, such revisions become very difficult (Hoffman 1999: 54).

Denying that she nurtures patriotic sentiments for the country of her birth, Hoffman reflects on how the place that she first knew nonetheless remains ingrained in her. Despite the fact that she knows that to her and her kin Poland was "also hostile territory" (84), as noted above, she accepts that "the country of my childhood lives within me with a primacy that is a form of love" (74). Poland and Cracow represent to her "the landscapes that we saw as the first, and to which we gave ourselves wholly, without reservations" (74-75). In her post-1989 travelogue *Exit into History: A Journey Through the New Eastern Europe*, she remarks: "Poland – and by extension, Eastern Europe – remained for me an idealized landscape of the mind" (Hoffman 1993: ix).

The expulsion from the "Paradise" of childhood is followed by "Exile" in foreign lands. The transitional voyage by sea and rail brings the Hoffman family to Vancouver, a city that will forever remain the place in which she "fell out of the net of meaning into the weightlessness of chaos" (151). This middle part of her memoir dwells on the feeling of loss – the loss of home, existential grounding, and her former self. During her first difficult years of

---

Macpherson (2006: 68-69). It should be noted that, in *Shtetl: The Life and Death of a Small Town and the World of Polish Jews* (1997) and *After Such Knowledge: Memory, History and the Legacy of the Holocaust* (2004), Hoffman addresses this dark side of Polish history and the moral responsibility of later generations concerning the Holocaust.

acculturation she experiences pangs of nostalgia, but the predominant narrative mood is that of alienation. The overarching focus is directed at how she has to learn to speak, write, think, and even dream in a new language, while highlighting that this process involves constructing a new sense of self. This is poignantly brought out in her recollections of the moment she feels she is bereaved of her identity on her first day of school, as her own and her sister's names are Anglicized: from now on she will no longer be Ewa but Eve. She writes: "Our Polish names didn't refer to us; they were as surely us as our eyes or hands. ... We walk to our seats, ... with names that make us strangers to ourselves" (105). At the time her frustration remains unvoiced, but when reconstructing the episode in her memoir, she adds: "Alienation is beginning to be inscribed in my flesh and face" (110).

As a newcomer Hoffman also has to come to terms with "the unwritten rules for the normal" (147), which trigger the painstaking process of generating "A Life in a New Language". For instance, when people take a step back if she stands "too close, crowding them", she learns her lesson that, "Cultural distances are different". She finds that if she sits on her hands while talking, it will keep her from gesticulating, and that the codes of politeness dictate reserve, not allowing her to be direct in her comments to others or in venting her feelings. As she puts it, "I learn to tone down my sharpness". When her mother comments that she is "becoming 'English'" – the equivalent of her "becoming cold" – she feels hurt and protests, explaining: "I'm no colder than I've ever been, but I'm learning to be less demonstrative" (146). Becoming what she calls "a silent ventriloquist" (220), she learns to adapt to the cultural codes of her new environment, and to observe what she at a later point refers to as "subcutaneous beliefs, which lie just below the stratum of political opinion or overt ideology" (210).

From her description of this transitional period the reader gets a sense of how she feels locked in a void between her past and her present world:

> I can't afford to look back, and I can't figure out how to look forward. In both directions, I may see a medusa, and I already feel the danger of being turned into stone. Betwixt and between, I am stuck and time is stuck within me (116).

She feels existentially decentered, being translocated not only geographically, but also culturally and linguistically, as she is caught between her Polish self, articulated through her native language, and her new self, which she must construct by way of the English language. Borrowing the vocabulary of linguistic theory to express her being "Lost in Translation", she writes:

> But mostly, the problem is that the signifier has become severed from the signified. The
> words I learn now don't stand for things in the same unquestioned way they did in my
> native tongue (106).

Lying in bed at night waiting for the moment she refers to as her "nighttime talk with myself", she experiences that, "Nothing comes. Polish, in a short time, has atrophied, shriveled from sheer uselessness. Its words don't apply to my new experiences" (107).

While the text manages to convey the overwhelming emotional distress experienced by the adolescent self, the account of these episodes is at the same time clad in the self-reflexive vocabulary of the adult self looking back, allowing her to add comments such as: "I am becoming a living avatar of structuralist wisdom" (107). Thus the text draws attention not only to an emerging awareness in her former self that language is more than a transparent medium for thought, and that language and culture are vital to a person's identity and sense of self, but also to the fact that the intuition of such insight may come before theoretical explanation and intellectual learning. Hoffman ends her second part on a note that conveys her sense of a decentered or composite self:

> I cannot conceive of my story as one of simple progress, or simple woe. ... From now on,
> I'll be made, like a mosaic, of fragments – and my consciousness of them. It is only in that
> observing consciousness that I remain, after all, an immigrant (164).

Here she borrows the metaphor of the mosaic, widely adopted to denote Canada's multicultural society, which serves to signal that her old self will not be totally erased in the process of transition and translation into a new cultural environment.

The feeling of being culturally decentered is carried over into "Part III: The New World". While this section continues to play on the split self, the mood steadily changes from alienation to assurance, as the focus is gradually shifted from longing for the lost home and feeling lost in the new environment to arrival and the construction of a new self and a new home. Before making the full transition, however, Hoffman describes the doubleness she experiences, thus illustrating Aciman's contention that "exiles see double, feel double, are double" (Aciman 1999: 13). Hoffman represents this sense of doubleness as a split personality – a split between her Polish self and her American self – which encompasses language, culture, and sense of self. As several critics have observed, in some instances this split is staged as a dramatic dialogue,[6] for instance when her Polish self and her English-speaking self argue about love and marriage:

> Why should I listen to you? You don't necessarily know the truth about me just because you speak in that language. Just because you seem to come from deeper within.
> This is not the moment to lie to yourself.
> I'm not lying. I'm just not a child any longer. My emotions have become more complicated. I have ambivalences.
> …
> If you don't satisfy me, you'll always be dissatisfied.
> Go away. You're becoming succubus.
> I won't be so easy to get rid of.
> I don't need you anymore. I want you to be silent. Shuddup (199).

While the demon of her Polish self continues to haunt her for a while, Hoffman's English-speaking self gains the upper hand in the end. As Fjellestad perceptively notes, "Making a choice in Polish means following one's passion and a sense of duty to oneself; a choice in English entails reasoning and calculating", adding in parenthesis that "reasoning wins" (Fjellestad 1995: 139). Towards the end of the memoir, Hoffman confides: "When I talk to myself now, I talk in English" (272). Her efforts of translating herself have indeed rewarded her with "A Life in a New Language".

## Transplantation and Cultural Metamorphosis

In many respects Hoffman's memoir inserts itself into the tradition of American immigrant writing. She even evokes Mary Antin's *The Promised Land* from 1912, which has become a classic of the subgenre of immigrant autobiography, confiding that she has a special affection for Antin's tale, and observing that it reads like "a fable of pure success" (163). Antin's autobiography has been considered a prototypical enactment of the process of cultural transformation, aptly described by Thomas Ferraro in *Ethnic Passages*. In fiction as well as non-fiction by writers of immigrant origin, he says, we find "a ritual enacting of

---

6    Macpherson, for instance, finds that in these passages Hoffman draws on "contemporary theatrical performances" (Macpherson 2006: 72).

Americanization", as ethnic writers tend to "adopt the paradigm of cultural rebirth – 'from alien to American' – [and] then put it to the test of experience" (Ferraro 1993: 7, 1). The notion of "ethnic passage" as "cultural rebirth" is indeed inscribed in the opening words of Antin's autobiography, which read: "I was born, I have lived, and I have been made over" (Antin 1997: 1).

Both Antin and Hoffman adopt conventional tropes that figure in American tales of migration, and which hark back to an American classic from the time of the American Revolution. In his "Letter III: What Is an American?" from his *Letters from an American Farmer*, Crèvecœur suggests that, "Men are like plants" (Crèvecœur 1904: 56), and in the process of being transplanted to the New World they undergo a metamorphosis. He explains:

> … in Europe they were as so many useless plants, wanting vegetative mould, and refreshing showers; they withered, and were mowed down by want, hunger, and war; but now by the power of transplantation, like all other plants they have taken root and flourished! (Crèvecœur 1904: 52-53).

The plant imagery is repeated in a quotation from Antin's Introduction that Hoffman has inserted into her own tale. Antin writes: "All the processes of uprooting, transportation, replanting, acclimatization, and development took place in my own soul". But Hoffman is especially intrigued by the remarks that Antin has appended to this statement:

> I felt the pang, the fear, the wonder, and the joy of it. I can never forget, for I bear the scars. But I want to forget – sometimes I long to forget. … It is painful to be consciously of two worlds. The Wandering Jew in me seeks forgetfulness (Antin 1997: 3; qtd. in Hoffman 1998: 163).

Hoffman recognizes her own feelings in these comments, and wonders about what remains untold in Antin's tale, which otherwise appears to conform to the prototypical account of successful assimilation. Unlike Antin, she chooses *not* to "forget", and she makes "the pang, the fear" and "the scars" part of her own narrative. Already before her family's departure from Cracow, Hoffman is forewarned of the pains of exile by a family friend who tells her: "Delicate plants are more difficult to uproot and transplant. For a while, you'll feel like a plant with its roots exposed. You'll have to learn how to protect yourself" (82). Rather than repressing her feelings, Hoffman engages in the process of scrutinizing and "working through" her painful memories, as her memoir amply demonstrates.

Hoffman's memoir ends on a note that might suggest that she has finally "arrived", and that she comes close to having reenacted the ritual of the "self-made" woman by translating her old self into a Polish-American self. This suggestion of "arrival" is predicated on her realization that the cost of translocation is the transformation of self, but only up to a certain point, for she states: "But in my translation therapy, I keep going back and forth over the rifts, not to heal them but to see that I – one person, first-person singular – have been on both sides" (273). Apparently she comes close to shedding her old identity and embracing a new – American – identity. However, she repeatedly insists that the transformation is not complete, as when she writes:

> I only know that the hybrid creature I've become is made up of two parts Americana, that the pastiche has lots of local color. Despite my resistance, or perhaps through its very act, I've become a partial American, a sort of resident alien (221).[7]

In other words, the experience of border crossing leaves her with the sense of a composite self, which has been interpreted by many commentators as a symptom of her embracing a postmodernist constructivist perspective.[8]

While readings along these lines are compelling, I would like to draw attention to the formative effect of her experience of translocation and exile, and suggest that it has provided her with the "double perspective" that Saïd in *Representations of the Intellectual* considers to be one of the rewards of the exilic experience, resulting from the ability to see "what has been left behind and what is actual here and now" (Saïd 1994: 60). While exile implicates "deprivation" and "marginality", it also provides "a sort of freedom", he argues, as the perspective of marginality fosters the ability to consider "situations as contingent, not as inevitable" (Saïd 1994: 62-63, 60).[9] This reward – or "freedom" – is also recognized by Hoffman. Writing about the gap between her Polish and her

---

7    Hoffman's reference to "two parts Americana" could be read as an acknowledgement of her double relocation, first to Canada and subsequently to the United States.

8    Fjellestad, for instance, notes that while the text inscribes "poststructuralist wisdom" and the mixed reactions to "being thrown into the postmodern world of constantly shifting boundaries and borderless possibilities", at the same time "Hoffman's attempts to affirm a (poststructuralist) fragmented, decentered, and fictional self are subverted by outbursts of rage and an acute sense of loss" (Fjellestad 1995: 136, 143).

9    Basically the same point is made by Mikhail Bakhtin in his 1970 "Response to a Question from the *Novy Mir* Editorial Staff" in which he objects to the idea that the best way to understand a foreign culture is to immerse oneself in it: "In order to understand, it is im-

American self, or what she also refers to as the "Great Divide", she recognizes that it has left her with a new vision, a "chink" that offers a specific perspective on the world (272, 274), which allows her to declare: "Because I have learned the relativity of cultural meanings on my skin, I can never take any one set of meanings as final". Her experience of border crossing and transculturation has provided her with "an Archimedan leverage from which to see the world" (275). Nonetheless, she also admits:

> But for all our sophisticated deftness at cross-cultural encounters, fundamental difference, when it's staring at you across the table from within the close-up face of a fellow human being, always contains an element of violation (209-10).

That is to say that the perspective of marginality enables Hoffman to recognize even the distance that may exist between theoretical insight and lived experience, not only concerning her own past, but also in her encounter with others.

This perspective of marginality could be taken as a signal of how Hoffman resists sharing Antin's notion of "hav[ing] been made over", which also means that her memoir may not entirely conform to the structures of Ferraro's "paradigm of cultural rebirth" referred to above. Interestingly, Ferraro's model finds a parallel in religious initiation rituals as described by scholars such as Victor Turner. Building on Arnold Van Gennep's seminal writings, Turner makes reference to how "all rites of passage … are marked by three phases: separation, margin (or *limen*, signifying threshold in Latin), and aggregation" (1977: 94). The three parts of Hoffman's memoir could to some extent be said to match the three phases of the rite of passage: the initial phase in which the *initiand* undergoes separation or detachment from the former group, the liminal period characterized by the state of "betwixt and between", and the final stage of crossing the threshold to take one's new position in the social structure (Turner 1975: 232). However, her outsider origin as "migrant foreigner" sets her apart as one of Turner's "marginals", who remain in a liminal position: "Marginals like *liminars* are also betwixt and between", Turner observes, "but unlike ritual liminars they have no cultural assurance of a final stable resolution of their ambiguity" (Turner 1975: 233). In other words, while Hoffman may have crossed geographical borders, her memoir suggests that culturally and mentally she retains a liminal position, arrested on the threshold, as it

---

mensely important for the person who understands to be *located outside* the object of his or her creative understanding – in time, in space, in culture" (Bakhtin 1986: 7).

were, rather than having "arrived" in the sense of being totally assimilated or immersed into majority culture. The notion of liminality could also be said to be inscribed in her reference to herself as "a partial American, a sort of resident alien", as cited above.

## Self-Narration: Constructing a "Home" in Language

In the title of her memoir Hoffman juxtaposes "loss" and "life", and the narrative she constructs bears out that the transition from an overwhelming feeling of loss to the affirmation of life has been a painful process, but that it has finally led to conciliation. In the second part of her memoir, entitled "Exile", she expresses her acute sense of disorientation and being lost between two worlds, as illustrated in the episode in which she is looking at a map of the world with her schoolmates:

> The reference points inside my head are beginning to do a flickering dance. I suppose this is the most palpable meaning of displacement. I have been dislocated from my own center of the world, and that world has been shifted away from my center. There is no longer a straight axis anchoring my imagination; it begins to oscillate, and I rotate around it unsteadily (132).

In the last part, entitled "The New World", the focus of her yearning appears to have been shifted, from nostalgia for the lost home of her early years, to longing for a sense of at-homeness in her adopted homeland. However, she states that a symptom of her not being entirely assimilated is that rather than embracing the generally accepted idea among her peers in the United States that each individual must face the "challenge of having to invent a place and an identity" for themselves, she still entertains a "residual nostalgia ... for the more stable, less strenuous conditions of anchoring, of home" (197). As has already been suggested, in this third part Hoffman gradually but steadily moves beyond the moods of nostalgia and alienation to the mood of acceptance and conciliation.

In *An Imaginary Life*, in which David Malouf imagines the Roman poet Ovid's exile, we find the statement cited in the epigraph: "Seeing the world through this other tongue I see it differently. It is a different world" (Malouf 1999: 59). As we have seen, in her memoir Hoffman has adopted the concept of translation to foreground how language shapes the world. A definition of the word "translation" from *The Oxford English Dictionary* reads: "Transference; removal or conveyance from one person, place, or condition to another"

(*OED* 2010: I.1.a.). Indeed, translation in Hoffman's case involves all three levels, of "person, place", and "condition". With reference to a critical point in the process of her acculturation, Hoffman dwells on the trope of translation when she writes: "… if I'm not to risk a mild cultural schizophrenia, I have to make a shift in the innermost ways. I have to translate myself". But as already noted above, she resists complete acculturation, or assimilation, which would entail her giving up her old self entirely, so she adds:

> But if I'm to achieve this without becoming assimilated – that is, absorbed – by my new world, the translation has to be careful, the turns of the psyche unforced. … A true translation proceeds by the motions of understanding and sympathy; it happens by slow increments, sentence by sentence, phrase by phrase (211).

The painstaking work of translation brings with it a new sensibility to language, as she realizes that she can move between her Polish and English languages "without being split by the difference" (274), based on the insight that, "Each language modifies the other, crossbreeds with it, fertilizes it. Each language makes the other relative" (273).

While language and translation figure as central tropes in Hoffman's life story of how she comes to terms with the traumatic experience of emigration and exile, the "talking cure" is also featured, especially in the final section, and apparently it proves to be an effectual path towards conciliation and finding a sense of at-homeness.[10] At one point, when the lack of language as a "means of ventilation" leads to frustration, she ventures the supposition that, "If all therapy is speaking therapy – a talking cure – then perhaps all neurosis is a speech dis-ease" (124). Towards the end of her narrative she confides that "the vocabulary of self-analysis" has provided her with a means of "gaining control" (270), and she comments:

> For me, therapy is partly translation therapy, the talking cure a second-language cure. My going to a shrink is, among other things, a rite of initiation: initiation into the language of the subculture within which I happen to live, into a way of explaining myself to myself (271).

---

10    Fjellestad notes that, "the homologue of her 'talking cure,' the cure of writing her book, turns out to be saturated with self-conscious reflections on her consciousness" (Fjellestad 1995: 142).

She also explains to her mother, who worries when she hears her daughter is seeing a psychiatrist, that "it only means that I've arrived; I've made it as a proper member of the American middle class" (267).

In fact, a telling indicator of the degree to which Hoffman has adapted to her new environment is that her memoir tends to conform to the structures of what she herself in "Life Stories, East and West" coins the "psychoanalytic" narrative mode. A "psychoanalytical narrative", patterned on the parameters provided by psychoanalysis, which she considers to be "one of the master discourses" of the Western world, is juxtaposed with a "political-historical" narrative, which she deems to be the typical "Eastern European narrative" (Hoffman 2000: 2, 5, 11). While the former "privileges individual subjectivity", the latter tends to be "framed so strongly by a common metanarrative … within which or against which everyone had to position themselves" (Hoffman 2000: 12, 11). Hoffman's analysis in "Life Stories, East and West" brings into focus how various forms of life writing involve a reconfiguration of life, adhering to conventional structures through which we conceive of different stages of a life process. In "Life as Narrative" Bruner observes that, "Indeed, one important way of characterizing a culture is by the narrative models it makes available for describing the course of a life" (Bruner 2004: 694), and in "The Autobiographical Process" he posits that, "Our Western version … emphasizes individuality, power and autonomy in explicating lives" (Bruner 1995: 166). In her memoir Hoffman comments that "I live in an individualistic society" (270), and it is indeed this society – not the society of her origin – that has provided the distinctive "psychoanalytic" framing of her life narrative.

Hoffman's memoir offers evidence that her "talking cure" somehow metamorphosed into a "writing cure", thereby confirming Adorno's proposition that for the exile "writing becomes a place to live" (87). Writing opens up for the possibility of self construction and world construction, of forming a new identity and a new home. Hoffman tells us how she is instructed by a fellow student that, "This is a society in which you are who you think you are. Nobody gives you your identity here, you have to reinvent yourself every day" (160). While her immediate reaction is to say that she has problems "figur[ing] out how this is done", the process of writing her life story – going over her past, and prospecting for a future – provides a viable path. In an essay aptly entitled "Narrative Identity", Paul Ricœur writes:

> We equate life with the story or stories that we can tell about it. The act of telling would seem to be the key to the sort of connection to which we allude when we speak … of the "coherence of life" (Ricœur 1991: 194-95).

Similarly, under the title of "The Narrative Construction of Reality", Bruner explores the ways in which cognitive psychology opens up for how to think of "narrative as a form not only of representing but of constituting reality", based on the premise that narrative "operates as an instrument of mind in the construction of reality" (Bruner 1991: 5, 6). Bruner also ventures to say that autobiographical writing provides a way in which individuals may locate themselves in relation to social and historical communities, and that it may even function as a "major prophylactic against alienation" (Bruner 1991: 20), which indeed appears to apply in Hoffman's case.

In a passage where Hoffman reflects on the implications of writing her memoir, she remarks that, "to some extent, one has to rewrite the past in order to understand it" (242). This statement echoes the same insight as that expressed by Ricœur in *Time and Narrative* when he proposes: "Subjects recognize themselves in the stories they tell about themselves" (Ricœur 1988: 247). Calling attention to the crucial significance of language and narrative for human existence in general, this statement has a direct bearing on the impetus behind – and the significance of – various forms of life writing. If, as Ricœur argues in another context, "the meaning of human existence is itself narrative" (Ricœur 1984: 17), Hoffman's undertaking to reconstruct her own self in the new language of her new environment is daunting. At one point she suggests that,

> being cut off from one part of one's own story is apt to veil it in the haze of nostalgia, which is an ineffectual relationship to the past, and the haze of alienation, which is an ineffectual relationship to the present (242).

Self-narration opens up a path towards reconciliation with the past, a perspective on the present, and hope for the future.

At the end of her memoir Hoffman reveals that she has found some grounding in the world, and that her command of language, enabling her to compose her life story, has played a vital part in bringing her to this point:

> If images, as some philosophers theorize, congeal out of the matrix of language, then perhaps I've had to wait to have enough linguistic concentrate for hope to arise. Or perhaps I've had to gather enough knowledge of my new world to trust it, and enough affection for it to breathe life into it, to image it forth. But once time uncoils and regains its forward dimension, the present moment becomes a fulcrum on which I can stand more lightly, balanced between the past and the future, balanced in time (280).

Under the title of "Narrative Identity" Ricœur ventures what he calls a "chain of assertions" regarding autobiographical writing:

> self-knowledge is an interpretation; self interpretation, in its turn, finds in narrative, among other signs and symbols, a privileged mediation; this mediation draws on history as much as it does on fiction, turning the story of a life into a fictional story or a historical fiction … (Ricœur 1991: 188).

By providing an account of the home she lost, and of the new home she made for herself through a laborious process of cultural translation, Hoffman's text testifies to how "self-knowledge" involves "self interpretation", mediated through language in self-narration.

Hoffman observes that Adorno "once warned his fellow refugees that if they lost their alienation, they'd lose their souls" (209), but she adds that, "if I don't want to remain in arid internal exile for the rest of my life, I have to find a way to lose my alienation without losing my self" (209). Her memoir represents an exercise of writing herself into existence, seeking a way to "reenter myself, fold myself again in my own skin" (274). In an interview Hoffman states: "In my writing, especially in *Lost in Translation*, there was an attempt to integrate, in a sense, the Polish and the American parts of the self" (Hoffman 2002: Part 5). As Aciman puts it, "an exile is continuously prospecting for a future home" (Aciman 1999: 13), and to Hoffman, the written word has provided a means for directing her attention away from nostalgic longing for the past, a healing cure for her exilic alienation, and a path towards and finding at-homeness. Life narration has brought her from "the weightlessness of chaos" (151) to the recognition, noted in the final pages of her memoir, that, "a succession of tomorrows begins to exfoliate like a faith" (279). "Right now", she declares, "this is the place where I'm alive" (280).

## Bibliography

Aciman, André. (1999). "Foreword: Permanent Transients" in: Aciman, André (ed.). *Letters of Transit*. New York: New Press, 7-14.

Adorno, Theodor W. (2005; 1974). *Minima Moralia: Reflections on a Damaged Life*. Jephcott, E.F.N. (trans.). London: Verso.

Antin, Mary. (1997; 1912). *The Promised Land*. New York: Penguin.

Bakhtin, Mikhail. (1986). "Response to a Question from the *Novy Mir* Editorial Staff" in: Bakhtin, Mikhail. *Speech Genres and Other Late Essays*. Emerson, Caryl & Holquist, Michael (eds.). McGee, Vern W. (trans.). Austin: University of Texas Press, 1-9.

Besemeres, Mary. (1998). "Language and Self in Cross-Cultural Autobiography: Eva Hoffman's *Lost in Translation*". *Canadian Slavonic Papers/Revue Canadienne des Slavistes,* 40 (3-4), 327-44.

Bruner, Jerome. (1991). "The Narrative Construction of Reality". *Critical Inquiry,* 18 (1), 1-21.

Bruner, Jerome. (1995). "The Autobiographical Process". *Current Sociology,* 43, 161-77.

Bruner, Jerome. (2004). "Life as Narrative". *Social Research,* 71 (3), 691-710.

Buell, Lawrence. (2005). *The Future of Environmental Criticism: Environmental Crisis and Literary Imagination*. Oxford: Blackwell.

Casteel, Sarah Phillips. (2001). "Eva Hoffman's Double Emigration: Canada as the Site of Exile in *Lost in Translation*". *Biography,* 24 (1), 288-301.

Crèvecœur, J. Hector St. John. (1904; 1782). *Letters from an American Farmer*. Carlisle, MA: Applewood.

Ferraro, Thomas J. (1993). *Ethnic Passages: Literary Immigrants in Twentieth-Century America*. Chicago: University of Chicago Press.

Fjellestad, Danuta Zadworna. (1995). "'The Insertion of the Self into the Space of Borderless Possibility': Eva Hoffman's Exiled Body". *MELUS,* 20 (2), 132-47.

Hirsch, Marianne. (1996; 1994). "Pictures of a Displaced Girlhood" in: Veeser, H. Aram (ed.). *Confessions of the Critics*. New York: Routledge, 121-40.

Hoffman, Eva. (1993). *Exit into History: A Journey Through the New Eastern Europe*. New York: Viking.

Hoffman, Eva. (1998; 1989). *Lost in Translation: Life in a New Language*. London: Vintage.

Hoffman, Eva. (1999). "The New Nomads" in: Aciman, André (ed.). *Letters of Transit*. New York: New Press, 35-63.

Hoffman, Eva. (2000). "Life Stories, East and West". *Yale Review,* 88, 1-19.

Hoffman, Eva. (2002). "Between Memory and History: A Writer's Voice". Interview with Harry Kreisler, 5 Oct. Conversations with History. Institute of International Studies, UC Berkeley.

Hoffman, Eva. (2005). "Eva Hoffman". Interview with Robert Birnbaum. *Identity Theory,* 14 Feb.

Kaplan, Caren. (2005). *Questions of Travel: Postmodern Discourses of Displacement*. Durham: Duke University Press.

Macpherson, Heidi Slettedahl. (2006). "'There is No World Outside the Text': Transatlantic Slippage in Eva Hoffman's *Lost in Translation*". *ARIEL: A Review of International English Literature,* 37 (1), 61-79.

Malouf, David. (1999; 1978). *An Imaginary Life*. London: Vintage.

*Oxford English Dictionary*. (2010; 1989). 2nd ed. Online version August 2010.

Ricœur, Paul. (1984). "The Creativity of Language" in: Kearney, Richard (ed.). *Dialogues with Contemporary Continental Thinkers*. Interview with Richard Kearney. Manchester: Manchester University Press, 17-36.

Ricœur, Paul. (1988; 1985). *Time and Narrative*. Vol. 3. Blamey, Kathleen & Pellauer, David (trans.). Chicago: University of Chicago Press.

Ricœur, Paul. (1991). "Narrative Identity" in: Wood, David (ed. and trans.). *On Paul Ricœur: Narrative and Interpretation*. London: Routledge, 160-99.

Saïd, Edward W. (1994). *Representations of the Intellectual: The 1993 Reith Lectures*. New York: Pantheon.

Saïd, Edward W. (1999). "No Reconciliation Allowed" in: Aciman, André (ed.). *Letters of Transit*. New York: New Press, 87-114.

Saïd, Edward W. (2000; 1984). "Reflections on Exile" in: Saïd, Edward. *Reflections On Exile and Other Literary and Cultural Essays*. London: Granta, 173-86.

Turner, Victor. (1975; 1974). *Dramas, Fields, and Metaphors: Symbolic Action in Human Society*. Ithaca: Cornell University Press.

Turner, Victor. (1977; 1969). *The Ritual Process: Structure and Anti-Structure*. Ithaca: Cornell University Press.

# Poems and Poets in Transit: Heterochronic Cross-Border Acts or the Aesthetics of Exile in 20th Century German-Jewish Poetry

*Sissel Lægreid*

For exile hath more terror in his look. Much more than death (Shakespeare: *Romeo and Juliet*, Act 3, Scene 3).

In her essay "A New Type of Intellectual: the Dissident" (Moi 1986:1), Julia Kristeva argues that writing "is impossible without some kind of exile", and follows up by rhetorically asking how one can "avoid sinking into the mire of common sense if not by becoming a stranger to one's own country, language, sex and identity?" In other words, Kristeva suggests that the act of writing requires the state of fundamental Otherness in terms of the perspective of the outsider who is not only a stranger and alien to others, but also and more importantly a stranger and alien to himself. In her book *Strangers to Ourselves* (Kristeva 1991) in which she analyzes the relation between the self and the other, she continues this line of thought with reference to Freud's concept of "das Unheimliche", which according to the semantics of the German adjective of "heimlich" means both "friendly comfortable" and something "concealed and kept from sight" as well as "deceitful and malicious" going on "behind someone's back".

In other words, "heimlich", in as much as "the familiar and the intimate are reversed into their opposites", may be said to harbour its own contrary meaning of "the uncanny strangeness" (Kristeva 1991:182). With reference to Schelling's definition of the word "unheimlich" as everything that should have remained hidden and secret but has come to light, Freud concludes that "unheimlich" somehow is a kind of "heimlich". Thus he indicates the ambivalent nature of a word transgressing its own semantic limits by merging into its opposite of the "unheimlich" (Freud 1982: 248-250).

In accordance with the etymology of this ambivalent word as demonstrated by Freud, Kristeva, in a chapter discussing the experience of exile and estrangement, argues that the foreigner "is the hidden face of our identity" (Kristeva 1991:1) and still his "so other" face "bears the mark of a crossed threshold that irremediably imprints itself as peacefulness or anxiety", indicating "the never regular image" of a face bearing the imprints of "the ambiguous mark of a scar – his very own well-being". Despite the uneasy doubling of the image of exile and alienation as "good or evil – pleasing or death-bearing", Kristeva argues that to the observer the foreigner's happiness "seems to prevail, *in spite of everything*, because something has definitely been exceeded: it is the happiness of tearing away, of racing, the space of the promised infinite". However, this happiness is "constrained …, since the foreigner keeps feeling threatened by his former territory, caught up in the memory of happiness or a disaster – both always excessive". Consequently, the "foreigner calls forth a new idea of happiness. Between the fugue and the origin: a fragile limit, a temporary homeostasis" (Kristeva 1991:4).

In accordance with the etymology of the Latin words *fuge* from *fugere* "to flee", indicating something driving away or out, and *origin* from *oriri* "to rise" and *origo* "beginning, source of a spring and birth", in sum indicating a time-spatial starting point, being a stranger living in exile in terms of its time-spatial dimension means being mentally in motion and never permanently fixed to a point in time or space. "Posited, present, sometimes certain", the happiness of the foreigner "knows nevertheless that it is passing by, like fire that shines only because it consumes. The strange happiness of the foreigner consists in maintaining that fleeing eternity or that perpetual transience" (Kristeva 1991:4).

In other words, the experience of exile implies coping with fragile boundaries and temporary equilibriums. And from the perspective of the crossed threshold, both existentially in terms of real-life experience and aesthetically this time-spatial state can be described as being in transit, always in between seemingly opposite positions. This is only seemingly so, since these positions are never permanently *there* as fixed entities, but are constantly moving, thus making it difficult to limit and draw lines in order to separate the one from the other. Instead, they seem to co-exist in a manner described by Ernst Bloch, author of *The Spirit of Utopia* (Bloch 1964) and The *Principle of Hope*,[1] emphasizing the role of hope as a human drive, as the concept of the "Gleichzeitigkeit des Ungleichzeitigen": the simultaneous co-existence of the simultaneous and un-simultaneous.[2]

---

[1]    Bloch describes the principle of hope as a way of dreaming forwards and hoping beyond the present day in *Das Prinzip Hoffnung* (Bloch 1959:7 and 9).

[2]    Bloch first coins the concept of the simultaneous/un-simultaneous in connection with his reflections on the rise of fascism and its consequences in *Erbschaft dieser Zeit*, which was first published in Zürich in 1935. In the 1960s he used the concept again in connection with cultural imperialism. Bloch, who regarded this principle as characteristic of modernity,

In my paper, keeping this perspective in mind, I will focus on examples of the aesthetic effects of the experience of exile and estrangement. More specifically, I will look more closely at the kind of estrangement, alienation and Otherness that Kristeva points to as both fundamental and productive to writing, which, as indicated in the title of my paper, can be found in 20th century poems written in exile by German-speaking Jews.

In the sense that the specific aesthetic manœuvers of these poems imply the transgression of borders, my point of departure is that they can be read as examples of heterochronic cross-border acts: Heterochronic both in the Bakhtinian sense of the term implicating that different kinds of time and time-spaces co-exist and are at work simultaneously, and in the sense used by Bloch as indicated above.[3]

From the perspective of the experience of exile, the aesthetics of exile may also be read as a consequence of a kind of deterritorialization both in the sense used by Deleuze and Guattarri and in the sense used by anthropologists, who use the concept of deterritorialization to refer to the weakening of ties between culture, cultural subjects and place in a globalized world. The idea is that when cultures are uprooted from certain territories, they change and gain both a special and different meaning in the new territory they are taken into. In other words, in a globalized world the process of deterritorialization is conceived of as a process of culture changing, where certain cultural aspects tend to transcend specific territorial boundaries.[4]

In our globalized world, where things seem to be constantly in motion, this is considered a fundamental condition, a result of inherent processes of mediatization, migration and commodification, which go hand in hand with the intensification of deterritorialization (Hernandez 2002). Since the mediatization (i.e. globalized mass media, mediatic and communicative nets) is omnipresent in everyday contemporary cultural experience, it therefore must be clearly decisive in deterritorialized cultural experience (Tomlinson 1999).

---

focused on its connection to technical progress, rationality and the mental rejection of modernity which was typical of National Socialism. Cf. also Bloch 1978. When nothing else is noted, in the following all translations from German are by me (SL).

3    Heterochrony or "Multitemporality" is a key element in Bakhtin's conception of history. He explored the development of the concept of temporal incommensurability in his books on Rabelais and Dostoevsky as well as in his essays on Goethe and the chronotope.

4    One of the most influential theorists on the connection between globalization and deterritorialization is the anthropologist Aranji Appadurai. See e.g. Appadurai 1990: 295-310; 1991:192 -210; 1996.

This is an experience in which the globalized mass media open the world up to amplifying cultural horizons. Consequently, the places we live in along with our cultural activities, experiences and identities are transformed. Since globalization is a feature of deterritorialization, with its growing presence of social forms of contact, the result is a movement beyond boundaries which transcends the limits of a specific territory. And as a kind of "weighing of anchors" (Giddens 1990), the result is a closer involvement with the external, at the same time generating a closeness in distance and a relative distancing from what is close (Hernàndez 2002).

The dynamics of this observation indicating a time-spatial simultaneousness of the unsimultaneous as fundamental to the phenomenon of deterritorialization, may prove relevant to the following investigation, where the focus is on heterochronic cross-border acts and the aesthetics of exile in poems by poets in transit. But before we get there, let us make a detour via Gilles Deleuze and Félix Guattari, who coined the term deterritorialization. In their book *Anti-Œdipus* (Deleuze & Guattari 1972), and later in their Kafka book (Deleuze & Guattari 1975), they use it in connection with its opposite, reterritorialization, to develop a model for conceptualizing minor literature where the aim is the creation of "revolutionary conditions for every literature within the heart of what is called great (or established) literature". And since "there is nothing major or revolutionary except the minor", readers are encouraged to "create a becoming minor" (Deleuze & Guattari 1993:163-164), an expression which refers to the hegemony of language. Deterritorialization constantly aims at the disruption of traditional structures of language and expression, whereas reterritorialization reinforces its traditional structures. So reterritorialization means securing the status quo of mimetic representation, whereas owing to its "possibility of invention" (Deleuze &Guattari 1993: 157) deterritorialization tries to upset the balance by way of using deterritorialized language. This is a kind of language which disrupts the logic of language by transgressing its semantic norms and limitations. In other words, as a strategy deterritorialization implies deterritorializing mimetic representation, as Kafka did in *Metamorphosis* when he let words become blurred through animal noises. According to Deleuze and Guattari, using deterritorialized language means stopping "being representative in order to ... move towards [the] extremities or limits" of language. The skill and will of being inventive, the "intensive utilization of language"(Deleuze &Guattari 1993: 159), is a way of resisting the lure of language hegemony and of becoming major by way of opposing the "oppressed quality of this language to its oppressive quality" (Deleuze & Guattari 1993: 163).

An interesting point in view of the subject of my paper, Deleuze and Guattari specifically focus on the way the concept of deterritorialization and reterritorialization affects the lives and languages of people living "in a language that is not their own", thus living in what they call the "disjunction between content and expression" (Deleuze & Guattari 1993: 156). This situation, as Deleuze and Guattari point out, is precisely that of the minor writer, who, because of his or her outsider position "in the margins or completely outside his or her fragile community" is able much more freely to deterritorialize language "to express another possible community and to forge the means for another consciousness and another sensibility" (Deleuze/Guattari 1993: 154).

Both from an anthropological and aesthetical perspective, the definition of deterritoralization and the strategy of becoming minor offered by Deleuze and Guattari is of relevance to the question of how alienated individuals and groups who conceive themselves and are conceived of as society's Other assert and preserve their identity. The question is of fundamental relevance to the situation of exile, since both situations are the result of removing cultural subjects and objects from a certain location in space and time, which implies transcending specific territorial and language boundaries or limitations. The result is the experience of loss by the individuals involved, and in poetry such as that of many 20th century German-Jewish poems written in exile, this loss is aesthetically dealt with by performing a series of heterochronic cross-border acts in order to both restore, regain and resist the loss of home and identity.

The common denominator of these poems is the kind of aesthetics of the transitory described by Kristeva as a fragile limit and temporary homeostasis; and as indicated in the title of my paper, they are poems in transit, which more often than not bear the mark of a crossed threshold with its imprint of peacefulness and anxiety – allegorically not symbolically speaking. For in the sense Walter Benjamin describes the term allegory in *The Origin of German Tragic Drama*,[5] they are not merely referring to the state of being in exile and the feeling of grief and sorrow, but rather imaginatively enacting the experience of exile, in the sense of representing a fragile boundary and temporary equilibrium. In other words, they are not merely referring symbolically to the idea of exile, but in a more concrete manner they are allegorical personifications enacting the fragile boundary and temporary equilibrium of the experience of exile. Thus they aim to make what is no longer here, but is in fact absent, seem present and by way of imagination, emerge as a manifest thing or object to be experienced here and now in a manner which corresponds to Walter Benjamin's

---

5    My reference is to the German original *Ursprung des deutschen Trauerspiels*.

concept of the dialectical image (Benjamin 1980: 701; 1985: 576-77), where the idea is a kind of border-crossing movement from the dream state into the state of being awake and conscious. The place where the dialectical image can be seen virtually as a mosaic of the past and the future in a glance swift as lightning is in Benjamin's conception of the threshold between dream or the subconscious and the conscious state of being awake. Bearing this perspective in mind, I will argue that poems written in the wake of the Holocaust may be read as examples of a kind of emblematic reification where the principle is what Benjamin describes, in his book about the German Tragic Drama (Trauerspiel), as "das Primat des Dinghaften", the dominance of things or "thinglyness" before sentiments (Benjamin 1980: 207-430). Benjamin situates the origin of the Trauerspiel with its focus on "Trauer" and "Spiel" or the demonstrative acting out of sorrow in the allegory, and stresses the reciprocal relationship between the concept of the allegory and melancholy. As is the case with the baroque experience of a world in crisis, which is enacted in the Trauerspiel, both the allegoric and the melancholic experience is one of fragmentation and decay; and unlike the symbol, the melancholy allegoric experience lacks and rejects the illusion of coherence (Benjamin 1980: 361). Benjamin consequently describes the allegorical gaze of melancholy at the world as a disillusioned and critical one, where in accordance with "das Primat des Dinghaften", the aim is the fragmentation of the world by way of an emblematic reification and revaluation of the world of objects. As in the tradition of melancholy (cf. Dürer's *Melencholia I*) in the world of allegory and melancholy, props and relics play a significant part as emblems, although not in the sense of "meaning" something specific, but by virtually "being" what they signify in the sense of being released into the bodily world (physis). As indicated above, examples of this kind of allegorical writing and reading the world in its fundamental "thingly" dimension can be found in poems written in the wake of the Holocaust. These poems are what Paul Celan called "dingfest gemachte ... Worte" and "Wort-dinge im Gedicht"(Celan 2005:146), words made rock solid or "wordthings in the poem", containing the time-spatial dimension of the fugue and the origin as described by Kristeva, where the transitory concept of being both on the move away from and back to a place and time that can be imagined or dreamt of as still being there and gone at the same time,[6] simultaneously hovering somewhere in between, indicating the time-spatial co-existence of a

---

[6]   "Die dingfest gemachten Worte, die Wortdinge im Gedicht – in einem einmaligen Prozess gestellt, sie halten auf ihr Ende zu, eilen ihm entgegen: sie stehen im Lichte einer Letzt-

Not-Yet- and Never-More-Land, is essential. The exile's fundamental experience of loss and being uprooted, where the only hope lies in the aesthetics of the transitory, can be seen in the following statement by Celan: "Where are we going. Always back home". They are. I'm not! I reside at that Back, which goes on and on".[7]

This statement is one of many examples where Celan, in the sense Adorno from his American exile describes as making the text his home,[8] plays with the boundaries and limitations of language and situates himself in his own linguistic play of neologisms and duplicate semantics. In accordance with the appeal made in one of his poetological statements of embarking on the act of delimitation "Away from the borders – or across, beyond it into the unlimited!",[9] in the example above Celan is playing with the duplicate semantics of the word "Back", thus stressing its time-spatial dimension. Instead of going "back home" ("nachhause") to the place he topographically came from and has left, he, unlike the others ("sie"), claims to be residing ("hause") somewhere else in an alternative time-spatial dimension "at that back" ("im Nach"), "which goes on and on" simultaneously as personifications of both a time and place of the past in a split second emerging as being present here and now – like Benjamin's dialectical dream image.

A similar play in and with language can also be seen in poems by Rose Ausländer, who like Paul Celan came from the city of Chernovitsy, the capital of Bukovina, a land which in itself may be said to be a prototype of deterritorialization in the border-crossing sense used by anthropologists. Throughout its history this land has been on the move back and forth across the borders of Rumania, Russia and Austria. It was once the heart of the Rumanian Principality of Moldavia, from 1775 to 1918 it was the easternmost Crown Land of the Austrian Empire, and it is now divided between Rumania and the Ukraine.

The city of Chernovitsy, currently the administrative centre of the province of south-western Ukraine, was the old capital. Rose Ausländer and Paul Celan had both belonged to the same group of writers in Chernovitsy, left it forever shortly after the war, but kept returning to it by way of imagination in their poems from their positions as exiles in Paris (Paul Celan) and New York

---

dinglichkeit' – ich sage <u>Licht</u> nicht <u>Dunkel</u>, aber bedenken Sie: den Schatten, den das wirft!" (Celan 2005: 146).

7    "Wohin gehen wir. Immer nachhause. Sie tuns. Ich nicht! Ich hause im Nach, das da geht und geht". (Celan 1975: 59).

8    "In seinem Text richtet sich der Schriftsteller häuslich ein". (Adorno 1997:152).

9    "Fort von der Grenze – oder hinüber, hinweg ins Unbegrenzte!" (Celan 2005: 95 f.).

and later the Nelly-Sachs-Haus in Düsseldorf (Rose Ausländer). To deal with the loss of "home" in the wake of the Holocaust, they imagine and virtually experience themselves to be living in two places in time and space simultaneously. In other words, they perform transgressions of time-spatial borders, corresponding to the concept of the simultaneousness of the un-simultaneous in the sense Ernst Bloch uses the term: when describing his idea as the spirit of utopia and the principle of hope, Bloch talks about dreaming and remembering forwards and backwards in time at the same time in a dialectical movement (Bloch 1959). This corresponds to Walter Benjamin's concept of the dialectical image, which as indicated above is conceived of as a kind of border-crossing movement from the dream state into the state of being awake and conscious. In accordance with his Marxist-Messianic conviction, the idea was that of trying to rescue the tradition and what is left of the past from disappearing into oblivion by using a kind of quotation technique where fragments of the past are drawn or blasted out of their context in the past and into the present where they merge into an image, with traces of the past being seen and virtually experienced as being present and rescued for the future.

A similar dream image construction of the past in order to make it alive in the present and preserve it for the future is illustrated brilliantly in the following two poems dealing with the fundamental loss of what used to be "home" by making a transition into No Man's Land. In the first one (Sachs 1986: 204) Nelly Sachs, who was born in Berlin in 1891 of Jewish parents and after 1940 lived in exile in Stockholm, presents exile as an option between life and death in the following way:

> You have already got your flight luggage
> across –
> the border is open
> but first
> they throw all of your "home"
> like stars out the window
> do not come back
> inhabit the uninhabited
> and die.

This poem performs the act of border crossing on two different levels: First as a kind of rescue operation in order to escape by stating that the border is open and the flight luggage is already across. In other words, life can seemingly still go on somewhere safe on the other side of the border. But this is only seemingly so because the prospect the option is the loss of "home", where the concept of home (in inverted commas) implying a place of origin and identification in a Benjaminian sense by way of being both reified as "stars [thrown] out the window" and personified as stars alluding to Jews wearing the yellow star, although lost and vanished, is evoked as something simultaneously present here and now as a result of a heterochronic cross-border act between past and present producing a dream image of what was – in a split second. In this respect, these lines can also be read as an illustration of Kristeva's statement about the exile and the foreigner whose happiness is a fragile limit and temporary homeostasis.

But instead of the happy feeling about the possible return back across the borders of "home" at some point in the utopia of a brighter future, the future is death or even worse: the total banishment of the lines "inhabit the uninhabited/and die". The utopian No Man's Land thus turns out to be a dystopia with borders which can only be crossed at the peril of death and oblivion.

In the second poem, "Nobody" (Ausländer 1985: 132), Rose Ausländer chooses a different and playful mode when she states:

I am King Nobody
carrying
my No Man's Land in my pocket

With my Foreigner's Pass Port I travel
from Ocean to Ocean

Water your blue eyes
your black eyes
the colourless

My pseudonym
Nobody
is legitimate

Nobody
suspects
that I am a king
carrying in my pocket
my homeless land

Despite the playful and seemingly more optimistic mode than in the poem by Nelly Sachs, where the inhabitants are banished into the uninhabited territories to die, "home" is no longer there, but in transit carried and hidden by "King Nobody" in his pockets with a new or no identity as "No Man's Land" and therefore conceived of as "homeless land". In other words, the land which has been deterritorialized in the sense that it has lost its expected significance as such. And even though the lyrical subject claims to be carrying it with her in her pocket, it can no longer be inhabited. Therefore it does not exist any more as a home offering a permanent shelter to its inhabitants.

The heterochrony of the examples above is illustrated in the following lines from the poem *Windgerecht*[10] (Celan 1992: 169) by Paul Celan: "(Not Yet Been and still There / both even, / go through the hearts)".[11] As in so many of the poems Celan wrote, the context of this poem is the Holocaust, which in this particular stanza presents itself audio-visually to the reader as synecdochic representations of the dead making them present here and now: "Songs: / Eyevoices, / in chorus, / read themselves sore".[12]

The kind of aesthetics where the experience of exile is both reified and personified corresponds with Celan's concept of the poem as words made rock solid and as word things in the poem;[13] and as indicated above, this is also typical of the poetry of Nelly Sachs. In one of her many letters to Paul Celan, she talked of her poems as things and children and described her metaphors as wounds and her books as orphans with reference to the destiny of the Jewish people.[14] This destiny is dealt with in poems like "In Flight" (In der Flucht) from the collection *Flight and Metamorphosis* (Sachs 1968: 204), which describes the metamorphosis of the world from the perspective of a butterfly changing into an inscription on a stone which the poem's lyrical subject ends up holding in her hand stating that "Instead of Home / I hold the Metamorphoses of the World".[15] Thus the final lines of the poem sum up the experience of exile as a consequence of a never-ending process of flight and metamorphoser. In addition to the aesthetics of the transitory, which by definition accompanies the metamorphosis on all levels in time and space, the poem is an example of the fragile boundary and temporary homeostasis as described by Kristeva.

---

[10]  The title reads both as "Windjust/righteous" and "Winderect".

[11]  "(Ungewesen und Da, / beides zumal, / geht durch die Herzen)".

[12]  "Gesänge: Augenstimmen/im Chor / lesen sich wund".

[13]  "Die dingfest gemachten Worte, die Wortdinge im Gedicht" (Celan 2005: 147).

[14]  See Wiedemann 1993:10 and 12.

[15]  "An Stelle von Heimat / halte ich die Verwandlungen der Welt" (Sachs 1968: 204).

A similar experience can be seen in the concluding lines from another of her poems, "When someone comes from afar",[16] which sums up the experience like this: "A stranger always has his home in his arms like an orphan, that he is maybe just trying to find a grave for".

Nelly Sachs, who like Rose Ausländer knew Paul Celan, identified with the feeling of loss and desperate sorrow as a survivor of the Holocaust, which he has most expressively depicted in his most famous poem, the "Death Fugue" (Todesfuge) with the famous lines:[17] "Der Tod ist ein Meister aus Deutschland", "Death is a Master from Germany".

Interestingly, in view of the lines quoted above from the poem by Nelly Sachs, and in a comment on the reception of this poem in Germany, on several occasions Celan said that it was the only grave his mother, who was executed in a Rumanian concentration camp, ever had. In other words, *Death Fugue* was written for and in remembrance of his mother and reads as follows in English:

Black milk of daybreak we drink it at evening
we drink it at midday and morning we drink it at night
we drink and we drink
we shovel a grave in the air there you won't lie too cramped
A man lives in the house he plays with his vipers he writes
he writes when it grows dark to Deutschland your golden hair Margareta
he writes it and steps out of doors and the stars are all sparkling he whistles
his hounds to come close
he whistles his Jews into rows has them shovel a grave in the ground
he commands us play up for the dance
Black milk of daybreak we drink you at night
we drink you at morning and midday we drink you at evening
we drink and we drink
A man lives in the house he plays with his vipers he writes
he writes when it grows dark to Deutschland your golden hair Margareta
Your ashen hair Shulamith we shovel a grave in the air there you won't lie
too cramped
He shouts jab this earth deeper you lot there you others sing up and play

---

16  "Ein Fremder hat immer/seine Heimat im Arm/wie eine Waise/für die er vielleicht nichts/ als ein Grab sucht" in: "KOMMT EINER/ (von ferne)", (Sachs1968: 117).
17  Translated by John Felstiner (Felstiner1995).

he grabs for the rod in his belt he swings it his eyes are so blue
jab your spades deeper you lot there you others play on for the dancing
Black milk of daybreak we drink you at night
we drink you at midday and morning we drink you at evening
we drink and we drink
a man lives in the house your goldenes Haar Margareta
your aschenes Haar Shulamith he plays with his vipers
He shouts play death more sweetly this Death is a master from Deutschland
he shouts scrape your strings darker you'll rise then as smoke to the sky
you'll have a grave then in the clouds there you won't lie too cramped
Black milk of daybreak we drink you at night
we drink you at midday Death is a master aus Deutschland
we drink you at evening and morning we drink and we drink
this Death is ein Meister aus Deutschland his eye it is blue
he shoots you with shot made of lead shoots you level and true
a man lives in the house your goldenes Haar Margarete
he looses his hounds on us grants us a grave in the air
he plays with his vipers and daydreams der Tod ist ein Meister aus Deutschland
dein goldenes Haar Margarete
dein aschenes Haar Shulamith

As indicated both by its title ("Death Fugue") and by the aesthetics of its composition, this poem can be read as a significant example of what Kristeva describes as characteristic of the transient happiness of the foreigner living in exile, which moves between "the fugue and the origin: fragile limit, a temporary homeostasis". In accordance with the etymology of fugue and origin stated above, the poem illustrates the principle of the transitory – both "fleeing eternity" and "perpetual transience". This notion is supported by the irony of metaphor of "the grave in the air", the only space granted to the grave-digging Jews by the man commanding them to work harder.

Instead of going into the details of this rich poem in the attempt to add yet another interpretation to the long list already in existence, I would like to focus on the translation made by the biographer John Felstiner of some central words, which is particularly interesting in relation to the concept of the simultaneous un-simultaneous. Felstiner does not once say "Germany", but keeps the word "Deutschland" from the original, the result being that the time-space dimension and its heterochronic aspect is emphasised in a way that keeps the memory of the tragedy alive and present here and now, which of course was what Paul Celan himself intended in his German version of the tragedy.

The same can be seen in the translation of the two allegoric metaphors, each in their synecdochic way referring to the very core of German and Jewish culture and tradition, and thus remembering it: "Dein goldenes Haar Margareta" and "Dein aschenes Haar Shulamith", "your golden hair Margareta" and "your ashen hair Shulamith". Here the translator keeps moving back and forth between the German and the English language, and even combines the two languages in different ways, before finally returning to the German original: "Dein goldenes Haar Margareta/Dein aschenes Haar Shulamith".

The aesthetic effect of this combination is increased in the verse prior to these two lines by the way the English translation keeps merging into the German original in a way that makes it difficult to keep the two apart. And because of this merging act, in which the two traditions, the German and the Jewish, which the tragedy on so many levels was all about, are represented by two pars pro totos, the names Margareta and Shulamith, this poem may be seen as a heterochronic cross-border act – in other words performed both in a linguistic and historical sense.

In addition to the loss of their home and native country, a common denominator of Jewish German-speaking poets living in exile was the experience of having lost their mother tongue, or more precisely their use of the German language as they knew it, the language they had identified with and used before the catastrophe. This led to a conflict which forced them to reflect on their relation to it, since it was now also virtually the language of the murderers. One way of solving the conflict between identifying with and rejecting this language was to stop using it. And another way was the one chosen by Paul Celan, who, as indicated above, played with transgressing its semantic limits by creating new words or playing with its etymology, thus both pushing against and crossing its borders. In the sense of Deleuze and Guattari, Celan chose the way of "becoming a minor" by constantly creating deterritorialized language, which functioned both as a resistance and a rescue operation to avoid having to surrender to the hegemony of the "master language" or as in the Death Fugue "der Meister aus Deutschland".

His play with the limitations of language was a way of coming to terms with the loss of home and native country, and a way to avoid having to give up his mother tongue, in German called Muttersprache as opposed to Vaterland, the father's country. Rose Ausländer playfully points to this significant opposition in the following poem, which also deals with the loss of homeland. She deliberately calls it "Motherland" ("Mutterland") (Ausländer 1985: 98):

My Fatherland is dead
They have buried it
in the Fire.
I live in my Motherland
Word.

A similar transition from native country as a geographical area and cradle of cultural identity to language as a substitute for the loss can be seen in the following statement made by Paul Celan: "Obtainable, close and un-lost in the midst of all losses only this one thing stayed: language".[18] Consequently, Celan addressed this problem of loss by transgressing the borders and limitations of the German language, as in the following poem (Celan 1985: 57):

BLACK,
like memory's wound mark,
the eyes are digging for you
in the crownland, –
bitten bright by heart's teeth –,
which forever will be our bed:
through this shaft you must come –
you come.

In the sense of the seed
the ocean out-stars you in your innermost, for ever,
naming has come to an end
over you I throw my destiny.

In this example remembrance of the past catastrophe is called memory's black wound, ("Erinnerungswunde") and eyes are digging for the poem's you, the beloved other, in the Crownland (Kronland), Celan's lost home of Bukovina, once part of Austria-Hungary, which, as is stated, forever will be their bed due to the fact that it now after the catastrophe is felt to be a land bitten bright by heart's teeth. The metaphor thus indicates the internalised pain of the poem's I and You, who are both suffering the consequences of the Jewish destiny, a notion which is indicated by the neologism "out star" ("aussternen") used in-

---

18   "Erreichbar, nah und unverloren blieb inmitten der Verluste dies eine: die Sprache" (Celan 1983: 185).

stead of "carve out", thus connecting to the context of history and the yellow star Jews were forced to wear during the Nazi regime.

This reading is confirmed at the end of the poem by the mentioning of the word destiny and in the line "the name giving has come to an end", in other words there will be no more naming, indicating the many nameless graves of the dead after the Holocaust. This destiny, which for the survivors implied not only the loss of "home" but also of identity, and as in Rose Ausländer's poem becoming a Nobody, is described by Celan in the poem called "TO STAND":[19]

TO STAND, in the shadow
of the wound mark in the air.

Stand-for-nobody-and nothing
Unrecognized,
for you alone
With everything, which has room in there,
also without language

As in the previous poem, the first line refers to and evokes the memory of the Holocaust: the neologism "Wundenmal" (wound mark) can be read as an equivalent to memory's black wound (Erinnerungswunde), since the German "Mal" in addition to "mark" also means memorial and commemoration. And in a heterochronic sense this can be read as a dialectical dream image where past and future merge into one here and now, rooted in the intention of preserving what was once there and thus rescuing fragments of it for the future. From a poetological perspective this may be read as a kind of utopian wishful thinking, a dream image, about something still being "there" where it has yet not been, as in the lines from the poem "Windgerecht" quoted above: ("Not been and still there, / Both even / go through the hearts)".

As a kind of a delimitating dream image where memory and remembrance play an essential part, some of this can also be seen in the following poems. The first one, "The Heritage I",[20] is by Rose Ausländer and reads like this in English:

---

19    "STEHEN", (Celan 1983: 23).
20    "Das Erbe I" (Ausländer 1985: 224 224).

Where
in this Austrialess time
is there a word still growing
in its roots

I am thinking
of Bukovina
uprooted word
birds presumed dead

also of Safed
where I am deaf and dumb
but perhaps heritage
is writing poetry there
for me.

The poem is written in memory of the lost home land of Bukovina, which like Rose Ausländer and the lyrical subject of the poem lives in an "Austrialess" time. In the anthropological sense of deterritorialization indicated above, it has been uprooted from its previous connection with Austria and in that sense like the lyrical I is searching for belonging and perhaps finding it in "heritage" represented by "Safed", an important place of learning in Jewish religious tradition. Safed was a centre of cabbalist mysticism, and alongside Jerusalem, Tiberias and Hebron was a holy Jewish city. In other words, it is the utopian time-spatial dimension of Jewish heritage and/or identity which Rose Ausländer is trying to inscribe herself into by mentioning its name, thus hoping to be part of its tradition and identity here and now, and perhaps and in accordance with the principle of hope, as a part of it, to be preserved for the future. This hope of preservation and still belonging by transcending time-spatial borders lies in the poem's last line: "perhaps heritage is writing poetry there for me".

A similar hope of being rescued by way of aesthetic manœuvers can also be seen in the poem "In the rivers" (Celan 1983: 13) by Paul Celan. Although it may seem very different, the same time-space dimension can be seen in these lines, which are intentionally insisting and hoping to be preserved for the future by way of making a heterochronic act of border crossing. In other words, as we can see from the very first line, to inhabit the utopian No Man's Land – beyond the limitations and boundaries of time and space:

In the rivers north of the future
I throw out the net which you
reluctantly burden
with shadows written
by stones.

Situating itself in the utopian time-spatial dimension "north of the future", the lyrical subject (I) hopes to get rooted in the moving element of rivers by throwing out a net which the poem's other (You) burdens. However, the rooting takes place not only "reluctantly" but also "with shadows written by stones". Consequently, since the shadows are mere reflections of stones representing in writing what is absent, despite the hope and intention of the poem's I of finding a place in a u-topian landscape beyond all time-spatial limitations, the actual rooting or re-rooting never takes place.

In this sense this poem may be read as a poem by a poet in transit. And its intention may therefore be said to correspond to a poetological statement Celan made about the poetics of poems, where he describes their intention as "Event, Movement, Being in transit". Poems, he said, are both wounded by reality and searching for reality, constantly trying to find the right direction and as such crossing borders, hoping at some point to be washed ashore somewhere, perhaps in the safe haven of heart land ("Herzland"), like messages in a drift bottle. For also in this sense poems are, according to Celan, in transit, always on the move searching for something out there – hopefully solid rock to hold on to, and simultaneously, as in the statement quoted above, moving towards their end in the light of a last thinglyness ("Letztdinglichkeit") (Celan 2005: 146).

In accordance with the appeal to poets quoted above "Away from the borders – or across, beyond it into the unlimited!", since it may be read as an expression of the experience of exile and alienation in the Kristevan sense of a fragile boundary and a temporary equilibrium, Celan's poem both illustrates and sums up the intention of this essay: As in the examples above by other poets in transit, it depicts the state of loss and perpetual absence which is fundamental to the experience of exile. And thus it illustrates how this implies being in transit, constantly on the move between repeated acts of de- and reterritorialization, where the only hope of finding a place like home lies in crossing borders into a u-topian landscape – for ever beyond boundaries.

# Bibliography

Adorno, Th. W. (1997). "Minima Moralia. Reflexionen aus dem beschädigten Leben" in: Tiedemann, R. (ed.). *Gesammelte Schriften*. Frankfurt a.M.: Suhrkamp Verlag.

Appadurai, A. (1990): "Disjuncture and Difference in the Global Cultural Economy" in: Featherstone, M. (ed). *Global Culture*. London: Sage.

Appadurai, A. (1991). *"Global ethnoscapes: Notes and queries for a transnational anthropology"* in: Fox, R.G. (ed.). *Recapturing anthropology: working in the present*. Santa Fe: School of American Research Press.

Appadurai, A. (1996). *Modernity at Large: Cultural Dimensions of Globalization*. Minneapolis: University of Minnesota Press.

Ausländer, R. (1985). *Gesammelte Werke in sieben Bänden*. Braun, H. (ed.). Frankfurt a.M.: Fischer Verlag.

Benjamin, W. (1980). *Gesammelte Schriften*. Tiedemann, R. and Schweppenhäuser, R. (eds.). Frankfurt a.M.: Suhrkamp Verlag.

Benjamin, W. (1985). *Das Passagenwerk*, Tiedemann, R. (ed.). Frankfurt a.M.: Suhrkamp Verlag.

Bloch, E. (1959). *Das Prinzip Hoffnung*. In fünf Teilen. Frankfurt a.M.: Suhrkamp Verlag.

Bloch, E. (1964). *Geist der Utopie*, Frankfurt a.M.: Suhrkamp Verlag.

Bloch, E. (1978). *Tendenz – Latenz – Utopie*. Frankfurt a.M.: Suhrkamp Verlag.

Celan, P. (1992). *Gesammelte Werke*. Allemann, B. and Reichert, S. (eds.). Frankfurt a.M.: Suhrkamp Verlag.

Celan, P. (1975). "Briefe an Alfred Margul-Sperber". *Neue Literatur* Jg. 26, H. 7, Bucarest.

Celan, P. (2005). *Mikrolithen sinds, Steinchen*. Die Prosa aus dem Nachlaß. *Kritische Ausgabe*. Wiedemann, B. & Bardiou, B. (eds.). Frankfurt a.M.: Suhrkamp Verlag.

Deleuze G. and Guattari F. (1972). *L'Anti-Œdipe*. Les Edition de Minuit: Paris

Deleuze G. and Guattari F. (1975): *Kafka. Pour une littérature mineure*. Paris: Les Editions de Minuit.

Deleuze G. And Guattari, F. (1993). "Minor Literature: Kafka" in: Boundas, Constantin V. (ed.). *The Deleuze Reader*. New York: Columbia University Press.

Felstiner, J. (1995). *Paul Celan: Poet, Survivor, Jew*. New Haven: Yale University Press.

Giddens, A. (1990). *The Consequences of Modernity*. Cambridge: Cambridge Polity Press.

Hernàndez, G.M. (2002). *La modernitat globalitzada. Anàlisi de l'entorn social*. València: Tirant lo Blanch.

Holmquist, B. (1986). *Das Buch der Nelly Sachs*. Frankfurt a.M.: Suhrkamp Verlag.

Kristeva, J. (1991). *Strangers to ourselves,* trans. Roudiez, Leon s. New York and London: Harvester & Wheatsheaf.

Mitscherlich. A. et al. (eds.). *Sigmund Freud. Studienausgabe*, vol. I-X. Frankfurt a.M: Fischer Verlag.

Moi, T. (1986). *The Kristeva Reader.* Oxford: Basil Blackwell.

Tomlinson, J. (1999). *Globalization and Culture.* Chicago: Chicago University Press.

Wiedemann, B. (1993). *Paul Celan/Nelly Sachs. Briefwechsel.* Frankfurt a.M.: Suhrkamp Verlag.

# The Threshold Returns the Gaze: Border Aesthetics in Disciplined Space

*Jørgen Lund*

The expression "border aesthetics" is likely to be accompanied by a nimbus stemming from the concept of avant-garde. Border aesthetics immediately triggers ideas of spatial movement with "front line" significance, accomplishments with the status of "border crossings". Art and aesthetic experience, as long as they are seen as valuable at all, are among contemporary culture's most likely candidates for top ranking when it comes to expectations of innovation and change, the capacity to transgress or transcend. The expression "border aesthetics" thus often seems to signify the sheer opposite of standing still and getting nowhere. The notion that we may encounter new and different people at the border also contributes to this air of heroism.

There is a danger that this could make the notion of border aesthetics amount to little more than a run-of-the-mill academic neologism, a verbal formula only suitable for selling in well-established, normative conceptions. In this essay, I will try to offer an alternative context for considering the aesthetic significance of the border, and thereby hopefully point out a different tendency inherent in the notion of border aesthetics. I will suggest a view that is concerned not so much with ideas like transgression or cultural exchange across borders as with the phenomenology of the border "itself". Maybe here – so to speak *on* the border or even deep *inside* it – one can find that border aesthetics doesn't necessarily end up recommending clichés about "positive thinking" and "crossover operations", as if there were no limits.

Borders have played an important role in mythology ever since Antiquity, as suggested by the well-known subject *rites de passage.* One of the authors who have gone into the richness of the border phenomenon and made it a decisive part of his thinking is Walter Benjamin. In works like *Berlin Childhood Around 1900*, "The Work of Art in the Age of Mechanical Reproduction", *One-way Street* and *Das Passagen-Werk*, the border occurs in a number of ways: *Gateways* and other in-between architectural zones like loggias, *clipping* as essential effects in film, unnoticeable transitions from one part of the city to the next experienced in the state of *flanerie*, mornings passing silently and irreversibly into afternoons. And of course: eventually the political and temporal barriers separating the exiled Jewish writer from his bourgeois adolescence and native city of Berlin. But – and this will be the focus here – the *threshold* seems eventually to stand out as the very middle of Benjamin's concern with borders.

In Benjamin's philosophy, the threshold can actually be seen as a kind of end in the double sense of the word. In this text, I will follow the significance of the threshold by regarding it as the very centre of Benjamin's critique of spatial thinking in a certain sense. Benjamin is actually but one among a number of modern thinkers who may inform border aesthetics in ways which resemble each other, but his contribution may be of special interest owing to its tendency to condense into what I will call thinking in "thingness". The threshold is where borders and what I will call "border discipline" change into *matter* in a certain sense.

Winfried Menninghaus's book from 1986, *Schwellenkunde. Walter Benjamins Passage des Mythos*, places the concept of threshold and a certain "threshold knowledge" as a kind of heading for Benjamin's philosophy in general. And indeed, borders and transitions are present in Benjamin's writing. In fact, they occur to such a degree that one could be tempted to say that they eventually gain contours and materialize *as* threshold. The threshold stands forth rather like an object of desire in the middle of it all. For instance, the experience of space and time in *flanerie* is characterized by Benjamin as *Durchdringungs- und Überdeckungstransparenz*, "transparency of blending and overlapping" (Benjamin 1983: 584). What can be called a formal principle of early avant-garde, developed in Siegfried Giedion's architectural thinking, is thus in Benjamin not simply a question of "new form" and new spaces, but indirectly a staging of something with the character of a material event. In the thematic of superposition, there is ultimately densification – spaces, volumes and positions coming together as a certain materiality or body.

What is at stake here? What could be Benjamin's reason to arrange a sense in which interest in the border ends up with the *object* threshold? Let us try to slow down this question by first asking about the border. Those who know about thresholds "know about waiting", Benjamin writes (Benjamin 1989: 25). Later, he remarks: "Threshold and border must be strictly distinguished: The threshold is a *zone*" (Benjamin 1983: 1025). Thus, in opposition to the threshold understood as a material object with an extension, the border is a *line*: Sometimes an extremely significant one, sometimes a question of life and death. Benjamin's own tragic fate at the border between France and Spain in 1940 is but one example of this.

## Border discipline

On the border, that which is most decisive and real, is something which exists on a higher level, so to speak above one's head. The border is where one experiences the power of abstract factors, whether politics, legislation or some age-old state of affairs between clans and families, as a dominant power, something superior to one's physical and empirical life. One could put it like this: The border is maximum discontinuity between the individual's fate on the one hand, and on the other the concrete sensory experience, the bodily *here and now*. Archetypical for the border in this sense is the child's hard lesson after crossing some kind of physical or symbolic border without understanding a bit of it until it is too late, when it is made feel the consequences of "ignorance", usually involving more or less shameful acts of correction or punishment. Accordingly, the phenomenon of the border is indistinguishable from a sense of being permanently a potential trespasser, or even – by virtue of the simple fact of possessing a body and thus always taking up space – being out of bounds.

In its Greek origin, the word *geometry* literally means to measure the earth, the art of measuring and surveying land. Hence, geometry and trigonometry shouldn't just be understood as formal operations related to certain systematic calculations and representations of reality. Geometry is historically linked to the positions of the landlord, the general and the war lord: the status and power needed to set borders, to survey the world as a structure of territories and estates, and not least the capacity to enforce this viewpoint. The geometer commands lines and borders, which includes a command to abstract from the here and now. This means to comply to the current state of affairs.

A primordial link between borders, territories and violence is expressed in the old saying that landlords used to bring their infant sons along the borders of the family possessions, and make a stop at every important point to give them a good beating. The result for the future might be an inerasable awareness of the premises, but more significantly it was probably a more or less suppressed sense of being an underdog, a sense of existential deficit necessarily followed by an intense desire to get the upper hand at last. In what I call *border discipline*, essential roles are played both by that which is openly imposed by authorities and by that which works unconsciously, by means of suppressed memories of acts of force.

The age-old idea of geometry as something "universal" and metaphysically elevated, free of historical contingence and social meaning, in itself tends to instantiate the very authority of abstraction, not least by means of the very difficulty of really understanding the relationship between geometrical figures and the reality they represent. The "universal" at play here is ultimately the absolute submission to the non-empirical and non-individual, to a state where sensory experience and individual questions don't matter while authority certainly does. Border discipline disregards the here and now in favour of abstractions, euphemisms and unquestioned imperatives, for instance the compulsion to "keep going", actually to be oriented in one direction, eventually *upwards*.

The power of counting and measuring can be felt indirectly whenever we are dealing with the act of overlooking, delimiting and putting numbers on things. Insight into this complex is retained in the fairy-tale of the goat which learned how to count, and which thereby caused fear amongst the counted, namely the rest of the livestock. Since humans are more likely than animals to deal with numbers, we tend to adopt, to take over the habit of counting, rather than to cry out in protest. This also means accepting and forgetting the original pain: the forming of relations and structures overshadows individual experience. Thus, the elevated position seemingly has no past, no history, it just consists of objective geometry. To operate from a position above communicates being in one's right precisely through acts and measures directed "downwards" – relations simply *exist*. This is the reason why numbers and geometrical figures could be said to have connotations that make them function like stop-signs for the impulse to deal with realty as an actual chain of events.

More light is perhaps shed upon this by M. Heidegger when he gives the word *mathematics* a specific meaning related to *learning* and *teaching*. The mathematical is, Heidegger says, originally that which can be taught and learned (Heidegger 1987: 53). The mathematical thus doesn't come down to the activity of dealing with numbers and figures, but to what could be called the original *lesson* per se, condensed in the roles appropriate to *schooling*, to what Heidegger calls *Schulbetrieb* (Heidegger 1976: 317): to know one's place according to the alternative of teacher versus pupil, the one who knows and the one who does not. This alternative is the learnable and teachable before everything else. In Edmund Husserl's phrasing, "the art of measuring paves the way for universal geometry and its 'world'" (Husserl 2002: 226), and we could add that this is the world as handed down by mathematics in Heidegger's sense, schooling meaning to adapt to a pattern which is never questioned itself.

## The disembodied eye

This is the world of border discipline: the world as readily surveyed, measured up and grasped as a substance in itself, and – in correlation to this – a certain elevated or would-be elevated way of being. Hence, the world is here not something to be experienced and questioned, but is rather Reality guarded by a full stop. One could say that this corresponds to thinking of it as something at *eye's distance*. Reality interpreted in this way has as its correlate the individual constituted as an anxiously gazing point which tries to survey everything and to keep the correct positions.

Thus, border discipline corresponds to what we may call the disembodied eye, famously instantiated in the Renaissance by Alberti's monogram of a winged eye, and by Cartesian conceptions of reason as a kind of visual intake in front of the world understood as a mathematically accountable "extension". Understood as part of border discipline, the disembodied eye thus isn't simply the decisive factor in a historical episteme or *Zeitgeist* initiated by Rene Descartes and scientific reason, but rather the correlate to the abandonment of the experiencing and feeling body in any part of history. The idea of the world as *res extensa*, a measurable object as it were in front of reason and vision, is not simply an interpretation of reality, but is rather part of the drama of trying to "stay up" by abandoning the body.

By swift association, this could be more or less the same as what is often termed instrumental thinking, or an attitude which treats everything and everyone as objects. However, the regular critical tenor which blames "subjection" and the act of "reducing others to objects" may actually be problematic. For instance, to try to pinpoint the guilty far too easily comes down to reproducing the obsession of locations and positions: the role of the judge is a means to stay up. What we tend to forget is that this desire for authority is itself something once imposed on us. What John Dewey once called "the spectator theory of knowledge" (Houlgate 1993: 87) is thus neither simply the theoretical idea that the world is something detached from us, nor the distanced gaze of a passively aggressive person. "The spectator" isn't really a privileged and comfortable position outside trouble, but rather the centre of distress. In accordance with what Michel Foucault put under the heading *panopticism* (Foucault 1977: 195f), "the spectator" is him- or herself in a situation of omnipresent observation, not knowing from where and by whom.

This state of universal "seen-ness" is part of the obsession of localities and positions in border discipline, a state of permanent attention which is never allowed to think and remember, as if something better is principally unattainable.[1] To reduce everything to objects isn't just something carried out by a malign attitude, but something handed down as a tradition in a certain way of life. The original meaning of the word "object" interestingly includes the verb to *throw*. With Heidegger, we could phrase the meaning of *obiectum* as "thrown-against-ness" (Heidegger 2006: 139). To treat everything as an object was in itself thrown against us. The archetypical "thrown-against-ness" could well be said to be the exterior position of the disembodied eye, thrown against us as an overwhelming fait accompli. We tend to forget that what is responsible and guilty is itself outcast, and that this is the very reason for its destructive function. Part of this function may be to keep at bay a historical understanding of how this tragic state of affairs came into being.

In border discipline, energy is directed into maintaining absolute borders between us and Reality outside and detached from us, between us and what M. Merleau-Ponty called "the big object" (Merleau-Ponty 2004: 31). Border discipline doesn't just proclaim the authority of "scientific facts" in an attitude often called positivism. It also proclaims the existence of a separate sphere of "ethics" and "values". For instance, engagement in high-tension discourses to confirm the existence of such entities is a crucial part of border discipline's effort to keep things straight. Borrowing a word from Bruno Latour, we can say that the bodiless eye, the distressed spectator, is thus involved in "factishism" (Latour 2007), with both physical reality and ethical values being something "out there". Facing the "factish", we *stand at attention* in such a way as to reproduce this very stance and the structure it is part of, the lesson to be learned and taught again.

Another way of putting this is to say that the being of positions is being without a body, without feelings and without memory. To continue to throw this on seems to be the only correct stance, as if we were ultimately bodiless, geometrical identifications, without any inner or outer depth. To pass on the obligation towards "the big object" is to take a stance against our historical and individual life, against our "flings", "dreams" and "fantasies", to reproduce life-draining blames against the individual in the name of what is really "out there". The only possibility in border discipline is to keep a certain position,

---

1   The critique of border discipline, then, is related to one of the important issues in the critical thinking of the 20th century, namely the critique of an ontology modelled on the visual, often associated with tough-minded scientism. As has been mapped by Martin Jay, a whole tradition of philosophy – including Bataille, Sartre and Derrida – has criticised "scopic regimes" of the rationalist and scientist making, stemming from Alberti and Descartes (Jay 1993).

and to talk and act as if everything is just locations and directions. This comes close to what Adorno called "topological thinking", "which knows where every phenomenon belongs but of no phenomenon what it is" (Adorno 1977: 24). To avoid the position of the suspect, one makes oneself identical to positions which either carry out acts of "evaluation" and assessment, or are evaluated and assessed themselves.

## "Threshold knowledge"

Are we after all left with hope of something like a *way out* of border discipline, probably almost a paradoxical idea? The possibly aporetic moment of this question may be the moment for Benjamin's threshold. As mentioned above, in Benjamin's writings the threshold singles itself out among borders and limits at large: it is the only example of border as an *object* or a thing. The moment of distress may be the new starting point for the body, matter, "thingness".

For being an object with physical and sensuous qualities, the threshold is not much. Often, it is but a flat outline on the floor, something close to a void. The threshold stays low in more than one sense. Appropriate to the feet rather than to the eye, it never actually becomes something in its own right, but remains an interruption, a bump. It may be somewhere behind our back or in the dark, maybe just centimeters from our toes. The threshold leaves the typically frontal location of "the perceptual object" empty, and rather evokes a kind of animation of materiality in space. It is possible to put one foot on either side of the threshold, to sit on it, or finally to stumble over it. It is thus not so much a *something* as a spreading sensitivity for what is there, a quest into *something* per se.

In this, the threshold corresponds to the last pages of Benjamin's "The Work of Art in the Age of Mechanical Reproduction". Here, Benjamin lets the positive "absent-mindedness" of the film audience be expressed in terms of the *haptic* and tactile typical of architecture. The haptic is an expansion without fixed points, the *touch* meaning both the sensitive body and what is being touched, and could thus be described by the sentence: "Close your eyes and see!" (Didi-Huberman 1999: 11). The threshold is an instance of delay and deferral, but therefore precisely the material world being allowed for at last. This also means allowing for exposedness and unpredictability, a being in the position neither of the subject nor of the object. The threshold is acknowledgement of being "not clever", of the lapse and the flaw, and involves regarding this as a productive element. It corresponds to the good reasons to be ill-located in time and space, as acknowledged in Benjamin's remarks on childhood experiences under the heading "magnifications" in *One-way Street* (Benjamin 1955: 59).

"Threshold knowledge" is the knowledge that knowledge stumbles, that to feel split and to not know where one stands is the way of both life and knowledge. It isn't so much a kind of cognition as a kind of *becoming* which eludes any surveillance or assessment. The threshold comprises a communication with what is currently just a possibility, maybe forgotten, maybe something of the future. It is so to speak the unmeasured middle. The threshold corresponds to that which has been suppressed and outcast, to the rudiment or that which might have been, all that which now might evoke "envy" towards the future (Benjamin 1977: 251). It is a kind of invitation or address to a different life and a different kind of being.

Certainly, the threshold is a dividing instance which is continuous with the world of universal geometry, with the system of limits and constrictions in border discipline. But as materiality, the threshold is exactly the moment when this very system takes on contours as *something*, so that the system is no longer just acted out and passed on, not longer only the unconscious vehicle of distressed being. The threshold is thus so to speak the geometer's own fate becoming visible and addressable in the midst of his big *res extensa*. So the threshold cannot be a theoretical object we try to envision or cognate in the normal sense, but is rather living "thingness", the *something* we *become*. The threshold is the immeasurable event of the eye starting to return into body and matter, "the spectator" regaining a body, getting emotion and feeling back. To melt into the semi-object of the threshold is the event when something arrives which is not observable "from above" or from eye's distance. If this waking up is at the cost of the visual in a certain sense, it cannot simply mean something like abandoning the visual altogether, but on the contrary must mean *regaining* the visual as something active and meaningful, so to speak as a vitalizing act of life.

The threshold thus indicates the moment when what was "object" starts to respond, when "seen-ness" is itself reacting, simply put: To *return the gaze*. The idea we are dealing with here, the object which starts to look, feel and think, is the possibility of the "spectator" or the bodiless eye to recognizing him- or herself as an – until now – unknowing part of material reality, of the suppressed and subjected. This change will be more or less the same as standing up against the chain of events which produced good reasons to stay "outside" in the first place. The threshold isn't something "different" or "somewhere else", but is the very moment of waking up to the knowledge that every surveyed *position* and *instance* was really a being kept down. To acknowledge "thingness" in this sense, as an alternative to border discipline, is not simply to look in a different direction or to become different, but to allow for a being of one's own.

This also means that the threshold is about recognizing historical fate as *specific* and *individual* fate, as something we are into and may possibly change. Thus, the threshold isn't really an "alternative", meaning something beyond or outside troubled reality, but rather an acknowledgement of real attachments to history, which also, in effect, means forms of complicity with what has been and what may become. This complicity is however not one of guilt, leaving us so to speak in the role of the "bad", but rather a *methexis* or participation in forces and energies which may take a different turn at last. Threshold knowledge then, although well acquainted with the sad tradition of victimization and sacrifice, is something very different from regression into a passive or tragic state, that which tends to be judged as "the role of the victim". As has been pointed out by Ernst Cassirer, the threshold has been central in the history of border mythology. For Cassirer it is related to a "mythic-religious *Urgefühl*" (Menninghaus 1986: 28). Maybe this should be taken rather literally, as the beginning of feeling and *aisthesis* anew.

## "Thingness"

The self-acknowledgement of being which is activated here is the same as a good ignorance of traits, positions and characteristics which can be observed from an elevated position. Another way of putting this is to say that the threshold is even a stubborn non-acceptance of space and time in a certain sense. Space and time, often regarded as "transcendentals" or a priori categories, the strange phenomena which Kant once called "existing un-things" (Cassirer 2006: 489), are found in Benjamin's writings to be taking on individual and literal qualities, and are thereby made less powerful in the negative sense. In his writing on film, space, movement and time are described as entities which both "widen out" and "concentrate", even in a way that makes it possible to "snatch" them (Benjamin 1963: 36).[2] In *Das Passagen-Werk,* a time of the day – the afternoon – almost becomes a living creature when Benjamin speaks about to "catch the afternoon in the net of the evening" (Benjamin 1983: 533); and in *Berlin Childhood around 1900*, time has the material-like capacity to become

---

2    On this point, I am indebted to Per Kvist, who made me aware of the suggestive German filmic term *Zeitraffer* which is used by Benjamin, equivalent to the English expression "time lapse".

"aged", *veraltet* (Benjamin 1989: 12). In his Berlin memoirs, time and space "lie down at the feet of the city god" (Benjamin 1989: 13).

Heidegger has written: "It stays undecided in which way space *is*, or if it can be granted a being at all" (Heidegger 1969: 7). Something of the same goes for time: According to a later comment by Heidegger on the title of his famous *Being and Time,* time is that which is "given up" (Heidegger 1998: 157). The utopian air which comes along with the idea of space and time at rest comes down to an immense reduction of the total weight of the "this is simply how it is". This could be described as a good ignorance capable of encouraging a kind of emotional intelligence and a free-floating historical sensibility, all at the expense of dry knowledge and intellectualisms, such as cheeky remarks about "accepting the difference between now and then". The threshold means an increase in vitality with and *by* good reasons to let space and time stay in the background.

Giving priority to the thing rather than to the whereabouts of everything is also involved when Heidegger would reduce the significance of *locus* and measured space in favour of the Greek concept *topos,* something defined by *what* is there: "The place belongs to the thing itself" (Heidegger 1998: 50). This increased significance on the part of the thing needn't be understood as one of domination or possession. Rather, this priority at the cost of *where* and *when* comes along with a sense of acceptance, smallness and vulnerability as if there's no anchorage for being at all.

The tendency for the threshold to be a minimum, being less also in terms of space and time, should actually work as a yielding of space, of spaciousness, for that which has been left out. The threshold must remain vague, small in a variety of meanings. The un-located position of the threshold could be identified as always beyond itself, *nomadic,* the living fact of "thingness" in advance of any interpretation and contextualization. This may communicate with the emphasis Benjamin puts on the *flaneur.*

To allow for this roaming character and to let it speak may be precisely what is needed to avoid the distressed acting-out of the obsession of locations and topological thinking. This may also address the well-known, apparently indestructible capacity for love of what is small, what is *smaller* than a reality experienced as too big and frightening. Positive emotive impulses are instinctively triggered not only by the presence of children, but also by animals and pets, teddy-bears and actually by small material items of any sort.[3] This

---

[3]  I try to develop these thoughts further in the article "Villa Wannsee: The distance to the crime scene", in print.

life-giving source, operating through and by what Benjamin in the context of photography called a "technique of diminishing" (Benjamin 1963: 61), is also at play in our historical imagery, in the mental images which are not just snap-shots of the past, but also a kind of working through it in order to find a better future. In this imagery, Adolf Hitler represents not only extremely hateful actions towards humans, but also the emotional attachment to his dog.

\*

The problems I have dealt with in this text in terms of topological thinking, the disembodied eye and the obsession of locations, correspond more or less to Benjamin's criticism of historicist notions of evolution and enlightenment in capitalist culture. It must be remembered that for Benjamin, the optimistic idea of history as a kind of objective continuum, a domain of constant progress and improvement, was part of the blindness of the politics which ended in fascism. One can say that Benjamin's philosophy is an experiment aimed at staging a transformative "threshold experience" or even "threshold magic" for modernity, at a moment when the possibility of a shift was crucially important. If we grow too sure that such moments "belong to the past", we may be indulging in an idea belonging to the kind of border discipline which for good reasons triggered Benjamin's scepticism.

We cannot *know* to which degree Benjamin failed or was wrong in some sense of the words, or to which degree we fail in our readings today. But there certainly still are reasons to be concerned about the tendency for the body, its individual sensations and history, to be forgotten and outcast, not least in the middle of anxious eagerness to learn and teach the proper lessons. In our context – by means of the threshold – the border may be exposed as something *absurd* that is precisely *felt* and *remembered* as absurd. The repertoire of signs and marks, even fences and check-points, which are regularly found on state borders, cannot but underline the fundamental phoniness of the abstract line as a judge of individual fate. If border aesthetics may acquire significance as aesthetics of the threshold, this significance could be the very process of waking up to, remembering and standing up against, this absurdity. Instead of throwing oneself headlong into the struggle for border crossings and transgressions, and instead of seeking a safe or neutral position as it were outside it all, it might be possible to linger so to speak at the border, maybe to find a space where one doesn't have to move on anywhere or "think differently": Border discipline at last beginning to be experienced and felt, gaining a new *aisthesis,* on the threshold.

# Bibliography

Adorno, Th.W. (1977). "Kulturkritik und Gesellschaft". *Prismen*. Frankfurt a.M: Suhrkamp.

Benjamin, W. (1955). *Einbahnstrasse*. Frankfurt a.M: Suhrkamp.

Benjamin, W. (1963). *Das Kunstwerk im Zeitalter seiner technischen Reproduzierbarkeit*. Frankfurt a.M: Suhrkamp.

Benjamin, W. (1977). "Über den Begriff der Geschichte". *Illuminationen*. Frankfurt a.M: Suhrkamp.

Benjamin, W. (1983). *Das Passagen-Werk*. Frankfurt a.M: Suhrkamp.

Benjamin, W. (1989). *Berliner Kindheit um neunzehnhundert*. Frankfurt a.M: Suhrkamp.

Cassirer, E. (2006). "Mythischer, ästhetischer und theoretischer Raum" in: Dünne & Günzel (eds.). *Raumtheorie. Grundlagentexte aus Philosophie und Kulturwissenschaften*. Frankfurt a.M: Suhrkamp.

Didi-Huberman, G. (1999). *Was wir sehen blickt uns an: zur Metapsychologie des Bildes*. München: Wilhelm Fink Verlag.

Foucault, M. (1977). *Discipline and Punish. The Birth of the Prison*. London: Penguin.

Heidegger, M. (1969). *Die Kunst und der Raum. L'art et l'éspace*. St. Gallen: Erker-Verlag.

Heidegger, M. (1976). "Brief über den Humanismus". *Wegmarken*. Frankfurt a.M: Vittorio Klostermann.

Heidegger, M. (1987). *Die Frage nach dem Ding*. Tübingen: Max Niemeyer Verlag.

Heidegger, M. (1998). *Einführung in die Metaphysik*. Tübingen: Max Niemeyer Verlag.

Heidegger, M. (2006). *Der Satz vom Grund*. Stuttgart: Klett-Cotta.

Houlgate, S. (1993). "Vision, Reflection, and Openness" in: Levin, David Michael (ed.). *Modernity and the hegemony of Vision*. Berkeley: University of California Press.

Husserl, E. (2002). *Phänomenologie der Lebenswelt. Ausgewählte Texte I*. Stuttgart: Reclam.

Jay, M. (1993). *Downcast Eyes. The denigration of vision in twentieth-century French thought*. Berkeley: University of California Press.

Latour, B. (2007). *Elend der Kritik. Vom Krieg um fakten zu Dingen von Belang*. Zürich-Berlin: Diaphanes.

Lund, J. (in print). Villa Wannsee: The distance to the crime scene.

Menninghaus, W. (1986). *Schwellenkunde. Walter Benjamins Passage des Mythos*. Frankfurt a.M: Suhrkamp.

Merleau-Ponty, M. (2004). *Das Sichtbare und das Unsichtbare*. München: Wilhelm Fink Verlag.

# Authors' Biographies

**Knut Ove Arntzen**, b. 1950. Professor of Theatre Studies at the Department of Linguistic, Literary and Aesthetic Studies, University of Bergen. His primary research interests and recent publications are on postmodern theatre, drama and performance art in geo-cultural perspectives. He is currently visiting professor to the State College of the Arts in Oslo and Vytautas Magnus University in Kaunas, Lithuania.

**Jørgen Bruhn**, b. 1968. Associate Professor at the Linnæus University, Sweden. Bruhn has written monographs on Marcel Proust (with Bo Degn Rasmussen), M.M. Bakhtin and various articles on the theory of the novel, on medieval literature and culture and on intermediality. Recent work include "Heteromediality" in Lars Elleström (ed.), *Media Borders, Intermediality and Multimodality* (Palgrave-MacMillan 2010), *Lovely Violence. The Critical Romances of Chrétien de Troyes* (Cambridge Scholars Publishing 2010).

**Steven G. Ellis**, b. 1950. Professor and Head of History, School of Humanities, National University of Ireland, Galway. His primary research interests focus on British state formation, regions, and frontier societies. He has published widely on British and Irish history and his most recent books are *The making of the British Isles: the State of Britain and Ireland 1450-1660* (Pearson/Longman, London, 2007) and (ed. Iakovos Michailidis) *Regional and Transnational History in Europe* (Edizioni Plus-Pisa University Press 2011).

**Per Olav Folgerø**, b. 1958. Associate Professor at the Department of Linguistic, Literary and Aesthetic Studies, University of Bergen. His main field of research is Byzantine iconography. Most of his scientific work deals with the iconography in S. Maria Antiqua, Rome.

**Lillian Jorunn Helle**, b. 1949. Professor of Russian literature at the Department of Foreign Languages, Russian Studies, University of Bergen. She has published numerous articles on Russian 19th century literature and culture, Russian Symbolism and Modernism, Social Realism and literary theory (Belyj, Bakhtin, Lotman, Jakobson). She is currently preparing a book on Tolstoy's last novel, *Resurrection*.

**Øyunn Hestetun**, b. 1949. Associate Professor of American Literature at the Department of Foreign Languages, University of Bergen. Her main area of research is literary and cultural theory, including postcolonial theory and ecocriticism, and her most recent publications focus on Native American literature, migrant writing, and environmental issues.

**Helge Vidar Holm**, b. 1947. Professor of French Literature and Culture Studies at the University of Bergen. Co-leader of the interdisciplinary research group "The Borders of Europe". His main research focus is on narrative theory and French novels from the 19th and 20th centuries. His most recent book is *Moeurs de Province. Essai d'analyse bakhtinienne de Madame Bovary* (Peter Lang SA 2011).

**Siri Skjold Lexau**, b. 1951. Professor at the Department of Linguistic, Literary and Aesthetical Studies, University of Bergen. Her primary research interests are architecture and urban studies. She has published widely on architectural and urban history, and her most recent book is *Norsk arkitekturhistorie* (A History of Norwegian Architecture), published at Det Norske Samlaget 2008.

**Jørgen Lund**, b. 1965. Associate Professor at Department of Art and Media Studies, Norwegian University of Science and Technology, Trondheim. His primary research interest is contemporary visual culture and art. His recent works center on the relationship between the philosophy of history, aesthetic experience and psychological trauma.

**Sissel Lægreid**, b. 1952. Professor of German Literature and Culture Studies at the University of Bergen, currently co-leader of the interdisciplinary research group "The Borders of Europe". Her research projects and recent publications are within the fields of the aesthetics of exile, hermeneutics, modernism, German-Jewish exile literature and Rumanian-German literature. Her most recent publication is on Herta Müller, *Diktatur og diktning. Herta Müllers foratterskap*. Sissel Lægreid & Helgard Mahrdt (eds.) (Tiden 2012).

**Kåre Johan Mjør**, b. 1973. Postdoctoral Research Fellow at the Uppsala Centre for Russian and Eurasian Studies, Uppsala University, Sweden. His primary research interests are Russian historiography, Russian philosophy, and Russian intellectual history. His most recent book is *Reformulating Russia: The Cultural and Intellectual Historiography of Russian First-Wave Emigré Writers* (Brill 2011).

**Torgeir Skorgen**, b. 1967. Senior Researcher and University Librarian at the University of Bergen. His primary research interests are German literature and philosophy; in particular hermeneutics, dialogism, multiculturalism, nationalism and racism.

**Gordana Vnuk**, b. 1956. Founder of and Artistic Director of "Eurokaz" theatre festival since 1987. Lecturer at the Theatre Academy in Zagreb, Croatia. Post-graduate studies on cultural politics in France (University of Bourgogne). Former Artistic Director of Kampnagel in Hamburg, Germany and Theatre Programmer in Chapter Arts Centre in Cardiff, Wales.

**Jardar Østbø**, b. 1974. A scholarship holder and auxiliaire teacher at the Russian Section at the Department of Foreign Languages, University of Bergen 2007-2011, he defended his PhD thesis *The New Third Rome. Readings of a Russian National Myth* in 2011. His field of interest includes nationalism, imperialism, national identity, geopolitical thought, history of ideas, historiography and national stereotypes.

**Sigrun Åsebø**, b. 1972. Associate Professor of Art History at the Department of Linguistic, Literary and Aesthetic Studies at the University of Bergen. Her research interests are feminist historiography and theory, and questions of gender, sexuality and women artists from modernity until today. She defended her PhD thesis *Femininitetens rom og kvinnekroppens grenser. Å lese kunstens historie med A K Dolven og Mari Slaattelid* (The Spaces of Femininity and the Boundaries of the Female Body: Reading the History of Art with A K Dolven and Mari Slaattelid) in spring 2011.